Pelican Books
Unequal Shares

A. B. Atkinson is Professor of Economics at the
University of Essex. He was educated at
Churchill College, Cambridge, and was a Fellow
of St. John's College, Cambridge. He has written
*Poverty in Britain and the Reform of Social
Security* as well as a number of articles in
academic journals. He is editor of the *Journal of
Public Economics* and a member of the London
and Cambridge Economic Service. He is
currently engaged in research on the distribution
of income and wealth in Britain.

A. B. Atkinson

Unequal Shares

Wealth in Britain

Revised edition

Penguin Books

Penguin Books Ltd, Harmondsworth,
Middlesex, England
Penguin Books Inc., 7110 Ambassador Road,
Baltimore, Maryland 21207, U.S.A.
Penguin Books Australia Ltd, Ringwood,
Victoria, Australia
Penguin Books Canada Ltd,
41 Steelcase Road West, Markham, Ontario, Canada

First published by Allen Lane, The Penguin Press, 1972
Revised edition published in Pelican Books 1974

Copyright © A. B. Atkinson, 1972, 1974

Made and printed in Great Britain by
Richard Clay (The Chaucer Press) Ltd,
Bungay, Suffolk
Set in Monotype Times

For Judith

Contents

List of Tables   xi

List of Figures   xii

Preface   xiii

Introduction   xv

Part I: Wealth in Britain

1   Wealth in Britain   3

   The Meaning of Wealth   3
   Distribution of Personal Wealth in Britain   8
   Comparison with the Distribution of Wealth in
      Other Countries   19
   Changes in the Distribution of Wealth over Time   21

2   The Advantages of Wealth   25

   The Concept of Ownership   25
   Income from Wealth   31
   Wealth and the Control of Industry   38

3   The Accumulation of Wealth   45

   Accumulated and Inherited Wealth   45
   The Accumulation of Wealth   47
   The Yield from Wealth   53

4   Inheritance and the Distribution of Wealth   59

   Factors Influencing the Transmission of Wealth   59
   The Quantitative Importance of Inheritance   68
   Inheritance in Three Families   73

5   The Case for Greater Equality   77
   Intrinsic Arguments Against Greater Equality   78
   Consequential Arguments Against Greater
      Equality   88

Part II: The Reform of Wealth Taxation

6   Wealth Taxes – An Introduction   99
   Types of Taxes on Wealth   99
   Redistributive Effect of Taxation –
      Appearances and Reality   103
   Basis for Comparing Taxes   106
   Taxes on Wealth in Other Countries   108

7   The Impact of the Present Tax System   113
   Estate Duty   113
   Avoidance of Estate Duty   120
   Taxation of Income from Wealth   129

8   A Wealth Tax for Britain?   135
   A Wealth Tax in Britain   135
   A Wealth Tax to Replace Surtax?   142
   A Redistributive Wealth Tax   149
   Reform of Capital Gains Taxation   157

9   Taxing the Transfer of Wealth   163
   Strategy for Wealth-Transfer Taxation   163
   The Government Green Paper on Inheritance Taxation   175
   A Lifetime Capital Receipts Tax in More Detail   179
   The Consequences of a Lifetime Capital Receipts
      Tax   184

Part III: Wealth for All

10   The Social Ownership of Wealth   195
    The National Debt and a Capital Levy   196
    Nationalization   207
    Denationalization   216

11   Spreading Personal Wealth   220
    Saving Incentives   220
    Pensions and Wealth   226
    Capital Growth-Sharing Schemes   234

Part IV: Conclusions

12   A Programme for Reform   249

Notes on Sources and Further Reading   254
References   262
Index   269

List of Tables

1 Total Personal Wealth in Britain 1966   7
2 Distribution of Wealth – Inland Revenue Estimates for 1968   11
3 Adjusted Estimates of the Distribution of Wealth – 1963–7   14
4 Top Investment Incomes 1967–8   16
5 Changes in the Distribution of Wealth 1911–13 to 1960   21
6 Wealth and the Composition of Portfolios 1957–9   30
7 Concentration of Ownership of Different Assets 1954   31
8 Inequality in Wealth and the Distribution of Income 1959   38
9 Owners of Quoted Ordinary Shares   42
10 Inequality by Age – Great Britain 1963–7   52
11 Rate of Interest and the Accumulation of Wealth   54
12 Return to Ordinary Shares 1919–69   55
13 Degree of Assortative Mating in Britain in 1949   66
14 Marriages of Children of Dukes 1330–1934   67
15 Changes in Estate Duty 1894–1972   116
16 Revenue from Death Duties as a Percentage of Total Personal Wealth   126
17 Effective Rate of Tax on Different Types of Income   132
18 Rates of Wealth Tax   137
19 Effect of Replacing Surtax by a Wealth Tax   143
20 Impact of a Redistributive Wealth Tax   150
21 Rate Schedule for an Integrated Gift and Estate Tax   166
22 A Lifetime Capital Receipts Tax   171
23 Redistributional Impact of the 1968 Special Charge   198
24 Scale for a Capital Levy   199
25 Savings of Retirement Pensioners   233

List of Figures

1 The Distribution of Wealth and Income in Britain and the United States 1953–4   20

2 Wealth and Age – A Stylized Model   51

3 Relationship between Estates of Fathers and Sons   69

4 Estates of Fathers and Sons in 1924–6 and 1956–7   71

5 A Classification of Wealth Transfer Taxes   102

Preface

This book owes a great deal to other people. Firstly, there are those who have read and commented on different versions of the manuscript. J. M. Atkinson, C. J. Bliss, C. D. Harbury, G. Hughes, J. E. Meade, D. M. G. Newbery, W. D. Nordhaus, J. R. S. Revell, A. Roe, A. Shorrocks, Z. A. Silberston, C. Spencer, O. Stutchbury, P. Townsend and G. S. A. Wheatcroft all read either the whole manuscript or substantial parts. Their critical comments led to many improvements in the argument and in its presentation, and suggested new approaches to be explored. I am extremely grateful to them for their help, without which writing this book would have been both more difficult and less pleasant. Peter Wright of Penguin Books first suggested that I write this book and has encouraged me throughout. His advice and patience have been much appreciated. Finally, I should like to express my gratitude to Miss Jill Adlington, who typed the final version with great efficiency and goodwill.

My debt to published work will be clear to the reader, and I should like to take the opportunity of acknowledging the extent to which my thinking has been influenced by the (rather few) economists who have written on the subject of the distribution of wealth. I should also at this point explain the treatment of references. These presented some difficulty, since I was anxious to steer a course between the dangers of detailed footnotes, which are distracting to the general reader, and of complete absence of documentation, which is irritating to those with an academic interest. The compromise adopted is to give brief references in the text for all tables, diagrams and major quotations, and to give a more detailed description of sources (and a bibliography) at the end of the book. The references in the text are given in the form of the author's name and the date of publication – e.g. (Smith, 1971) – which will allow the source to be identified from the bibliography.

The manuscript of the book was essentially completed early in 1971. Since that date there have been a number of important developments in government policy. In the 1971 Budget, the Chancellor of the Exchequer announced plans for a reform of personal income taxation, which were further elaborated in the Budget of 1972. These plans are described in the Postscript to Chapter 7, and I have included a number of footnote references to their likely consequences. In September 1971, the government outlined its proposals for pension reform. The principal implications of their proposals are discussed briefly in Chapter 11. Finally, the Chancellor announced in his 1972 Budget that the government 'believe that the time has come for a thorough-going review . . . of death duty', and in its Green Paper *Taxation of Capital on Death* (discussed in the Postscript to Chapter 9) called for 'a full public discussion of the possibilities'. It is my hope that this book will contribute to this discussion and will demonstrate the need for radical reform.

University of Essex   March 1972

Preface to the Pelican Edition

In this paperback edition I have taken the opportunity of revising Chapters 7, 8 and 9 in the light of the changes in income and estate taxation introduced in the Budgets of 1971–3, and to incorporate the material previously included in postscripts to these chapters. Apart from a few minor corrections, the rest of the book is unchanged.

Introduction

One of the most marked inequalities in our society is that in the distribution of wealth. The evidence available shows that over a quarter of the total personal wealth in Britain is in the hands of the richest 1% of the adult population and that as much as three quarters belongs to the top 10%. In 1969, 19 people died leaving estates of over £1 million, an amount which it would have taken the average manual worker a thousand years to earn. While the ownership of wealth is not everything (indeed John Ruskin once claimed that 'there is no wealth but life'), there can be little doubt that wealth makes a great deal of difference to people's lives. The lives of the 19 people who left £1 million or more must have been quite different from that of the average manual worker. Wealth provides security and freedom of action; it allows a person to retire early (or not to work at all); it allows his children to complete their education without financial worries. A person inheriting £1 million can spend £400 a week for the next fifty years. Alternatively he can control the operations of a large company and the jobs of hundreds of workers. Wealth may not be essential to human happiness, but its unequal distribution has profound consequences for our society.

The extreme concentration of wealth in Britain has given rise to a great deal of concern – a concern which has not been limited to a small minority on the left of the Labour Party but shared by people of widely differing political views. The need for measures to bring about a more equal distribution of wealth has been accepted by successive Chancellors of the Exchequer, and there have been a number of attempts to increase the effectiveness of death duties. Many people feel, however, that these measures have been quite inadequate and that more far-reaching reforms are required. The proposals put forward have included new taxes, such as a wealth tax or a gifts tax (those who like their taxes in mnemonic form can choose between G.E.T. (Gratuitous Enrichment Tax) and P.A.Y.A. (Pay as You Accumulate.)) Others have argued for a capital levy or for wider nationalization. Finally, a number of schemes have been proposed for encouraging saving among those with little wealth, including contractual savings schemes (like Save As You Earn), wider share-ownership plans, and proposals to include a capital element in wage negotiations.

Recognition of the concentration of wealth-holding and pressure for reform have raised many important questions:

Do the figures quoted above mean what they appear to? Or are we, as has been suggested by *The Times*, 'proceeding through mis-leading statistics to false conclusions'?

If wealth is in fact concentrated in a relatively few hands, what does this mean in terms of people's lives and in terms of economic power?

What are the main forces causing inequality in the distribution of wealth? Is it the result of inheritance, or do some people just accumulate more than others during their lifetimes? Have death duties succeeded in bringing about greater equality?

If we are concerned to reduce the degree of inequality, should this be done by reducing wealth at the top or by increasing wealth at the bottom?

If we are going to tax the rich, would it be best to have a wealth tax or a tax on gifts? What would be the effect of new taxes on the incentives to work and save? Would they even be administratively feasible?

Would further nationalization reduce inequality in the distribution of wealth? What is likely to be the effect of savings incentive schemes such as Save As You Earn? What role can the trade unions play in achieving a redistribution of wealth?

The aim of this book is to try to provide answers to some of these questions: to assemble the evidence about the distribution of wealth in Britain and to examine the consequences of reforms. The book is divided into four main parts:

Part I is concerned with the present distribution of wealth in Britain and the causes of inequality. In chapter 1 the available evidence is presented about the degree of concentration and the way in which it has developed over time. This evidence is often quoted but rarely examined very carefully, and I have tried to go behind the statistics to see just what they mean and how reliable they are likely to be. Chapter 2 is concerned with the 'advantages of wealth', and the way in which inequality in wealth-holding affects the distribution of income and economic power. Chapters 3 and 4 deal with the factors leading to concentration in the distribution of wealth, and in particular with the role of inheritance. This analysis of the causes of inequality provides the basis for the discussion in chapter 5 of the arguments for greater equality.

Parts II and III of the book deal with the various measures that have been proposed with the objective of securing greater equality. In Part II, I examine the contribution which could be made by reforming the present taxes on wealth or by introducing new taxes. Chapter 6 outlines the different ways in which wealth could be taxed and describes briefly the types of wealth tax in force in other countries. In chapter 7 I discuss the impact of the present British tax system and the effectiveness of estate duty (how far is it in fact true that it is only a 'voluntary' tax?). Proposals for reform are considered in chapter 8, which deals with the introduction of an annual wealth tax and the extension of capital gains taxation, and in chapter 9, which is concerned with new taxes on the transfer of wealth and the scope for a lifetime capital receipts tax. Part III ('Wealth for All') considers non-fiscal measures for bringing about greater equality: a capital levy to redeem the National Debt, nationalization and denationalization, savings incentive schemes, pension reform and union-negotiated capital growth sharing schemes.

Part IV of the book is only a few pages long and attempts to summarize the conclusions of Parts II and III in a programme of the reforms which I should like to see introduced.

This plan for the book may appear over-ambitious, and I should emphasize here that it does not provide answers to all the questions outlined above. In some cases, the knowledge required to answer them satisfactorily is simply not available, a situation which reflects the serious neglect by economists and other social scientists of wealth-holding and the causes of inequality. In 1926 Lord Stamp outlined a programme for research into the role of inheritance, which is clearly an institution of central importance in our society. Forty-five years later very little progress has been made and (with one or two notable exceptions) the subject has been largely ignored. In other cases, the answer to the question depends on the objectives pursued and on attitudes towards inequality. A person who saw nothing wrong with the present distribution of wealth would not consider that any reform was necessary. Those people who agree that the present distribution is unjust may disagree about the costs (for example, in terms of a fall in savings) which they would be willing to bear in order to reduce inequality.

The fact that a number of the questions raised involve judgements about values does not, however, mean that nothing can be said, and one of the central themes of the book is the importance of clarifying the precise nature of the objectives of reform. This arises particularly in the context of the distinction drawn in chapter 3 between inherited and accumulated wealth, the former relating to wealth that a person has received from others in the form of bequests or gifts, and the latter to wealth that he has himself accumulated. If we are concerned with 'unequal chances in life', it is chiefly inherited wealth which is relevant, since it represents the advantage with which a person starts life (whereas inequality in accumulated wealth may simply reflect differences in savings patterns). On the other hand, when we consider inequality in control over production both accumulated and inherited wealth are relevant: the man who has built up a business from nothing may have as much as or more economic power than the man with a legacy. In assessing the contribution which can be made by different reforms, the distinction between these different sources of wealth plays an essential role. Certain schemes would contribute towards a reduction in the concentration of inherited wealth, but have no impact on control over production; whereas others would lead to greater equality of control but have no effect on inheritance. A programme for reform clearly has to contain a balance of such measures.

The emphasis of the book is on *reform*. This reflects two important considerations. Firstly, in my judgement there is a strong case for the introduction of reforms in Britain designed to bring about greater equality of wealth-holding. This case is developed in Part I, but it is only fair to say at this stage that one of the principal motivations for writing this book was the belief that new measures are seriously needed. Secondly, I have focused on reforms rather than remedies involving the revolutionary overthrow of political or economic organizations. The measures discussed would represent radical changes in government policy but would operate within the framework of present economic institutions. It could be argued that such reforms can achieve nothing and that the only solution lies in changing the basic economic structure, but this is not an opinion I share. While a radically different form of economic organization might well be desirable, it is not in my view the only means by which greater equality can be brought about. In Parts II and III, I have tried to demonstrate that there are a number of reforms which could do a great deal to reduce the present concentration of wealth.

There are inevitably a number of aspects of wealth-holding which are not covered in the book. In particular, I should draw attention to the fact that I have not considered two means which have been suggested for achieving greater equality: the spread of home-ownership, and the formation of 'human capital'. For people in the middle of the wealth range, ownership of their home represents a major part of their wealth, and is one of the most important factors separating them from those at the bottom of the wealth distribution. Moreover, home-ownership has in the past offered a relatively high rate of return (see chapter 2). It has therefore been argued that wider home-ownership would have an equalizing effect on the distribution of wealth and would tend to narrow the differences which exist among the bottom 90% of the distribution. Measures to encourage owner-occupation involve, however, many complex questions of housing policy which are outside my field of competence, and for this reason they are not discussed. The question of 'human capital' requires some explanation. It has been argued that in assessing a person's wealth we should include not only his physical and financial assets, but also the investment which he has made in the form of education and training. Suppose that instead of going to work immediately on leaving school, a person spends three years training as a student or apprentice. During this period he earns less than he otherwise would have done and has various other costs, but these are (presumably) compensated for by higher earnings when qualified. In this way, he can be said to be 'investing in education' by sacrificing immediate income, and this investment can be seen as parallel to that in physical or financial assets. Moreover, apart from the investment which the individual (and his parents) are making in his education, the state is also investing a great deal: teachers' salaries, the cost of providing and running schools, universities and technical colleges all represent investment in education. 'Human capital' is clearly of considerable importance, both with regard to the transmission of wealth between generations (for a rich man the education of his sons at Eton may be just as effective a means for passing on wealth as a straightforward gift) and with regard to the equalization of wealth through state-provided education. However, this particular aspect of wealth is not one to which I can do justice in this book, and I shall consider only 'non-human' wealth.

Part I
Wealth in Britain

1. Wealth in Britain

Millionaires are still alive and kicking, and it takes a good deal of ignorance to assert the opposite. – *J. Pen*

The Meaning of Wealth

What we mean by wealth may best be demonstrated by considering what would happen if the government were to carry out a national survey of wealth-holding. Suppose that a person finds that he has been selected to take part in this survey, and that he has to give details of his total wealth. What should he fill in? The first things that would probably occur to him are tangible possessions: his house, furniture, car, clothes, etc. It appears then to be quite a simple task – all he has to do is to make a list of everything he sees around him. However, the government wants not just a list of all the people who have refrigerators, but the total *value* of a person's assets, so that it is not enough to write down 'refrigerator', for some value has to be placed on it. Valuation of household contents is probably not too difficult because they are mostly replaceable; a person will know what a new refrigerator costs and can work out from this roughly what his five-year-old one is worth. When we come to his house, valuation becomes more difficult, since its location is unique; and while estate agents can make a reasonably informed guess on the basis of prices paid for similar houses in the same area, the true value would not be known unless the house was actually sold.

In addition to those items of wealth that a person can see physically around him, he is likely to hold financial assets. These mean that the person does not own physical assets himself, but rather claims against someone else who does. These claims transfer ownership of physical assets without transferring the location of the assets: the depositor in a building society has a claim against the society, which in turn has a claim on the houses occupied by borrowers. Financial assets may take a wide variety of forms. They may represent claims against the government (pound notes, National Savings Bank deposits, government bonds, etc.), claims against financial institutions (bank deposits, building society deposits, etc.), claims against companies (e.g. shares), or claims against other people (e.g. a loan to one's brother-in-law). A person may also have financial liabilities: money borrowed from a bank or building society, for example. As with physical assets, there are problems of valuing these claims and liabilities. For assets such as currency or bank deposits, valuation is straightforward. In the case of company shares quoted on the Stock Exchange, the market valuation can be adopted, although, as we shall see, it may not be fully satisfactory. Where the shares have no quotation, as with many small family businesses, valuation may give rise to serious difficulties. Similarly there are problems with assets such as annuities or life insurance: how much is a policy maturing in twenty years' time worth now?

On the assumption that these problems of valuation can be resolved (if in some cases in a rather rough and ready way), we can draw up a balance sheet of a person's wealth. For an 'average' couple (combining their wealth) the position might look something like this:

	Value (£)	
Assets:		
House	5,000	
Contents and personal belongings	1,000	
Car	750	
Cash and money in bank	100	
Savings in building society	150	
Life assurance policies	500	
		7,500
Liabilities:		
Mortgage	−1,600	
H.P. loan on car	− 500	
		−2,100
Net Worth		5,400

The last line shows the value of the couple's net worth – or the total value of their assets less the value of their liabilities. This allows, for example, for the fact that part of their house belongs in effect to the building society rather than to them. In what follows, when I refer to a person's wealth I mean his net worth.

At this point, the relationship should be clarified between *wealth* and *income*, about which confusion sometimes arises. This confusion is the more understandable in that classical writers used the terms virtually synonymously. Adam Smith's *Wealth of Nations* was – despite its title – chiefly concerned with the determinants of the level and distribution of incomes. In current usage, the essential difference is that wealth is a *stock*, whereas income is a *flow* over time: wealth is measured in pounds, but income in pounds per year (or whatever period is chosen). The personal balance sheet drawn up above would clearly represent a person's *stock* position, and although he might derive flows of income from this stock (interest, dividends, etc.) it would be a quite different dimension. The term 'distribution of wealth' refers to the distribution of the ownership of physical and financial assets, whereas the 'distribution of income' refers to the receipts accruing from the ownership of assets (and from other sources such as earnings) in a given period.

The balance sheet which we have drawn up covers all the assets normally included in figures for wealth-holding, but there is another class of assets that should not be overlooked: the value of rights to occupational and state pensions. A person may be in employment covered by an occupational pension scheme, under which he (or his employer) has saved part of his income and in exchange will receive a pension when he retires. These pension rights undoubtedly constitute part of his wealth. Since these rights are not marketable there are problems of valuation, but it is possible to make some estimate of the actuarial value of the pension earned. There is, however, no reason why we should stop at occupational pensions: we ought also to include the rights which a person has acquired to National Insurance pensions. It might be objected that since the future rates of state pensions are unknown we cannot estimate their actuarial value; but we can at the very least make a valuation based on the conservative assumption that they remain at their present level. Finally, carrying this argument to its logical extreme suggests that we ought to include the value of rights to sickness and unemployment benefits (both state and private). The fact that a person can claim sickness benefit has a value to him and should (in theory at least) be allowed for. However, the value of these latter benefits is for most people much smaller than that of rights to occupational and state pensions, and they will be ignored in what follows.

So far I have focused on the wealth of a single person (or couple). If we add up the net worth of all households in the country, we arrive at the *total personal net worth*. In the course of this adding-up there will be a lot of cancelling: if a person lends his brother-in-law £500 his financial assets include this loan, but the brother-in-law's wealth position includes a corresponding liability, and when we add the two together the asset and liability cancel. What remains will be physical assets and financial claims on other sectors (banks, firms, the government and the rest of the world). The estimated value of total personal wealth (excluding rights to state pensions) in 1966 was £106,600 million (see Table 1). About half of this was in the form of physical assets and about half in financial assets. The largest proportion of physical assets consisted not surprisingly of houses and land, although consumer durables added up to a sizeable amount. The financial assets consisted of three main types: bank and building society deposits, life insurance policies (and occupational pensions), and company shares.

The total of personal wealth relates to the wealth owned directly by individuals, and must be distinguished from the total wealth of the *nation*. In order to arrive at the latter figure, we have to add in the net worth of the company sector and of the government. In the former case, it might be expected that if we took the total physical and other assets of the company sector, subtracting any loans or other debt outstanding, what would be left would equal the Stock Exchange valuation of the outstanding share capital. Since a company belongs to its shareholders, the net value of its assets should be exactly equal to the value of its shares, and it would have no independent net worth. However, the work of J. R. S. Revell has shown that in fact this is not the case: the total stock market value of all company shares is considerably less than the total net value of the assets of companies. If a person could buy the average company at its stock market valuation, he would, according to Revell's estimates, be getting a good bargain. The reason for the existence of a positive net worth for the company sector is that the stock market price for company shares represents only their value to a 'marginal' holder, and the bulk of shareholders are not willing to

Table 1: Total Personal Wealth in Britain 1966

	Total (£ million)	Average per adult* £ (approximate)
1. Physical assets:		
Houses and land	32,600	800
Consumer durables	5,800	150
Other	11,700	300
Total	50,100	1,250
2. Financial assets:		
Cash and bank deposits	8,100	200
Building society deposits	10,200	250
Government securities	8,900	225
Company shares	16,200	400
Life policies and occupational pension rights†	20,600	525
Other	7,600	200
Total	71,600	1,800
3. Financial liabilities:		
Total	15,100	375
4. Net Worth (1 + 2 − 3)	106,600	2,675

*Throughout the book 'adult' should be taken to mean a person 18 or over, unless otherwise indicated.

†State pension rights are not included.

Source: Roe (1971). See also Notes on Sources.

sell their shares at that price. The 'intramarginal' holders might be happy to retain their shares even if the price rose considerably, either because they consider that the firm has good prospects or because their holding gives them control over its operations (a factor discussed further in the next chapter). It is for this reason that takeover bidders have to offer a 'premium' over the current stock market price. As a result, holdings of company shares should be valued at a higher figure than the stock market price; indeed it may well be reasonable to attribute the whole difference, i.e. the company sector net worth, to the shareholders as a body (which would in 1966 have increased total personal wealth by about a quarter).

The net worth of the public sector (the central government, local authorities and the nationalized industries) may be positive or negative. If, for example, the government finances capital formation in the public sector out of tax revenue, it acquires a positive net worth. On the other hand, if it issues bonds to finance current expenditure, it acquires a liability to the personal sector without any corresponding physical assets, and the public sector's net worth becomes negative. In fact during the period 1957 to 1966 the wealth of the public sector swung from a net debt of £8,000 million to a net worth of £6,000 million – both small figures in relation to total personal wealth.

The relationship between these different concepts may be summarized as follows:*

	1966 (£000,000,000)
Total personal net worth	107
Net worth of company sector	25
Net worth of public sector	6
Total national wealth	138

Distribution of Personal Wealth in Britain

If one could have taken the total personal wealth in 1966 (with some allowance for the fact that company shares are worth more than their market value) and divided it equally among the adult population, it would have given an average wealth for a married couple of around £6,000. Today (1971) the figure would be nearer £8,000. But the fact that this is the average wealth does not mean

*Non-profit-making bodies (such as friendly societies, trade unions and charities) are ignored.

that most people possess that amount. Many own much less, and a small minority own very much more. It is with these differences that this book is primarily concerned.

Unfortunately, the evidence we have about the distribution of wealth is both extremely limited and subject to substantial error. There is an enormous gap between the information that we should ideally like to have and the evidence that can be brought to bear. The situation has been well described as follows: 'Despite the various attempts that have been made to discover the facts about the distribution of capital in Britain, the most striking aspect of the subject is the statistical darkness which surrounds it.' (Lydall and Tipping, 1961, p. 83.) This statistical darkness has not become any clearer over time, and there is at present little prospect of additional illumination.

Ideally, we should like an annual census of wealth giving details of the wealth of all households or individuals for each year – the kind of information described above. This would provide evidence about the distribution of wealth, as well as allowing us to examine the relationship between individual and family wealth and the relationship of wealth-holding to age. A survey approach of this type was adopted a number of years ago by the Oxford Institute of Economics and Statistics, and in 1953 and 1954 they carried out two sample savings surveys in which they collected details of the net worth of households. There are however two major difficulties in using this information. Participation in the survey was voluntary and a third of the households refused to co-operate. This would not have been serious if the refusal had been spread uniformly across the population, but in fact it was the very wealthy who were significantly under-represented. There was also a definite tendency for those responding to understate their wealth, particularly in the case of financial assets (which they may simply have forgotten about). The survey data currently available is, therefore, both out of date and subject to considerable error. This situation might be changed if the government decided to revive these surveys and make participation compulsory (as is the case with the Population Census and certain industrial inquiries). This does not seem very likely, however, and we shall probably have to continue to rely on alternative methods.

Estate Duty Method

Under our present system of taxation, the only occasion when a person's total assets and liabilities are revealed is at his death. The estate duty returns are, therefore, an important source of information about the distribution of wealth; in effect they allow us to use the dead as a sample of the living. The basic method of estimating the distribution of wealth from this source is straightforward. In its Annual Reports the Inland Revenue presents details of estates classified by the age and sex of the deceased. We then assume that those people of a particular age and sex who died in that year were a random sample of the living population: if the mortality rate for a particular male age group is 1 in 1,000, we assume that for every man who died at this age in a given year there were 999 alive in similar circumstances and we multiply the numbers and values of estates in this age group by 1,000. In other words, the estimates of the distribution of wealth are reached by 'blowing up' the estate figures by the reciprocal of the mortality rate – the 'mortality multiplier' as it is called. The choice of the correct mortality multiplier is a matter for some care (for example, allowance should be made for the fact that wealthier people tend to die later than those with little wealth); but once it has been made the estimation of the distribution of wealth becomes a matter of simple arithmetic.

The most recent estimates using this method of the distribution of wealth in Britain are those made by the Inland Revenue for 1968 (see Table 2). From this we can see that some 20,000 people owned wealth in excess of £200,000 in 1968, with an average of £390,000 each. (Unfortunately we cannot work out how many are millionaires, since they are not separated from those with a mere £200,000.) These 20,000 people represented a very small fraction of the adult population (0·05%), yet they owned 9% of the total wealth recorded by the Inland Revenue. The top 1% of the adult population (which included those in the top part of the £25,000–£50,000 range) owned 32% of total wealth; and the top 5% (which included people down to £9,000) owned 59%. In other words, only about a third of total wealth was left for the remaining 95% to share. Over 90% of the adult population owned less than £5,000.

Table 2: Distribution of Personal Wealth – Inland Revenue Estimate for 1968

Range of net worth	Total number of people	Percentage of adult population (18 and over)	Average wealth (£)
Over £200,000	20,000	0·05	390,000
£100,000–£200,000	40,000	0·10	135,000
£50,000–£100,000	121,000	0·30	67,000
£25,000–£50,000	326,000	0·85	34,000
£15,000–£25,000	436,000	1·10	20,000
£10,000–£15,000	598,000	1·55	12,000
£5,000–£10,000	2,191,000	5·60	7,000
Total over £5,000	3,732,000	9·55	17,000

Source: Inland Revenue (1970) Table 123 and *Annual Abstract of Statistics.*

The estimates made by the Inland Revenue indicate a very high degree of concentration in the distribution of wealth in Britain. There are, however, a number of major reasons why these estimates may not be very accurate. Firstly, in the classification of estates by age and size, some of the 'cells' contain very few estates: in 1968–9 only one man died aged 25–34 with wealth above £200,000. This means that there may be wide variation in the estimates from year to year, particularly in the younger age groups. A wealthy young man crashing his sports car could add 1,000 to the estimate of the number of people with wealth over £200,000. Secondly, not everyone has to pay estate duty. In 1968 estates below £5,000 were not liable for duty, and as a result the estate duty statistics only provide adequate coverage of the upper part of the wealth distribution. This means that total personal wealth is likely to be underestimated, which leads in turn to an overstatement of the share of the top wealth-holders. Thirdly, certain classes of property are excluded from the estate duty statistics because they disappear on death. The most important of these are rights to pensions and annuities, neither of which forms part of a person's estate, although if he were alive they would constitute part of his wealth. Since property of this kind forms a major part of the wealth of most people, its omission undoubtedly leads to an overstatement of the degree of concentration.

The last two considerations both cause the degree of inequality to be exaggerated; however, there are a number of factors working in the opposite direction. Among the most important are those resulting from the avoidance of estate duty by the wealthy. This subject is discussed at greater length in chapter 7, but I should point out here the principal ways in which avoidance affects the estimates of the distribution of wealth obtained from the estate duty returns. In some cases, property escapes estate duty altogether: for example, discretionary trusts (although these were brought within the scope of estate duty in the 1969 Budget), property settled on a surviving spouse, and the benefits from certain pension schemes. In other cases the estate duty law allows assets to be treated as separate estates: for example, certain types of settled property, growing timber, and certain life assurance policies. Since this property is likely to be concentrated among the top wealth-holders, the degree of inequality is clearly understated by the estate duty statistics. Another well-known means of avoidance is through gifts, but this does not mean that this wealth is omitted from the estate duty statistics. If a person aged 65 transfers part of his wealth to his son aged 40, this wealth will still appear in the estate duty estimates (since some of those aged 40 die and their estates are blown up by the appropriate mortality multiplier).* However, the widespread use of gifts to avoid estate duty *is* important when we consider the interpretation of the evidence, and we return to this question later. A final factor leading to an understatement of the degree of inequality is that the valuation of estates for estate duty purposes is in general based on market values. This means that no allowance is made for the excess of the net value of the assets of the company sector over its share valuation. Since the proportion of total wealth held in the form of company shares rises with the level of wealth, this is particularly important for the very wealthy, and may be expected to lead to an understatement of their share of total personal wealth.

*In fact the wealth may be counted *twice*, where the donor dies within seven years of death, so that the gift is included in his estate (as well as in the wealth of the recipient).

Adjustments can be made to the estate duty figures to correct for some of these deficiencies, and in Table 3 adjusted estimates are given for the period 1963–7. Although the adjustments made are necessarily approximate, and a great deal of further research needs to be done on them, the estimates given in this table should provide a more reliable indication of the degree of inequality than the Inland Revenue figures. Three main adjustments have been made. Firstly, to reduce the problems arising from the small numbers in certain cells, the estate duty figures for a number of years have been combined to give a single estimate covering the period 1963–7 (it can be taken therefore as representing the picture in the mid 1960s). Secondly, an allowance has been made of £750 for every man and £250 for every woman not covered by the estate duty returns (these amounts do not include the value of pension rights).* Thirdly, allowance has been made for certain types of property missing from the estate duty statistics: settled property (including discretionary trusts) and pensions. In the latter case, the adjustment for the value of *state* pension rights is a very approximate one and the assumptions on which it is based probably lead to their value being overstated, and hence the degree of inequality understated (since state pensions are much more equally distributed than other property). Two estimates are given, therefore, in Table 3 of the overall distribution of wealth: the first excluding, and the second including, the value of state pension rights.

The results of Table 3 show that, with these corrections for some of the major deficiencies of the estate duty approach, the degree of inequality remains very substantial. If the value of state pension rights is not included, the top 1% own 29% of total personal wealth and the top 5% own more than half. When state pension rights are included, the distribution is more equal, but the top 5%

*It seems unlikely that the average wealth of those not appearing in the estate duty statistics would exceed £1,000. For a person not to appear means either that no property was left (or that he died in debt) or that the assets were of a kind where small amounts could be transferred without probate (principally National Savings and deposits in building and friendly societies). It was estimated by H. F. Lydall and D. G. Tipping that in 1954 the average wealth of those excluded from the Estate Duty statistics was under £300.

still own over 40% of total personal wealth. These figures are still subject to considerable error, but there are two reasons for expecting them to err in the direction of *understating* the degree of concentration. Firstly, no correction has been made to the figures given in Table 3 for the undervaluation of company shares, which

Table 3: Adjusted Estimates of the Distribution of Wealth 1963–7

Percentage of population over age 25	Share of total personal wealth%*	
	Excluding state pensions	Including state pensions
1%	29	22
5%	54	41
10%	67	52

*Of those aged over 25.

Source: see Notes on Sources.

are in large part held by the very rich. Secondly, as noted above, the value of state pension rights is probably overstated. On this basis, it seems safe to conclude that the conventional wisdom that the top 1% own at least a quarter, and the top 5% at least a half of total personal wealth, is not too wide of the mark.

Investment Income Approach

The estate duty method has been the most popular in recent years, but an alternative approach was used by early workers in this field, notably by Sir Robert Giffen in the latter part of the nineteenth century. This takes as its starting point the statistics for investment income, and works back from these to the capital from which the income must have been derived: the estimates are obtained not from the recorded wealth of the dead but from the recorded investment income of the living.

The essence of this approach is to use a 'yield multiplier' to convert the distribution of investment income to a distribution of wealth. If, for example, the yield is thought to be 5%, then the multiplier would be $\frac{1}{\cdot 05} = 20$ – it would be assumed that an investment income of £5,000 corresponded to wealth of £100,000. The crucial factor in this calculation is the yield multiplier, and just as with the mortality multiplier of the previous section, the final estimates are very sensitive to its choice. The investment income corresponding to a given level of wealth will depend on the type of asset held, and the normal procedure is to calculate a weighted average yield based on the composition of wealth indicated by the estate duty statistics. The method is further refined by allowing for variation in the composition of assets with the size of the wealth-holding: e.g. cash and bank deposits tend to be held more by those with low wealth and company shares more by those at the upper end of the distribution. The yield multiplier will therefore vary with the level of wealth. The following figures (which relate broadly to 1963) may help illustrate the method of estimation. — According to the estate duty statistics, estates of over £500,000 were made up as follows:

Company shares (yield 4·6%)	60%
Government securities (yield 5%)	10%
Land and buildings (yield 2·5%)	12%
Cash, etc. (no yield)	8%
Other (yield 4%)	10%

This gives an average yield of 4% for the estate as a whole, so that an investment income of £24,000 would be expected to correspond to wealth of £600,000.

This method was used by *The Economist* a few years ago to estimate the degree of inequality in wealth-holding from the investment income data for 1959–60. Their results showed a significantly greater degree of concentration than that exhibited by the corresponding estate duty estimates. The share of the top 5% was estimated by *The Economist* to be 72% of total personal wealth, and the share of the top 10% to be as high as 91%.

The distribution of wealth obtained using this method differs from that derived from the estate duty statistics in that it relates to *income units* as defined for tax purposes rather than to *individuals*. Under income tax and surtax the income of a married couple is aggregated, so that the investment income approach is closer to a family basis than in the case of the estate duty method (where husbands and wives appear separately). There are in fact good reasons for taking the family as the basic unit for analysis. The wife and children of a wealth-holder share many of the benefits of his wealth and, as was argued by G. W. Daniels and H. Campion, 'it would obviously be misleading to place the wives and children of persons with £50,000 in the same category as paupers'. If it is the case that property tends to be vested in one of the partners in a marriage, the estate duty estimates of wealth-holding will tend to exaggerate the degree of inequality among families. In an extreme case where men owned all the property, the estate duty statistics might show the top 5% of the adult population as owning 50% of all wealth, but these would make up some 10% of all families, so that in terms of families the degree of concentration would be less. The fact that the investment income returns show a *higher* degree of concentration suggests, however, that this tendency is out-weighed by the other deficiencies of the estimates.

Use of the investment income approach allows us to examine further the wealth of those at the very top of the scale on the basis of the statistics showing the amounts received under the 'special charge' on investment incomes imposed in the 1968 Budget. The figures for the top investment incomes in 1967–8 are shown in Table 4. At the very top there were 92 people with reported investment incomes of an average £196,000 each. Assuming a return of 5% (N.B. this relates only to income subject to income tax and does not include capital gains), this would imply wealth-holdings of nearly £4 million; and a return of $7\frac{1}{2}\%$ would still imply wealth of over £2½ million.

Table 4: Top Investment Incomes 1967–8

(Chargeable) investment income range	Numbers in that range	Average investment income (£)	Average wealth (£ million) assuming yield of:	
			5%	$7\frac{1}{2}\%$
£ 40,000 –	238	44,700	0·9	0·6
50,000 –	224	60,000	1·2	0·8
75,000 –	78	88,000	1·8	1·2
100,000 –	92	196,000	3·9	2·6

Source: calculated from Inland Revenue (1970), Table 43.

The Distribution of Wealth in Perspective

The available evidence suggests that wealth in Britain is at present shared very unequally. According to the estimates derived from the estate duty statistics, the top 1% of wealth-holders own over a quarter, and the top 5% over a half of total personal wealth; and if the estimates based on the investment income returns are to be believed, the degree of inequality may be even greater. Presented in this way the significance of these statistics may, however, be rather difficult to grasp, and we need to try to put them in perspective.

Let us begin with the bottom 90%. Although they constitute a large majority of the population, they own less than a half of total personal wealth and possibly as little as a third. Moreover, even this is quite unequally shared. Those in this group range from the bankrupt to the married couple worth some £12,000 or more, who are likely to have considerable savings in addition to owning their house and their pension rights. Most people come somewhere in between. Where exactly they come depends particularly on two factors: whether they own their house, and whether they have rights to an occupational pension. Both of these become more important as they get older – as the mortgage is paid off and as they approach retirement. At present about half the householders in the country are owner-occupiers; and about two thirds of men are covered by occupational pension schemes (although there are wide disparities in the value of the rights).

Turning to the top 10%, it can be clearly seen that they are all much better off than the average person. However, it would be quite wrong to regard them as a homogeneous group. Indeed the disparities between people in the top 10% are as wide as those in the whole bottom 90%. The couple worth £12,000 who are just at the dividing line are comfortably off, but their wealth is less than 1/200th of that of those people at the top of the wealth distribution. This is not to deny the importance of their wealth – since in total they account for a sizeable fraction – but it would be fallacious to regard the top 10% as consisting of millionaires only. In a world where most people own very little a man worth £15,000 appears a long way up in distribution.

When we come to the very top of the wealth distribution, we have seen that there are probably 92 people worth at least £2½ million. In some cases they must be worth very considerably more: the reported wealth of the industrialist Lord Cowdray is some £100 million, and that of the property developer Mr H. Hyams is estimated at £27 million. The significance of these sums may be hard to realize, but it helps to remember that it would take the average worker about 2,000 years to earn £2½ million. A more graphic way of putting this in perspective is suggested by the example of Robert Cecil, who as the Treasurer of James I was ordered to give a large sum of money to the King's favourite, Viscount Rochester. Cecil, who thought that the sum was too large to give away lightly, had it laid in silver on tables in the gallery of Salisbury House when the King was coming to dinner. The King was struck with the appearance of such a large quantity of silver and asked what the money was for. On discovering, he immediately reduced the amount that was to be paid to less than half, not having previously appreciated the 'value' of the gift. If the same experiment were conducted with 50 new penny pieces, stacking them 3 inches high on tables 2 ft 6 ins. wide, we should need a table a quarter of a mile long to set out the average wealth of one of the top 92 wealth-holders. Lord Cowdray's table would stretch for some ten miles!

The extreme degree of inequality in the distribution of wealth can be seen clearly from a comparison with the distribution of income. As is well known, incomes are far from being equally distributed and the existence of inequality in before-tax incomes is the chief justification for our system of progressive income taxation. Yet the distribution of wealth is very much *more unequal* than the distribution of before-tax incomes. In 1967, the share of the top 1% of income receivers in the total income was 8% – very much less than the share of the top 1% in total wealth. The same picture emerges from a comparison of the distance between those at the top of the earnings scale and the average man. The top 92 managing directors in Britain today probably earn an average of around £60,000, which is some 40 times the earnings of an average worker; but the top 92 wealth-holders own over 1,000 times the wealth of the average man. The difference between the top wealth-holders and the average person (let alone those whose wealth is below the average) is much greater than in the case of earnings. The magnitude of the gap is in fact quite staggering.

Comparison with the Distribution of Wealth in Other Countries

It is interesting to compare the degree of concentration of wealth-holding in Britain with that in other advanced countries – in particular the United States. One might well expect that the United States, with the vast fortunes of the Carnegies, Rockefellers and others, would exhibit at least as much inequality as Britain.

Such comparisons are in general very difficult to make, since the statistics in different countries are usually collected on quite different bases. However, an attempt has been made to compare the distribution of wealth in Britain with that in the United States by H. F. Lydall and J. B. Lansing, using information from sample surveys of wealth-holding.* Although the results are rather out of date (relating to 1953–4), they are nonetheless of interest. The principal findings are presented in Figure 1 in the form of 'Lorenz' curves showing the proportion of total net worth owned by the bottom x% of households (the corresponding curves for the distribution of income are also included). These indicate firstly (as we have seen earlier) that wealth is very much more unequally distributed than income. Secondly, while there is little difference in the *income* distributions between the two countries, the distribution of *wealth* is significantly more unequal in Britain. This very surprising conclusion must be treated with caution in view of the substantial errors to which the estimates are subject (some of the deficiencies of the Oxford savings survey results were described on page 9). However, the authors are probably right in concluding that 'the differences between the net-worth curves shown here are so large that it is impossible to believe that they do not reflect a real underlying difference between the two countries'. This conclusion is further supported by the independent estimates of R. Lampmann for the distribution of wealth in the United States in 1954 which showed that the share of the top 1% was 24%, whereas

*In the case of Britain this was the Oxford savings survey referred to on page 9.

a comparable figure for Britain was over 40%. He concluded that 'inequality of wealth distribution is considerably greater in Great Britain than in the United States.'

A comparison of the distribution of wealth in Britain with that in the United States suggests, therefore, that wealth is considerably more unequally distributed in Britain. Moreover, comparisons

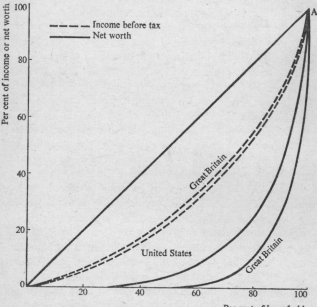

Figure 1: The Distribution of Wealth and Income in Britain and the United States 1953–4

Note: These curves show the proportion of total wealth (or income) owned by the bottom 20%, 40%, 60%, etc., of households. If there were complete equality, the curves would follow the straight line OA: the bottom 20% would own exactly 20% of the total wealth, and so on. The further away from the line OA the curve is, the more unequal is the distribution of wealth.

Source: Lydall and Lansing (1959), Chart 1.

with such countries as West Germany, Denmark and New Zealand show a similar picture. It seems quite possible that, as far as the distribution of wealth is concerned, Britain has the doubtful distinction of leading the international inequality league.

Changes in the Distribution of Wealth over Time

We have seen that there is a very high degree of concentration of wealth-holding in Britain today. Is this the outcome of a long-run trend towards greater inequality, or was wealth even more unequally distributed at the beginning of this century? Since this is one of the rare fields where information is available over a long period of years, this appears to be a relatively straightforward question to answer. However, in interpreting the results it is important to bear in mind the major social, economic and demographic changes that have taken place over the course of the century.

Table 5 summarizes the various estimates that have been made of the degree of inequality at different dates, beginning with 1911–13 (the earliest available). At first sight, these figures suggest that there has been a marked lessening in the degree of concentration since 1911. The share of the top 1% fell from nearly 70% to about

Table 5: Changes in the Distribution of Wealth 1911–13 to 1960

Year	Proportion of total wealth owned by top:		
	1%	5%	10%
1911–13	69	87	92
1924–30	62	84	91
1936–8	56	79	88
1954	43	71	79
1960	42	75	83

Note: For consistency, these figures are all obtained using the same method; they are based on the estate duty returns, relate to the population over the age of 25 in England and Wales, and are derived using mortality multipliers for the general population. As a result, the estimates for 1960 differ from those of the Inland Revenue, which use mortality multipliers adjusted for social class (and are therefore likely to be more accurate).

Source: Revell (1965), Table 6.

40% in 1960. More careful examination of these figures shows that the redistribution taking place has been of a rather special sort. Although the share of the top 1% fell markedly, that of the next 4% actually *increased* from 18% to 33%:

| | Share in total wealth | |
	1911–13	1960
Top 1%	69%	42%
Next 4%	18%	33%
Top 5%	87%	75%

This means that although the share of the top 1% fell, the gainers were those just below them in the wealth scale: of the 27% of total wealth they 'lost', only 9% went to the bottom 90%. It seems therefore that what redistribution there has been is not between the rich and the poor, but between the very rich and the rich.

These changes in the distribution of wealth can be interpreted in a number of ways. The popular interpretation would be that they reflect the equalizing effect of estate duty, which has been in force throughout the period with increasingly high rates. The large amounts of tax paid once per generation must, it is felt, have had a major effect on the distribution of wealth. This view overlooks, however, the opportunities for avoiding estate duty, which mean that the effective rate of duty may be very much lower than appears. As we shall see in chapter 7, the exemption from duty of gifts made more than seven years before death, the special treatment of property such as agricultural land or growing timber and the provisions for discretionary trusts and other settlements mean that the rich can (with good advice) maintain their wealth substantially intact for a number of generations.

The high nominal rates of duty cannot therefore be taken as demonstrating that estate duty must have led to a reduction in inequality; we have to look at how much is actually paid. On this basis an approximate indication of the effectiveness of estate duty can be obtained as follows. Over the period 1910–60, estate duty receipts averaged about 0·4% of total personal wealth each year. If we suppose that this was all paid by the top 1%, and that the revenue was used to reduce the National Debt, then over fifty years the share of the top 1% would have fallen on this account from 69% to 61%.* (This calculation is only rough and involves assumptions about what would have happened in the absence of estate duty – these questions are considered at greater length in chapter 7.) These figures suggest that it is unlikely that estate duty could have been responsible for the marked decline in the share of the top 1% – the annual revenue has been too small as a percentage of total wealth for it to have had a major impact.

Moreover, the straightforward estate duty interpretation does not explain why the share of the next 4% *increased*. It is, however, possible that this phenomenon can be attributed to the *indirect* effect of estate duty working through measures taken to avoid duty. One of the principal methods of avoidance has been that of passing on wealth before death in the form of gifts to one's heirs. A simple example illustrates the effect this would have on the distribution of wealth. Assume that Mr Smith Senior used to retain ownership of the family fortune until he died, when it passed to his son, Smith Junior. During his life Smith Senior appeared in the top 1% of wealth-holders, and his son, who had received legacies from other relatives, had sufficient wealth to appear in the next 4%. Suppose that with the increase in estate duty rates, Smith Senior decided at the age of 55 to make over part of his fortune to his son. His wealth would fall (although it is assumed that he would remain in the top 1%) and that of his son would rise (so that the share of the next 4% would increase). This is exactly what has been observed. Further evidence for this interpretation is provided by the fact that among male wealth-holders the share of younger age groups has increased. Whereas the average man of 65 plus used to own more than six times as much as the average man under 45, he now owns only three times as much. This again points to the conclusion that the redistribution of wealth over this century has not been between the rich and the poor, but between successive generations of the same family.

A further social and demographic consideration is the increased importance of wealth-holding by women. Between 1927 and 1960

*The total paid in Estate Duty would be 50 × 0·4%. The share of the top 1% would fall to $\frac{69\% - 20\%}{100\% - 20\%} = 61\%$.

the share of total wealth owned by women rose from 33 % to 42 %. This may in part simply reflect the increased longevity of women relative to men, but it may also be attributable to an increased tendency for husbands to leave part of their property to their wives, rather than passing it directly to the children. Moreover, since the estates of husbands and wives are not aggregated for estate duty purposes, there is clearly a strong inducement for the property to be shared more equally while both partners are alive. Many couples, for example, have the title of their house registered jointly. This tendency for wives to have a more equal share of wealth has the same effect as increased gifts *inter vivos* of splitting up wealth within a family, and hence creating the impression of greater equality without there being any genuine change in the position of the family as a whole.

The evidence regarding changes in the distribution of wealth may be summarized by saying that they suggest some decline in inequality, but that there are reasons for believing that this reflects in part the rearrangement of wealth *within* families rather than re-distribution *between* rich and poor families. Although transfers from older to younger members of rich families may represent some diminution of inequality, this is not what most people have in mind when they refer to redistribution and it makes no difference to the amount of inherited wealth passed from generation to generation.

2. The Advantages of Wealth

Wealth is not without its advantages and the case to the contrary,
although it has often been made, has never proved widely persuasive. –
J. K. Galbraith

We have seen in chapter 1 that a large fraction of total personal
wealth in Britain is concentrated in the hands of a few wealth-
holders, but we have not yet considered the implications of this
extreme degree of concentration. Just what difference does it make
that the top 5% own over half the wealth in Britain? What benefits do they derive from their wealth, and what economic power
does it convey? The answers to these questions will depend on the
rights associated with property and the form in which wealth is
held. To begin with, therefore, we need to consider the meaning
of 'ownership' and the different dimensions of property – particularly the income which it provides and the control which the
owner can exercise over its use.

The Concept of Ownership

The essence of ownership in our society is the possession of a
legally enforceable title. When in chapter 1 we considered a hypothetical person making an inventory of his wealth, he was assumed
to include all those items to which he had a legal claim. In the case
of financial assets, this legal claim is clearly of central importance.
A claim against a bank or a company is valueless if it is not enforceable, and without the backing of the legal code such assets could
not exist. The legal code determines such matters as the means by
which a claim may be enforced* and the classes of assets over
which claims can be established. Our legal code does not, for
example, recognize a claim to the ownership of another person:

*In some cases these may be rather bizarre: it is said, for instance, that a
bee-keeper can lay claim to a swarm so long as he keeps it within sight.

one cannot even sell oneself voluntarily into slavery. (This is one important feature distinguishing 'human' from 'non-human' capital: a person who has invested in his education cannot later sell out his stake, and it is in general very difficult to borrow on the strength of future earnings.) Similarly a person cannot establish claims to the atmosphere or to the sea.

The dependence of the concept of ownership on the legal code is of great importance, since the legal code in turn reflects the values of society, and is modified as these values change. The nature of property rights and the way in which they may be exercised is not absolute, and may be expected to vary between countries and to change over time.

The dependence of property rights on social values is well brought out by John Stuart Mill in the following passage:

The laws and conditions of the production of wealth partake of the character of physical truths . . . It is not so with the Distribution of Wealth. That is a matter of human institution solely. The things once there, mankind, individually or collectively, can do with them as they like. They can place them at the disposal of whomsoever they please, and on whatever terms. Further in the social state, in every state except total solitude, any disposal whatever of them can only take place by the general consent of society. Even what a person has produced by his individual toil, unaided by any one, he cannot keep, unless it is the will of society that he should. . . . The distribution of wealth, therefore, depends on the laws and customs of society. The rules by which it is determined are what the opinions and feelings of the community make them, and are very different in different ages and countries; and might be still more different if mankind so chose. [1891, pp. 143–4]

In considering the implications of inequality in property ownership, we must, therefore, bear in mind that the associated rights are not absolute, and could be changed if society chose to do so.

The concept of ownership comprises a number of different elements. As was pointed out by R. H. Tawney, property:

covers a multitude of rights which have nothing in common except that they are exercised by persons and enforced by the State. Apart from these formal characteristics, they vary indefinitely in economic character, social effect, and in moral justification. They may be conditional like the grant of patent rights, or absolute like the ownership of ground rents, terminable like copyright, or permanent like freehold, as comprehensive as sovereignty or as restricted as easement, as intimate or personal as the ownership of clothes and books or as remote and intangible as shares in a gold mine or rubber plantation. [1921, chapter 10]

In considering the ownership of property in Britain, however, it is sufficient for our purposes to distinguish three main dimensions of ownership: the right to income, the right of control, and the right to convey property.

The first dimension represents the return that a person derives from holding an asset, which consists primarily of the money income which the owner receives from it. Thus a man with £50 in the National Savings Bank receives an income of £1·75 a year; a man with £1,000 in company shares receives dividends; a man with an occupational pension has the right to receive a certain income when he retires. In some cases there may be no income, and in others there may only be the right to be considered for income (as with discretionary trusts). The income may be certain or it may be contingent (for example, on the firm in which a person has shares making a profit or on ERNIE choosing his number). The extent to which different assets yield income of different types is discussed further below. A broad interpretation of the notion of the return on wealth must allow for two further elements: security and freedom of manoeuvre. In addition to the money income which a person's wealth yields, he may also derive security from the knowledge that unforeseen expenditure can be met from his capital. If he should lose his job, he would be able to maintain his present standard of living by drawing down his wealth. Many of the risks which were important in the past, such as sickness or unemployment, are now covered at least in part by state social security or other benefits, but there are still enough contingencies for security to remain an important consideration. Secondly, wealth may be of importance in allowing freedom of action. Given our present institutional arrangements, it is often hard for people to borrow and this may be a severe constraint on their activities. Suppose, for example, that a man decided at the age of 35 that he wanted to go back to full-time education to train for a different job, and he was not eligible for a state grant. If he could borrow to support his family while he was training, he might well be able to pay it back later out of his increased earnings. However, in many cases he would find it very difficult to borrow, since it is not in general possible to mortgage future earnings. A person with wealth, on the other hand, would be able to lend it to himself by supporting himself out of capital. The process of wealth may therefore allow people to take advantage of opportunities which other people are prevented from using because they cannot borrow; wealth allows freedom of manoeuvre in the face of imperfect capital markets.

The second dimension of property rights concerns the *control* that ownership conveys. This may be interpreted in a number of ways. Narrowly, it can be seen in terms of the right to the withdrawal of capital. A man investing in a bank, a building society or the National Savings Bank can withdraw his capital (at some specified notice). A shareholder in a publicly quoted company can also withdraw his investment, although on rather different terms, since the selling price is not guaranteed and depends on the price he can get on the stock exchange. In the case of unquoted companies, withdrawal may be much less easy in that it may be difficult to locate a buyer. Finally, with certain assets the owner may not have any power to withdraw his capital. This is the case with the rights to an occupational pension, where the expected stream of income has a value, but it cannot be transferred and the individual cannot withdraw it (except by leaving the scheme). However, the power of withdrawal is only one aspect of control, and we are also concerned with the extent to which ownership of an asset allows the owner to influence the use to which it is put. With most financial assets there is no control over the use of the funds. The man with money in the bank has no say in whether it is lent to ABC Manufacturing to build a new plant or to Mr X to buy a yacht. The person with a life insurance policy has no control over whether his money is held in government securities or whether it is lent to property companies to buy office blocks. There are in fact only two main classes of assets which convey any significant degree of control – real assets and shares in companies. The control exercised by the owner of real assets is quite clear: the owner-occupier decides who lives in his house, the man with his own business can plan its production policy, and so on. The position of the shareholder is more complex. The shareholders in a company have the right to elect the directors and in this sense they have a power of vote over the firm's policy. However, many consider that the fragmentation of shareholdings and the development of a class of professional managers has led to a weakening of shareholders' influence, so that they now only exercise a minimal degree of control. This issue is discussed later in this chapter.

The third dimension of property rights concerns the right to *convey property*. The existence of a legal claim to the income from an asset does not imply that a person has the right to transfer that claim to someone else. For example, a person may enjoy the income from a trust for life, but be unable to control its disposition after his death. More generally, the existence of socially recognized rights to the income from property, and to control over its use, does not by itself imply the acceptance of the legitimacy of the right to convey property. It would be possible for a society to allow people to enjoy the income from property while alive without allowing them the right to dispose of this property. The transmission of wealth is essentially a social phenomenon, and the extent and direction of transfers depend heavily on the laws and customs of the society with which we are concerned. In the case of inheritance, the fulfilment of the testator's wishes depends on the existence of procedures for establishing the legitimacy of claims which are closely regulated under most legal codes. Moreover, the testator is undoubtedly influenced by the social customs regarding the division of his estate – whether, for example, primogeniture is customarily practised. For this reason, we need to explore the influence of legal provisions and social customs on the pattern of wealth transmission.

The three dimensions of property described above – the right to income, control over the use of capital and the right to convey property – are all central to understanding the implications of inequality. The remainder of this chapter explores in more detail the consequences of the first two aspects (the conveyance of property forms the subject of chapter 4). Before doing so, however, it may be useful to examine the composition of the wealth held by the very rich, since the importance of the different aspects of ownership depends crucially on the type of asset held.

Portfolios of the Rich

In the previous chapter, I discussed the differences in total wealth between those at the top of the wealth distribution and the average man, but did not consider the differences in the form in which wealth is held. This affects not only the income which is derived, but also the extent to which wealth gives rise to economic power.

Information about the portfolios of the wealthy can be derived from the estate duty returns in the same way as the estimates of the distribution of wealth. Some of the results obtained by J. R. S. Revell from this source for the years 1957–9 are reproduced in Table 6. (The composition of wealth changes with age, so that the

Table 6: Wealth and the Composition of Portfolios 1957–9

	Range of wealth (£)			
Percentage of wealth in form of:	3,000 –	10,000 –	50,000 –	250,000 –
Cash and bank deposits	20	13	9	8
Building society deposits	10	10	6	1
Insurance policies	10	7	3	5
British government securities	9	7	9	4
Company securities	3	24	44	38
Land and buildings	34	20	13	22

Source: Revell (1962), Table II.

figures given relate only to one age group: men aged 55–64 in 1957–9.) The most striking difference was in the proportion of wealth held in company securities (quoted and unquoted). Over a third of the wealth of the man owning £250,000 or more was in this form, whereas the man with £3,000 (which would then have represented about double the average wealth) held only 3% in company shares. The wealth of those in the bottom 90% was much more likely to be in the form of cash, bank deposits, building society deposits, and an owner-occupied house. Further evidence of the differential pattern of asset-holding is provided by a 1968 survey of investors in Britain, carried out for the Association of Building Societies. This showed that whereas manual workers (and pensioners) made up 69% of the population, they accounted (in number) for only 15% of all shareholders and 30% of unit trust holders. In contrast to this, they held 64% of National Savings Bank accounts and 74% of trustee savings bank accounts. H. G. Wells's statement at the turn of the century that 'the waiter one tips probably has a hundred or so in some remote company' seems a long way wide of the truth – even today.

The tendency of the very wealthy to hold their wealth in a quite different form from those at the bottom means that the distribution of holdings of particular assets is even more unequal than the distribution of wealth as a whole. This is brought out by the figures in Table 7, which is based on a study by H. F. Lydall and D. G. Tipping. Cash, bank deposits and land are held more equally than wealth as a whole; government securities show about the same degree of inequality as the overall distribution; but company shares are much more unequally distributed. The inequality in the case of shares is really remarkable – the top 1% appear to own four fifths, and the top 5% nearly all the company shares which are owned directly by the personal sector.

Table 7: Concentration of Ownership of Different Assets 1954

	Percentage owned by top:		
	1%	5%	10%
Cash and bank deposits	23	48	64
Government securities	42	71	83
Land, buildings and trade assets	28	58	74
Company stocks and shares	81	96	98
Total personal wealth	43	68	79

Source: Lydall and Tipping (1961), Table V.

Income from Wealth

It might well be thought that there can be little ambiguity about what we mean by the 'income' from wealth, but there is in fact a long history of controversy over this question. At a theoretical level, the debate has largely been resolved (economists being for once more or less agreed) in favour of the definition of income as the net accretion of real purchasing power over the course of the year (or whatever period is chosen). In other words, income represents the amount that a person could have spent over the year while leaving the real value of his wealth intact. This definition was adopted by the Minority Report of the Royal Commission on the Taxation of Profits and Incomes in 1955, which stated that: 'We know of no alternative definition that is capable of satisfying society's prevailing sense of fairness and equity.' (Para. 5.)

The chief feature that distinguishes this 'ideal' definition from the practice of the British income tax system is its comprehensiveness. Any receipt that represents increased purchasing power should in theory be included, whereas under the income tax there are a number of important classes of receipt that are not treated as income. Two in particular are of great importance: capital gains and the services individuals derive from physical assets in their possession (especially owner-occupied houses). A capital gain, or an increase in the value of an asset, means that a person can spend more while leaving the value of his wealth unaffected (abstracting for the moment from the consequences of inflation). If his holding of Marks and Spencer shares increases in value from £500 to £600 between 1 January and 31 December he can spend £100 more during that year without reducing the value of his wealth. This capital gain (even if not realized) should be regarded as part of his income in the same way as dividends or interest (and, conversely, capital losses should be subtracted from his income). The presence of inflation complicates matters, since part of the capital gain will then simply reflect the general rise in prices. Suppose prices increase by 10% during the year. For the holding of Marks and Spencer shares to represent the same purchasing power it would have to increase to £550; so that the *real* capital gain made is only £600 − £550 = £50. Recognition of the role of inflation brings out the fact that capital gains and losses are not simply associated with assets such as shares or real capital. If a person puts his money in the bank at an interest of 6%, and prices rise by 8% over the year, he will make a real capital loss of 8%; with the result that his net real income will be 6% − 8% = −2%. In real terms he is paying the bank to look after his money for him! The second important element of income excluded from income tax is the real return received by owner-occupiers. Owning a house does not provide a cash income, but in that it saves the owner from paying rent it has the same effect (a return should be 'imputed'). He is in essence letting the house to himself, and this provides an income just as much as if he let it to someone else and received a cash rent.

With these considerations in mind, we may examine the income associated with the principal types of asset held in personal portfolios:

Cash and Bank Current Accounts yield no money return, although a benefit is presumably derived from the ability to use these assets for transactions (and bank charges may be saved). The value of these assets is fixed in money terms, so that there will be a real capital loss equal to the rate of inflation.

Deposits in Building Societies, Trustee Savings Banks, Bank Deposit Accounts and the National Savings Bank yield a money return, but again their capital value is fixed in money terms, so that inflation causes a real capital loss. In April 1971 building society rates of interest (net of income tax) were some 5%, which with inflation at a rate of 8% represented a negative real return of -3%.

Government Stocks, unlike the previous two categories, do not have a guaranteed encashment value except at maturity, so that allowance must be made for the changes in money capital value. For stocks with no redemption date such as War Loan, these changes have been considerable (and notoriously in one direction). The rates of interest on government securities are currently high by historical standards (around $9\frac{1}{2}\%$), although the real after-tax return may well be negative.

Pension Rights are rather different from the assets listed above, since they provide no money income at all before retirement. The return on pension rights is in the form of a pension paid during retirement, and possibly a lump-sum payment on retirement (or on death while in employment). In view of the widely differing terms of occupational pension schemes, no general statement can be made about the level of the return. Similarly, the extent to which the return is protected against inflation (a factor of great importance with such a long-term contract) depends on the formula by which pensions are determined. If the pension entitlement is fixed in cash terms (e.g. £10 a year pension for each year of service) there is no protection against rising prices. On the other hand, those based on a fraction of salary at the date of retirement will keep up with increasing money incomes until retirement (although there are not necessarily provisions to protect it afterwards).

Land, Buildings and Other Real Assets can mean anything from an owner-occupied house to the holdings of a property millionaire. The former generates no money income, but, as we have seen, provides an imputed return in that the owner-occupier does not have to pay rent (the same is also true of consumer durables). Moreover, the price of houses has been rising steadily for many years. Between 1961 and 1969 the average price of new houses rose by about 70% and, although part of this reflected improvements in quality, the capital gains on existing houses were probably of much the same order. The return provided by an owner-occupied house is further increased by the concessions allowed under the present tax treatment of income from this source. Although the imputed rent used to be taxed under Schedule A of the income tax (a feature of our tax system that was frequently praised by foreign tax experts), this practice was abolished in 1963 and income from this source is now tax free. On a house which would fetch a market rent of £8 a week, this concession is worth some £3·10 a week to a standard rate taxpayer. Secondly, no capital gains tax is payable on owner-occupied houses. At the other extreme in scale from the owner-occupier is the millionaire with large holdings of office property or building land. He does not benefit from the tax concessions on imputed rent in the same way as the owner-occupier, but is likely to enjoy capital gains and these may be very much larger, as we shall see in the next chapter. Similarly, a high return can be made by successfully building up a business (in some cases borrowing money at negative real rates of interest) and then floating it as a public company, providing large capital gains on the holdings retained.

Company Shares convey a right to the profits of a company after the prior claims of debenture holders and creditors have been met. These profits may either be distributed as dividends or retained for further investment. The former clearly represents income to the shareholder; the latter may also do so if it gives rise to capital gains. At present (April 1971) the average dividend yield is around $4\frac{1}{2}\%$ (allowing for the standard rate of income tax), which means that the return to the holders of ordinary shares is similar to that obtained by investors in building societies. However, unlike building society deposits, shares may give rise to capital gains. These accrue irregularly. Between May 1967 and May 1968 the *Financial Times* Actuaries' Index of 500 Industrial shares rose from 111 to 160 (April 1962 = 100), but by May 1970 the index had fallen to around 125. Prediction of the capital gains (or losses) likely in the next few years is, therefore, extremely difficult.* The determinants of share prices are in many respects mysterious, with 'expectations' and 'confidence' playing an important role. All the same, while short-run movements may be heavily dominated by such factors, in the long run it seems reasonable to suppose that share prices must bear some relationship to the real profits of the company. If the average company is ploughing back a large proportion of its profits (as has been the case) and these retained profits are invested profitably, then its potential profits are increased, and this may be expected in the long run to lead to capital gains. Unless retained profits are invested unprofitably (and unless there is a permanent fall in the rate of profit on real capital) we may expect shareholders to receive eventually substantial capital gains in addition to the dividend. Certainly this has been true in the past: an index prepared by the firm of stockbrokers de Zoete and Bevan of the shares of thirty leading industrial companies over the period 1919–68 showed an average annual appreciation of $4\cdot7\%$ – or $2\cdot7\%$ in real terms.†

Discussion of company shares raises the question of the *riskiness* of income, which has not so far been considered. It is commonly held that assets with a fixed capital value represent a 'safe' investment, and the same is thought to be true of government securities;

---

*It may also be dangerous. In the introduction to *The Great Crash 1929*, J. K. Galbraith describes how his life was threatened by angry shareholders after he happened to discuss the manuscript of the book at a Senate hearing on the day that the stock market had one of the severest falls for years!

†It has also to be borne in mind that capital gains are taxed at a lower effective rate than other income. This subject is discussed in chapter 7.

whereas company shares are a 'risky' investment (not to be held by widows and orphans). It is certainly fair to say that company shares do involve a considerable risk of a short-term loss in capital value, just because the prediction of share prices is very difficult. Moreover, there is the long-term risk that the company may go bankrupt. Even the man who would never have contemplated buying shares in Rolls Razor might still have got into trouble with Rolls-Royce. However, it must be remembered that the presence of uncertainty about inflation may transform the relative riskiness *in real terms* of different assets. When the rate of inflation is unknown, money in the National Savings Bank has an uncertain capital value in terms of purchasing power, and the person who invests in traditionally 'safe' assets is in fact gambling on the rate of inflation. Moreover, there are reasons for expecting these assets to be more exposed to the risks of inflation than company shares. If wages rise and prices are increased by the same percentage, money profits also rise, so that real profits are maintained. This either permits the real dividend to be preserved or else generates (eventually) capital gains corresponding to the increase in money profits. (Where the company is borrowing money at a fixed interest rate, an acceleration in the rate of inflation may actually allow it to increase its real profits.)

The Distribution of Income from Wealth

The results of this discussion may be brought together in an examination of the distribution of income from wealth. For this purpose we can draw on the figures given by J. E. Meade for the distribution of income from wealth before tax in 1959:

Percentage of income tax units	Share of total income from wealth
Top 1%	60%
Top 5%	92%
Top 10%	99%

Source: Meade (1964), Table 1.

These figures suggest that the distribution of income from wealth is even more unequal than the distribution of wealth itself, with the top 1% receiving more than half the total investment income. This implies that the rich obtain on average a substantially higher return from their wealth than the poor. It can, however, be argued that the concentration of income shown by these figures is simply a statistical artefact, since the Inland Revenue information from which they were drawn omits a large part of the income accruing to the kind of asset that tends to be held by those with little wealth. We have seen that this is true of the imputed rent from owner-occupied houses, of the return from holding consumer durables and cash, and of the income accruing to pension funds (which belongs in theory to the employees but is not treated as part of their income). These considerations all mean that the real income accruing to small wealth-holdings is greater than indicated by the figures quoted. On the other hand the figures also exclude an important element of income accruing to the top wealth-holders – capital gains – and in quantitative terms these may be at least as significant. If allowance were made, therefore, for all the income excluded from the Inland Revenue figures, the higher return earned by the wealthy would quite possibly turn out to be a genuine phenomenon. It has certainly been true in the past that the return on the kind of financial asset held by small savers has been considerably lower than that on the company shares which form a large part of the portfolios of the rich.

The unequal distribution of wealth-holding, combined with the probably unequal returns on wealth, has major implications for the overall distribution of personal income. Suppose that the income from wealth were in fact equally distributed. On the basis of the average wealth figures given in the previous chapter (extrapolated forward to 1971) and of an assumed average return of 6% before tax, this would provide a married couple with an amount equivalent to over £9·00 a week. The effect of an equal distribution may be seen another way by drawing again on figures given by Meade – see Table 8. In 1959 the top 5% of income receivers collected 66% of the total property income,* and their share of

*The figure of 66% may appear to be inconsistent with that of 92% given on page 36. However, the latter refers to the top 5% with incomes *from wealth*, whereas the former relates to the top 5% with incomes *from all sources*. The top 5% shown in Table 8 will not be the same group of people – it will include some with very high earnings but little investment income.

total personal income was 26%. If investment incomes had been equally distributed, however, their share of total income would have fallen by almost a half to 14%, which would have been a quite marked movement towards greater equality.

Table 8: Inequality in Wealth and the Distribution of Income 1959

Top % of income receivers	Share of total investment income (%)	Share of total earnings (%)	Share of total incomes (%)*	Share of total incomes *if income from wealth equally distributed* (%)*
1	47	6	14	6
5	66	17	26	14
10	73	27	36	24

*These calculations are made on the assumption that the share of profits equals 20%.

Source: Meade (1964) Table 2, and my own calculations.

Wealth and the Control of Industry

A substantial part of the wealth of the very rich consists of company shares, and the top 5% of wealth-holders appear to account for virtually the entire total of personally held shares. In this section we explore briefly the extent to which this gives them control over the operation of British industry. Is it true, as some writers have suggested, that ownership and control are so separated in the modern corporation that the shareholder has no more influence than the man with money in the bank? How has this been affected by the growth of institutional shareholdings?

Where a company is controlled by one majority shareholder, there can be little doubt that he possesses considerable control over its activities. It has been argued, however, that in the typical modern corporation shareholdings are so fragmented that such control rests almost entirely in the hands of the managers (who often have no shares or only a small holding). I begin therefore by examining the evidence about the degree of concentration of shareholdings within firms. One of the best-known studies of this subject in Britain was that by S. Florence based on an investigation of large industrial and commercial companies in 1951. He found, as one would expect, that there were typically a large number of individual shareholders – the average being about 12,000. When he examined the distribution of holdings among individuals, he found that:

The salient characteristic disclosed by the facts of vote concentration among voters is the extreme inequality of holdings and votes in the typical large company . . . Twenty voteholders formed about one-sixth of 1% of all shareholders, and yet they held on average . . . about 30% of the votes. [Florence (1961), pp. 66–7]

This means that in general no single person had anything approaching majority control (the single largest shareholder held on average 12% of the votes), but the large number of individual holders may also have meant that it was possible to control the company with a relatively small holding. If there were only two shareholders, one would have needed 51% for control; but where there were a large number of small shareholders, it may have been possible to control a company with 30% or even 15% of the shares. (For instance, suppose that there were one block of 15% opposed to the major holder, but that the rest were small holders, who could not easily be organized and who were likely to vote at random. Then a holding of 25% would give control, since on average half the remaining 60% of small voters would support you.) In trying to determine what proportion of companies were in fact owner-controlled, Florence took, therefore, a number of indicators apart from the percentage of votes held (including the type of large shareholder and the holdings of directors). The conclusion he reached on this basis was that about one third of large companies in 1951 were probably owner-controlled.

This conclusion needs for at least two reasons to be interpreted with care. The coverage of Florence's study was limited to industrial and commercial companies and did not include such sectors as brewing, shipping or shipbuilding, which would probably have had a higher degree of owner control. It was limited to large companies, and smaller companies are more likely to be owner-controlled. In their survey of shareholdings in 1962–3, Revell and

Moyle (1966) commented that: 'in the smaller companies the degree of concentration is even greater: in three-quarters of these companies the twenty largest shareholders hold more than half the company's total market value.' It also excluded private companies, and although these tend to be small, there are a number of major private companies such as Sainsbury's and Ferranti, where the family retains control. Secondly, the findings are now 20 years out of date. Florence himself compared the situation in 1951 with that in 1936 and found that the proportion of owner-controlled firms was falling, and there are good reasons to expect that this trend has continued since then. However, a more recent study by M. B. Brown of the top 120 quoted companies (in terms of assets) showed that in 1966 30% were controlled by boards which either consisted almost entirely of members of the founding family (for instance, the Salmons and Glucksteins of J. Lyons) or were 'really only adjuncts to a dynamic tycoon like Wolfson or Clore'.

It appears that about two thirds of the major public companies in Britain are not owner-controlled in the sense that a single individual or family has a dominant shareholding. From this evidence it has been concluded that control over industry has to a considerable extent passed from shareholders to a class of professional managers. C. A. R. Crosland expressed the view in his *Future of Socialism* that 'The economic power of the capital market . . ., and hence *capitalist* financial control over industry . . . are much weaker. This change alone makes it rather absurd to speak now of a capitalist ruling class.' (1964.) In this view, capitalism has been replaced by managerial capitalism. To quote Joan Robinson (1966, p. 64):

In the main, industry and trade are now dominated by *managerial capitalism*, that is by companies nominally owned by a shifting population of shareholders and actually run by salaried staff . . . The return on shares from his [the shareholder's] point of view, is merely an alternative to interest on a loan, and his role in business is simply that of a *rentier*.

However, while the power of the capital market undoubtedly has weakened, it does not follow that shareholders as a body have no control over the policy of a company. The management of a company may enjoy considerable discretionary power, but it cannot act totally without regard to the interests of the shareholders. If it pursued a policy unacceptable to the owners, they could vote the management out and appoint new directors, although in view of the difficulties of organizing effective opposition this can only be expected to happen in rather extreme circumstances. It is more likely that where the shareholders are dissatisfied with the policy of the management they will sell their holdings, thus depressing the share price of the company. A depressed share price makes it difficult for the management to raise new finance, and is likely to invite a takeover bid. The existence of these constraints on the management of a company has been recognized by those taking the managerial view; and Joan Robinson, for example, qualifies her earlier statement by saying that:

The freedom of managers is, however, circumscribed by the legal fiction that the shareholders own the company. The group of rentiers who, at any particular moment, hold the company's shares regard them merely as an eligible placement for a fraction of their private wealth. They see no objection to selling their holdings to anyone who offers favourable terms. Thus when . . . the stock exchange value of a company falls below the potential profitability of its real assets, it is in danger of a *take-over bid* from another company or an individual tycoon who can buy up the business behind its own back, throw out the board of directors, prune the management . . . [1966, p. 67]

The modern firm may be characterized by managerial capitalism, but it is still *capitalism*, and there can be little doubt that the shareholders as a body are still able to impose constraints on the policy of a company. Moreover, the fragmentation of shareholdings, while reducing the power of the shareholders as a body, may allow the individual owning 5% or 10% of a company's shares to exercise considerable influence. This influence may be most obvious at the time of takeover bids, but it is latent at all times and the views of such shareholders no doubt weigh with the management when they are considering major changes in policy.

The issue of control has so far been discussed in terms of personal shareholdings, but it is also important to consider the role of institutional holdings (by insurance companies, pension funds, unit trusts, etc.). The extent of their holdings in 1957, 1963 and

1970, as indicated by the surveys carried out by the Department of Applied Economics, Cambridge, is shown in Table 9. In 1970 institutional holdings accounted for a third of quoted ordinary shares. This proportion represented a considerable increase over that in 1957, when it was less than one fifth. The insurance companies and pension funds are one of the largest sources of new capital, and in recent years their acquisition of ordinary shares has

Table 9: Owners of Quoted Ordinary Shares

	Percentage of market value		
	1957	1963	1970
Persons, executors and trustees	66	54	47
Insurance companies	9	10	12
Pension funds	3	6	9
Investment and unit trusts	6	9	12
Total institutional holders	18	25	33

Note: The other holders are principally non-financial companies and foreigners.

Source: see Note on Sources.

exceeded the total of new issues. In many cases institutional investors (individually or collectively) have a substantially larger investment in particular companies than the single most important shareholder, and they are in a position to influence its policy. The potential economic power which this conveys to the institutions has been criticized by a number of writers, including R. M. Titmuss, who has described the situation as follows: 'It is power concentrated in relatively few hands, working at the apex of a handful of giant bureaucracies, technically supported by a group of professional experts, and accountable, in practice, to virtually no one.' (Titmuss, 1963, p. 238.) Even those who have otherwise criticized Titmuss's views are agreed that this power is latent and that it has on occasion been exercised. For example, A. Seldon has written that:

It is common knowledge that some insurance companies own controlling interests in manufacturing and trading companies. The life offices' reply is that these exceptions are bound to be few, because to make the practice general would be to become involved in management, which would require staff and expertise they do not possess: the primary purpose, it is said, is investment, which dictates small holdings of shares in order to avoid involvement and to be able to abandon without major disturbance or publicity companies in whose managements confidence has been lost.

This position is feasible. Even so, it may be that holdings of only 10 per cent may occasionally require more than a passive role if the interests of the prospective pensioners are to be served. For while tacit control might be exercised by selling or indicating the intention to sell holdings, it may not always be easy to sell blocks of shares when the only likely buyers are other institutional investors. [Seldon, 1960, p. 19]

The growth of institutional shareholdings may mean that insurance companies and pension funds now possess some of the power that individual shareholders have lost, which is a rather different aspect of the separation of ownership and control. The holdings of the institutions are undoubtedly growing rapidly; whether the power they choose to exercise will increase correspondingly is yet to be seen. It is clear, however, that the control does not rest with the small savers whose wealth is invested in insurance policies and pension rights.

The Advantages of Wealth – Conclusions

In this chapter I have examined two principal dimensions of the ownership of wealth: the right to income, and the right to control over the use to which wealth is put. The importance of these depends on the way in which wealth is held, and for this reason the evidence about the portfolios of the rich is very significant. Not only do the top 1 % own a disproportionate share of total wealth, but also they hold it in a form which gives them a higher than average return and conveys a significant degree of control over industry. The small saver, typically holding his wealth in a bank or building society or in the form of life insurance, receives a low (and possibly negative) real return, and control over the use of the funds is in the hands of the financial institutions. The top 1 %, on the other hand, hold a large proportion of their wealth in real property and company shares (they account for four fifths of the personally-held company shares). In the past they have received substantial capital gains and have enjoyed protection against inflation. Moreover, despite the separation of ownership and control in the modern corporation, the wealthy shareholder may well be in a position to exercise considerable influence over a company's policy, and in a substantial number of cases the owners retain full control.

3. The Accumulation of Wealth

At the historical dawn of capitalist production – and every capitalist upstart has personally to go through this historical stage – avarice and desire to get rich are the ruling passions. But the progress of capitalist production not only creates a world of delights; it lays open in speculation and the credit system a thousand sources of sudden enrichment. – *K. Marx*

The present concentration of wealth in Britain is the product of a number of forces operating over a long period of years. In this chapter and the next I shall examine these processes and try to isolate those responsible for the extreme inequality that we observe. If it would take the average worker 2,000 years to earn £2½ million, how can people acquire such an amount? Why is it that there has been no marked decline in the degree of inequality?

Accumulated and Inherited Wealth

There are essentially two ways by which a person can acquire wealth. He may either accumulate it from his income or receive it in the form of gifts or bequests. In order to distinguish these two basic ways of becoming rich, I refer to the former as *accumulated wealth* and to the latter as *inherited wealth* (although some of it may not be strictly inherited: e.g. in the case of gifts *inter vivos*). This distinction plays an important role in the analysis that follows. It is not only central to the discussion of the processes underlying the distribution of wealth, but also of great importance in considering possible reforms. Before we can assess the desirability of a particular change we need to know whether inequality is primarily due to inherited or accumulated wealth: death duties, for example, are only relevant if inheritance is an important factor. Indeed, the means by which wealth is acquired may well affect attitudes towards inequality – 'first generation' wealth possibly being regarded more favourably than inherited wealth. A principal aim of the analysis is, therefore, to assess the relative importance of accumulated and inherited wealth in leading to concentration.

The spirit of the distinction between accumulated and inherited wealth should be quite clear: we are distinguishing between that part of his wealth a person would have owned if he had received no bequests or gifts, and that part which is not attributable to his own saving. However, the application of the distinction is less straightforward. Suppose that a person is now worth £25,000, and that he inherited £10,000 ten years ago. It would clearly not be correct to say that all the difference of £15,000 represented accumulated wealth. Without the inheritance, his income would have been smaller and he would probably have been unable to save as much. Moreover, the inheritance may have raised not only his income, but also the return which he could obtain from his own savings. It is commonly the case that entry into business is facilitated by a medium-sized bequest, giving a return to capital which is likely to be much higher than on institutional savings. In order to make some allowance for these factors, we could say that the man's inheritance would yield a return of 7%, and that if all the return were accumulated this inheritance would have doubled in value in ten years. On this basis his accumulated wealth would be £25,000 − £20,000 = £5,000, rather than £15,000. However, the assumptions about the return and the ploughing back of the interest would be arbitrary. Since we are trying to compare the actual position with a hypothetical one (where he received no inherited wealth), there is no precise way in which to draw the distinction between the two types of wealth.

If we had information about the amounts people had received in bequests and gifts, the difficulties described in the previous paragraph would be important in practice. However, we are 'rescued' from this problem by the fact that little such information exists. Instead we have to rely on more fragmentary sources of evidence. This evidence is of two main types. Firstly, in this chapter, I examine the factors underlying the accumulation of wealth – the motives for accumulation and the influence of the yield on wealth. In an attempt to see how far accumulated wealth could be responsible for the concentration of wealth, I explore what would happen in a hypothetical society with no transmission of wealth between generations through inheritance or gifts (so that everyone's wealth had its origins in accumulation). Under what circumstances (if any) could the accumulation of wealth by itself generate a degree of inequality similar to that observed in Britain? Could the observed concentration be explained in terms of self-made millionaires? Since there clearly is inherited wealth in Britain, this kind of 'mental experiment' may not seem very illuminating, but it provides a way of measuring the quantitative importance of accumulated wealth and allows us to reject certain explanations of the observed inequality. The second type of evidence, that relating directly to the transmission of wealth through inheritance, is considered in chapter 4.

The Accumulation of Wealth

In *The General Theory of Employment, Interest and Money*, Keynes discussed no fewer than eight different motives for saving, which he characterized as Precaution, Foresight, Calculation, Improvement, Independence, Enterprise, Pride and Avarice. These motives do not apply equally to all types of saver. It is those towards the beginning of the list, for example, that apply more to the small saver, with whom I begin here.

The meaning of the precautionary motive should be clear: it is simply a question of putting something away for a rainy day – the pound notes in the teapot. Most people try to acquire some saving which can be drawn on in emergencies (for example, illness of the breadwinner), so that by drawing on their savings they may be able to tide themselves over the fall in income. However, it seems unlikely that the amounts involved would be substantial or that this motive would be an important factor explaining the inequality in the distribution of wealth, since we should expect the holding of assets for precautionary purposes to be fairly evenly spread. For this reason, I do not discuss it further.

The motive of 'Foresight' is important in view of the fact that income does not necessarily coincide with a person's needs over his lifetime. An obvious illustration of this is that when a person retires he will cease earning, but will still need to provide for his consumption. As a result he will save while he is working so as to provide a pension during retirement. Alternatively, he may have greater needs when he marries or when he has young children, and hence people may 'save up to get married'. Under this approach, commonly referred to as 'life-cycle savings', the individual plans his saving so as to spread his consumption in some desired way over his lifetime: he saves or not according to some lifetime plan. In fact this planning is probably only carried out in some rough and ready way because of the high degree of uncertainty involved. The individual is not certain about his future needs (about how long he will live, the likelihood of his being ill, etc.), or about his future income (earnings, interest, and capital receipts such as inheritances and windfall gifts). However, despite this degree of uncertainty, life-cycle factors are undoubtedly of some importance in explaining individual savings behaviour.

Probably the most important aspect of life-cycle saving is that of saving for retirement. Now that people live longer, retire earlier, and are less likely to be supported by their children, saving for retirement (particularly in the form of contractual saving such as occupational and state pensions or endowment insurance) is an almost universal phenomenon. We may characterize the process roughly as follows. During his working life, a person saves for his old age. This process may be slower initially, when the man has family responsibilities, but when the children are leaving home he is able to put more aside (and is probably more aware of the need to do so). His wealth increases steadily until he retires; after that it is likely to fall as he draws down his savings. This kind of pattern is in fact exhibited by the evidence from savings surveys.* H. F. Lydall, for example, summarized the results of the Oxford savings surveys as follows:

Young men and women before marriage spend what they earn very freely, with little thought for the future. Immediately before and after marriage, however, they begin to set aside what surplus they can for building up a home. In the next twenty years or so they are usually pre-occupied with supporting their children, and their savings are not, on

*In interpreting the evidence from these surveys, it has to be remembered that incomes are rising, so that the wealth of people now aged 50 may not be a good indication of what people now aged 30 plan to have saved in twenty years' time.

balance, very great. After middle age, the number of dependants declines more rapidly than income, expenditure on durables also falls away, and people begin to put aside larger sums for their old age. After retirement they usually draw down their capital in order to supplement their shrunken income. [Lydall, 1955 (b)]

Wealth and Age

Insofar as the life-cycle theory provides a valid explanation of personal savings behaviour, we should expect to find that age was an important factor in explaining the distribution of wealth. Those at the point of retirement would have much greater wealth than those commencing their working career or those retired for a decade or more. This was pointed out clearly in an editorial in *The Times* on 28 September 1968:

Quite obviously in the most egalitarian of societies one would not expect the new-born babe and the man on the point of retirement to have identical savings, or even the fifty-year-old and the sixty-year-old, and there must therefore be a concentration of wealth in a minority of hands in any society one can conceive of.

The editorial goes on to argue that:

This effect is more marked than most people would suppose. If one calculates the probable pattern of savings in a hypothetical society with total equality of male incomes and total prohibition on inheritance, and if one assumes that the savings will belong to men as the main earners, then in that most egalitarian society over 80 per cent of the total private wealth would be in the hands of men over fifty who would comprise less than 15 per cent of the population. Where inheritance is not allowed, only the old can be rich.

It is not clear, however, that these factors are as quantitatively important as suggested. If one does as *The Times* proposed and calculates the 'probable pattern of savings in a hypothetical society with total equality of male incomes and total prohibition on inheritance', the results are rather different from those described by the editorial. This may be illustrated by a simple (if unrealistic) example. Suppose that a man starts to plan his lifetime consumption at the age of 25. He expects (confidently) that he will work until he is 65 earning an average of £1,500 a year. He will then retire, after which he expects (again confidently) to live until he is 75. If we suppose that he wants to spread his income evenly over his lifetime (leaving no bequests) and that the real rate of interest is zero, then he simply divides his total lifetime income – £60,000 – by the number of years in which he is going to consume it, arriving at an annual consumption of £1,200. If he adopts this plan, he consumes only 80% of his income while he is working, and so accumulates assets, on which he will then draw when he is retired – see Figure 2. If we suppose that the population consists of people just like him apart from their age, and that population and earnings are constant, then the distribution of wealth at any moment will have the same triangular pattern. In particular, if we look at the wealth of the richest 10% of the population over 25 we can see from Figure 2 that these are the people at the apex of the triangle – those aged 62–6. As *The Times* said, in this society 'only the old can be rich'. If we calculate the wealth of this group, it amounts to some 19% of the total personal wealth in this hypothetical society.*

This simple example leaves out a number of important features. No allowance is made for the desire to save to receive interest (Keynes's Calculation motive), for the wealth held by women, for expectations of increasing earnings, or for a preference for a rising rather than a constant standard of living (the Improvement motive). However, calculations which allow for these factors give rather similar results, suggesting that the share of the top 10% in such a hypothetical egalitarian society would be 25% of total wealth (rather than 19%), and that the share of the top 15% would be around 40% of the total.

*This figure is reached as follows: Wealth at the point of retirement is £12,000. The average wealth of those at work is £6,000 × 40N (where N is the number of people in each age group), the wealth of the retired population is similarly £6,000 × 10N, giving a *total* wealth of £300,000 × N. The wealth of those aged 62–6 is

$$
\begin{array}{r}
11,100 \\
11,400 \\
11,700 \\
12,000 \\
10,800 \\
\hline
57,000 \times N = 19\% \text{ of } 300,000 \times N
\end{array}
$$

These results differ from those reached by *The Times* editorial, which concluded that over 80% of total wealth would be in the hands of those over 50, who made up less than 15% of the population. There are two reasons for this difference. Firstly, *The Times* assumed that wealth belongs to men only, whereas in fact women own nearly 40% of all personal wealth (and this was allowed for in the figures quoted at the end of the previous paragraph). Secondly, *The Times* figure was based on the wealth of men over 50; and while they make up less than 15% of the population, they represent nearly a quarter of the total *adult* population, which is the base taken in most estimates of the degree of inequality (and which was the base for the figures given here). The conclusions reached by *The Times* are, therefore, misleading, and its suggestion that life-cycle differences can explain the observed inequality is a long way off the mark.

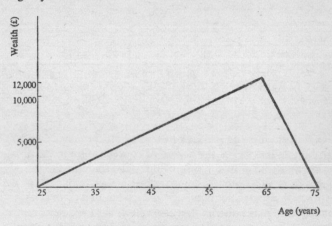

Figure 2: Wealth and Age – A Stylized Model

More direct evidence about the importance of life-cycle factors in explaining the observed inequality is provided by an examination of the distribution of wealth among people of the same age. If life-cycle considerations provided a major explanation, we should expect to find significantly less inequality among people of the same age than in the population as a whole: the inequality in the

latter would be attributable to differences in wealth between
people of different ages. Estimates of the distribution by age
groups can be obtained from the estate duty statistics in exactly
the same way as the overall distribution, and the results for the
period 1963–7 are summarized in Table 10 (no adjustments have

Table 10: Inequality by Age – Great Britain 1963–7

	Male			Female		
	Proportion of wealth in that class owned by top:					
Age	1%	5%	10%	1%	5%	10%
25–34	31	51	64	55	81	93
35–44	28	49	63	44	75	89
45–54	28	53	67	38	66	81
55–64	27	51	66	29	57	72
65–74	28	53	68	27	54	69
75–84	29	57	72	26	54	69
85–	30	60	75	28	57	72
Whole population*	32	58	73	32	58	73

*These figures are not adjusted for missing wealth, and therefore
differ from those given in Table 3. They relate to the population aged
over 25.

Source: Atkinson (1971), Table IV.

been made to these figures for pensions or other excluded wealth).
The bottom line shows the degree of concentration in the distribution as a whole. In the case of men, the share of the top 5%
ranges from 49% to 60%, compared with a share of 58% in the
distribution as a whole. In all age groups but one there is less inequality than in the distribution as a whole, but the differences are
slight. In the case of women, the share of the top 5% is actually
higher in three age groups than in the distribution as a whole, and
in no case is it more than 4% lower. If we were to take the shares
of the top 1% or top 10%, the result would be the same: inequality
among people of the same age is not markedly less than among the
population as a whole. These findings are not at all surprising,
but they confirm the view that we need to look elsewhere to explain
the observed inequality.

The Yield From Wealth

Of the motives for saving outlined by Keynes, three important ones remain – Enterprise, Avarice and Pride. The last, which he associated with the desire to bequeath a large fortune, is discussed in the next chapter. The difference between Enterprise and Avarice is that with the former accumulation is directed towards securing wealth 'to carry out speculative or business projects', whereas in the latter case it is a question of accumulation for accumulation's sake. Let us take the latter case first, and consider whether it is possible through pure accumulation to acquire the very large amounts of wealth that we have seen certain people own in Britain.

Accumulation – Can the Small Saver Grow Big?

The 1971 advertisements for Save as You Earn showed a man sitting proudly in a chauffeur-driven limousine, billed as 'the small saver grown big'. Whether it is in fact possible for the small saver to reach these heights is, however, very questionable. Suppose that a man earning £2,000 a year saves 5% of his income (or £100 a year) in addition to his contributions to state and occupational pension schemes, and that he accumulates the interest (which is assumed to be $4\frac{1}{2}\%$ in real terms). At the age of 65 he would have amassed £11,200 (assuming he started at 25). This is quite a handy sum, but nothing like the £200,000 or so required to appear in the top 20,000 wealth-holders. Even with a high level of earnings (£2,000 a year in 1970 would have put him in the top 5% of earners), and a substantial total savings rate, he would not accumulate enough at 65 to be accounted particularly wealthy.

This conclusion depends sensitively, however, on the rate of interest that we assume he can earn on his savings; and in this context it may be interesting to discuss a recent series of articles in *The Times* by Mr J. Carrington (14–18 October 1968). Mr Carrington asserts that 'by saving £2 a week it is possible to amass a capital of £100,000 within the space of a normal working lifetime', and indeed he shows that if a person saves £100 a year out of his earnings, as well as the whole of the interest, and is able to obtain a return of 12% on his saving, then in 42 years he can accumulate £108,086. However, 12% represents a very good return on his wealth. If instead of 12% he were only able to get 8%, then it would take him 57 years rather than 42 years to amass this amount – see Table 11 – which would take it outside the range of a normal working lifetime (starting at the age of 25, he would only be able to enjoy it at 82). With a return of 6%, it would take him 70 years, so that he would not get there unless he reached the ripe age of 95, saving all the way!

Table 11: Rate of Interest and the Accumulation of Wealth

	(Investing £100 a year and reinvesting the income)	
Rate of interest: % per year	Number of years required to reach £100,000	Amount accumulated over 40 years
		£
3	110	7,700
4½	87	11,200
6	70	16,400
8	57	28,000
10	48	48,700
12	42	85,900

Source: see Notes on Sources.

The second column in Table 11 shows the amount that a person would accumulate over a 'normal working lifetime' of forty years at different rates of return (again assuming that all the income is reinvested). With a return of 8% the amount is quite substantial – £28,000 – but if the return were only 3%, the amount accumulated at the end of 40 years would be less than £8,000.

A great deal turns, therefore, on the yield that a person can expect from his savings, and in his articles Carrington examines the past performance of ordinary shares to see whether his assumption of a return of 12% is realistic. As a basis for this examination, he takes the index prepared by the stockbrokers de Zoete and Bevan of the shares of thirty leading companies from 1919 to 1969 which I referred to in the previous chapter. Over the fifty-year period, the average annual yield was 10½% (of which just under half represented capital gains). The return varied between different

Table 12: Return to Ordinary Shares 1919–69

Period	Return in money terms (%)	Rate of price increase (%)	Real return (%)
1919–29	16·8	−2·7	19·5
1929–39	6·5	—	6·5
1939–49	7·2	5·2	2·0
1949–59	14·5	4·2	10·3
1959–69	14·2	3·5	10·7
1919–69	10·6	2·0	8·6

Note: The return is calculated on the basis of £100 invested each year and all gross income reinvested.

Source: de Zoete and Bevan (1971), pp. 7, 21.

periods (see the first column of Table 12), but nonetheless these results suggest that Carrington's assumption may not have been unduly optimistic. However, there are two very important factors that we have so far ignored – inflation and taxation. The return was 10½% in *money terms*, making no allowance for the rise in prices, and since prices have trebled since 1919 this is a very important omission. The average *real* return over the period was some 2% lower. Secondly, the amount that the person receives is reduced by taxation – by income tax and surtax on dividends, and (since 1965) by the capital gains tax (although this is not payable as long as the shares are retained, presumably the person will want to consume out of his wealth at some stage). Using figures from the same source, A. J. Merrett and A. Sykes have shown that the average return over the period since 1919, allowing both for inflation and taxation (income tax but not surtax), has been about 6%. When allowance is made for the long-term capital gains tax, this return is significantly less than half the amount assumed by Carrington.

This evidence suggests that by leaving out inflation and taxation – both of which are likely to be with us for some time yet – Mr Carrington painted too rosy a picture. With the kind of return that was historically to be earned on money invested in 'good' industrial shares it is not possible to amass £100,000 in a lifetime. A man saving 5% of his earnings of £2,000 (apart from his pension contributions) and receiving a return of 6% on his savings would

only be worth some £16,000 at the age of 65. As was argued by
J. Wedgwood:

> It is obvious, indeed, that mere 'thrift' never made a poor man rich.
> And for 'industry' to prove a philosopher's stone, it must take great
> risks and be combined with exceptional luck or exceptional talent. Both
> industry and thrift are certainly necessary qualities for the accumulator
> of property, but they are not in themselves the chief source of great
> fortunes. No poor man who sticks . . . to the securer forms of employ-
> ment for his labour and savings, can hope to leave much property to his
> descendants . . . however miserly his thrift. [1939, p. 175]

Enterprise and Self-Made Millionaires

It is clear from the preceding analysis that for a man to become a
millionaire in his lifetime, he has to obtain a return considerably
greater than that obtained by the average investor on the stock
exchange. That this is not impossible has been demonstrated by
the self-made millionaires who have become household names in
the postwar period: for instance, Charles Clore, Harry Hyams,
and Sir Jack Cohen of Tesco. However, it can in general only be
done by becoming an active and successful businessman, and the
opportunities are very limited.

Although the names of many self-made men are well known,
their activities have been less well documented and it is difficult to
assess the importance of different factors in contributing to the
establishment of their fortunes. Probably the best-known area
where large fortunes have been made in the postwar years is that
of property development, and the story of this period has been
well described by O. Marriott in his book *The Property Boom*.
This field was in many ways a rather special one. On top of the
acute shortage of office accommodation after the war and a
rapidly increasing demand, government planning controls were
imposed. These controls, although in many respects desirable,
brought with them the possibility of large capital gains. The intri-
cacies of the regulations were such that those with a thorough
knowledge could exploit loopholes such as the Third Schedule,
which could double the floor-space allowed for a development,
and hence double its value. One company is estimated by Marriott
to have made a profit of £2·2 million on one building alone as a

result of this schedule. The abolition of building licences in 1954 gave rise to enormous capital gains overnight: one site in Grafton Street bought by a developer for £59,000 a few days before increased immediately in value by 70%. The reversal of this policy with the ban on office building in London in November 1964 led to substantial increases in the value of completed office blocks such as the Euston Centre.

In the field of industrial investment there has been less scope for such spectacular capital gains, but nonetheless the postwar period has seen the creation of a number of substantial fortunes. In many cases this has been associated with products where there has been a rapidly expanding demand. One example of this is provided by a firm in the thermal insulation industry, which was started in 1963 by a man aged 22. Five years later, this firm floated its shares publicly with a market capitalization of £1½ million. The founder sold some £200,000 worth of shares and retained an interest of over £1 million. Similar records have been established in such fields as supermarket development.

In part these cases fit the picture described by Wedgwood of entrepreneurs taking risks to set up business in growing industries aided by substantial luck. However, in assessing the basis for their fortunes, it is important to bear in mind the effects of inflation. In many cases businesses were established on money borrowed at a fixed interest rate which was used to buy assets which were likely to maintain their real value. As prices rose, therefore, the real cost of borrowing fell. The institutions (insurance companies, banks and others) lending money to these incipient entrepreneurs were in effect paying them to take care of it, and this they did in a way that provided a substantial real return. Marriott commented 'How badly timed was the insurance companies' awakening to the property boom. In short, their participation was far better for the property developers than for them.' Moreover, as discussed earlier, the effect of inflation may be to reverse conventional notions of risk-taking: the entrepreneur holding real assets may have been taking less of a risk in real terms than the people lending at fixed interest rates and capital values. The origins of the fortunes of self-made men may therefore be traced as much to the opportunity of bridging the gap between the real return on investing in growing industries and the low real cost of borrowing, as to risk-taking and the ability to spot those industries in which demand is likely to grow. Imperfections in the capital market and restricted access to funds may also be important factors: the founder of the thermal insulation firm referred to earlier began with an inheritance of £10,000 from his father and he might well not have been able to enter the industry without such access to capital. Finally, we should draw attention to the role played by the generous tax treatment of capital gains under the British tax system. Until 1965 all long-term capital gains were free from taxation, which gave a great advantage to those who could choose to receive their income in this form. A large part of the return to building up a business, for example, is likely to be in the form of capital gains on the holding retained when the company is floated publicly. This position was changed substantially by the 1965 Capital Gains Tax, but, as is argued in chapter 7, the rates of tax are still appreciably lower than on other forms of investment income.

Self-made millionaires are undoubtedly exceptional men, but so are rich men; and what we would like to know is whether self-made men are the exception or the rule among the top wealth-holders. Do they account for most or only a few of the very large wealth-holdings? In the next chapter, an attempt is made to answer this question by investigating the wealth of the fathers of those men and women who have died leaving large estates.

Conclusion

The broad conclusion to be drawn from the analysis in this chapter is that it is possible for accumulated wealth to explain some of the very large holdings observed in Britain, but this can only be true of the active and highly successful entrepreneur, who is a rare individual. It is quite misleading to suggest that the ordinary man can save substantial wealth at the currently ruling rates of return, or that the observed inequality can be explained by life-cycle factors.

4. Inheritance and the Distribution of Wealth

Everyone knows that in all except the newest countries, the inequality in the amounts of property which individuals have received by way of bequest and inheritance is by far the most potent cause of inequality in the actual distribution of property. – *E. Cannan, 1905*

Inheritance in Britain is an extraordinarily neglected subject. As Cannan remarked, everyone recognizes that substantial amounts of wealth are transmitted from generation to generation, yet the implications for the development of wealth-holding have been largely ignored. In chapter 3 we saw that other explanations are unlikely to account for many of the large fortunes, and in this chapter we develop this line of argument by examining two major questions:

How does inheritance influence the development of inequality in the distribution of wealth? Does the transmission of wealth merely perpetuate inequality which already exists, or is it likely to intensify the degree of inequality?

How important is inheritance in quantitative terms in leading to inequality in the distribution of wealth? Do the top wealth-holders largely owe their fortunes to inheritance, or are they mainly self-made men?

Factors Influencing the Transmission of Wealth

There are three principal factors which determine the relationship between the wealth inherited by one generation (referred to as Generation I) and that received by the next (Generation II):

Accumulation or decumulation of wealth by Generation I. This generation may add to its inheritance or squander it, and the course chosen will influence the total amount transferred to the next generation.

Division of the estate (and of other wealth transmitted). The effect of a given estate left by Generation I depends on the way in which it is divided between the members of Generation II. This division reflects the laws and customs regarding the provision to be made for different members of the family (whether, for example, primogeniture is customarily practised), the extent to which charitable bequests are made, and the type of wealth taxes in force (discussion of this question is postponed to Part II).

Demographic factors. These include family size (which is clearly important where estates are shared equally) and marriage patterns (marriage can be seen from this point of view as the fusion of two transfers from the previous generation).

Inheritance and the Accumulation of Wealth

In the previous chapter we discussed a number of different motives for saving, but omitted one. Do people save in order to pass on wealth to their children and, if so, how is this related to the amount that they themselves inherited? The desire to provide one's children with a 'better start in life' is often referred to in connection with savings decisions, but it is hard to determine its quantitative importance. There have been a number of studies in the United States which have tried to throw some light on this question, particularly those carried out by the University of Michigan. For the population as a whole these studies suggest that the desire to make bequests is an unimportant motive for saving, but among high-income households it becomes more significant. In 1964, 20% of those with incomes of $10,000 and over mentioned this motive for saving and the proportion for those with incomes over $100,000 was about 50%.

This evidence suggests that the bequest motive for saving is important among those with the highest incomes. However, we are interested, not in the relationship with *income*, but in the relationship between saving for bequests and the level of inherited wealth. Do people who have inherited large estates save more or less for bequests than those who did not inherit? If those saving for bequest reasons were those who began life with nothing, and those who inherited spent heedless of bequests throughout their lives, we should expect the position of families in the distribution of wealth to change from generation to generation: the top 1% in the year 2000 would be made up of quite different families from the top 1 % in 1900. But, if those who inherit wealth save more than those who do not inherit, this would lead to increasing inequality and the perpetuation of the same families at the top of the distribution. Unfortunately, there is little concrete evidence about the relationship between saving for bequest motives and the level of inherited wealth. At an *a priori* level, arguments can be imagined in both directions. On the one hand, those who inherit wealth are also likely to inherit expensive tastes and may feel that there is little need for them to stint themselves by saving a large amount. On the other hand, reference is often made to the social pressures on the wealthy to maintain the family fortune, a consideration which applies most obviously to landed property and family firms, but may also be relevant to other forms of wealth.

The preservation of a family fortune depends, of course, on the abilities of the heir: he may wish to pass on his estate intact or enhanced, but not possess the skills required to do so. This leads to what may be called the 'clogs to clogs' argument that those who inherit large fortunes rarely inherit the abilities of those who created them, and consequently the heirs are likely to mismanage their inheritance (Leroy Beaulieu claimed, for example, that 'it is as hard to maintain a fortune as to acquire one'). However, while this may have been the case in the days when the maintenance of a fortune required careful management of an estate – when ownership and use of assets were coterminous – it seems unlikely that it is true today. By investing in a broad portfolio of equity shares, an heir should have little difficulty in the long run in preserving the real value of his inheritance. As Sir Hubert Henderson once said, 'the phenomenon which was such a familiar feature of the old-fashioned novel, a prosperous family reduced to sudden destitution, is becoming increasingly rare'. Or, as it has been put more forcefully by an American writer, 'The rich by inheritance have a position which they can lose only by a destructive tendency amounting almost to madness.'

The evidence about accumulation and the transmission of wealth is rather inconclusive, but on balance it seems reasonable to suppose that most heirs today do not dissipate their fortunes, so that inequality in wealth transmitted through inheritance is likely to be perpetuated. This conclusion does, however, depend on the extent of taxation on the income from wealth – a subject discussed in chapter 7.

The Division of Estates – Laws and Customs

Laws and customs regarding the division of estates vary greatly between societies and have changed considerably in Britain over the centuries. People in Britain today regard it as natural that the disposal of their property after their death is a matter to be decided as they please, but in many societies there are restrictions on the way in which it can be divided – or indeed on the extent to which property can be transmitted at all. The contrast often drawn in this context is that between the virtual freedom of bequest in Britain and the law of *legitim* (or reserved portion) found in France and other European countries, which places major restrictions on the freedom allowed to an individual in disposing of his estate. His descendants, if any, are entitled to a reserved portion depending on the degree of relationship. If, for example, he leaves only one child, one half of the estate goes to the child by right and one half can be freely disposed; if he is survived by two children, they each receive a third by right, and so on. Many writers have emphasized the importance of this contrast between Britain and France and have drawn conclusions for the development of wealth-holding in the two countries, arguing that the freedom of bequest in England, accompanied by the custom of primogeniture (or leaving the bulk of the estate to the eldest son), has led to greater concentration than in countries where, by law, estates have to be divided. Perhaps the most celebrated exponent of this view was de Tocqueville, who argued that:

Framed in one way, the law of succession combines and concentrates property and power in a few hands: it causes a landed aristocracy to flourish. But guided by other principles, and framed on other lines, its action is even more immediate, it divides, distributes and disperses both property and power . . . until by its incessant activity the bulwarks of the influence of wealth are ground down to the fine and shifting sand which is the basis of democracy. [Quoted in Wedgwood, 1939, pp. 94–5]

The effect of such differences in the degree to which estates are divided may be seen from a simple example. Let us assume that the distribution of wealth is initially such that the top 5% of families own all the wealth in the country, and that primogeniture is practised. If every family has two children, one boy and one girl, the estate passes entirely to the boy and the top 5% of the next generation own all the wealth, there being no change in inequality over time. If each family had more than two children, so that the population was growing, the wealth would still be concentrated in the hands of the same absolute number of people, but they would form an increasingly smaller proportion of the total. In this case inequality would increase under primogeniture, with the younger sons of the wealthy joining the ranks of the propertyless. If there were no sons in a family, so that a daughter inherited, two estates might merge (a son who was an heir marrying a daughter who was an heiress), and this would tend to accentuate the trend towards increased inequality. In the case of equal division among all children (male and female), on the other hand, the children of the top 5% would share the wealth equally between them. If they all founded separate families, the second-generation families would make up 10% of the population, so that it would now be the top 10% that owned all the wealth. On this basis, the effect of equal division would be for the distribution of inherited wealth to become more equal over time. This tendency would be reduced by the fact that some of the children of the rich would tend to marry other children with wealthy parents (we should expect this to happen even with random marriage and, as discussed below, there are good grounds for expecting the rich to intermarry); but this would serve only to dampen the equalizing effect and could not reverse it.* The quantitative importance of the difference between primogeniture and equal division in this form can be seen by supposing that a sixteenth-century Croesus had owned all the wealth in this country, and that it had been equally divided between his descendants at each stage (and that they had never intermarried). The distribution of his wealth would by now be completely equal; whereas under primogeniture it would still be in the hands of Croesus XV.

*An intermediate case is that where estates are equally divided among *male* children only (perhaps with the female children receiving a life interest). In the example given, this would maintain the *existing pattern* of inequality unchanged (whatever the family size).

So far we have discussed the influence of law and customs on the division of the estate among children; however, many people leave part of their estate to other relatives or to charities. In so far as they leave money to people outside the family this may have an equalizing effect, as with legacies to gardeners and chauffeurs. However, in many cases it may simply be a question of giving it to the children of other rich people or to equally wealthy friends. This was illustrated by the will of Alfred de Rothschild, who in 1918 left his estate to (among other people) Lord and Lady Carnarvon, Lord Porchester, Lady Curzon, Lord Esher and the Marquis de Soveral. A newspaper report at the time commented that 'it is seldom that a rich man distributes his money so widely or so generously', but it could hardly be thought that such bequests would lead to a substantial reduction in inequality. Charitable bequests, on the other hand, are clearly equalizing, although they are much less common in Britain than in America. This no doubt reflects the more generous treatment of charitable gifts under American tax law, although some commentators have suggested that it reflects a belief that 'good giving' expiates 'bad getting'. In Britain there is little evidence that charitable bequests exercise an important equalizing influence: a study by G. Z. Fijalkowski-Bereday showed that in 1944–5 only 9 out of 281 estates left the main bequest to charities. Similarly, J. Wedgwood estimated on the basis of a survey of wills published in *The Times* in 1925 that charitable bequests made up only about 4% of the total value of estates.*

Finally, there are those who leave their money to the government for the relief of the National Debt. This started in 1797 when Peter Thellusen left £700,000 which was to accumulate at compound interest during the lives of all his direct descendants living at the time of his death. If when the last died there was no direct heir, the accumulation was to go to the government for the redemption of the National Debt. In fact there were two direct

---

*Unfortunately, we have virtually no evidence about charitable *gifts* (as opposed to bequests). There are clearly some well-known examples (such as Lord Nuffield) where large sums have been given for educational and other purposes during a person's lifetime, but it is not possible to assess the quantitative importance of this factor.

heirs, but the estate had been largely eaten away by the law costs incurred by the family in trying to get the will set aside!

Marriage and Family Size

Examination of the effect of primogeniture and equal division brings out the influence of the patterns of intermarriage between families on the development of wealth-holding. If no property were vested in women, marriage as such would have little effect on the pattern of inequality and wealth would pass from father to son in the way described above. However, there have always been wealthy heiresses, and it has become increasingly common during this century for women to hold wealth in their own right. A good deal of the wealth held by women undoubtedly takes the form of property inherited by widows who in turn pass it on to their children, and as such does not really modify the process we have described, but we must also allow for wealth directly inherited by women from their parents, which is then transferred to their husbands or passed on to their children. An heir may receive a substantial part of his fortune through the mother's side of the family.

The influence of marriage patterns where women inherit equally with men can be seen in terms of the example discussed earlier. Suppose that we have equal division of estates among all children, and that the whole of the wealth of the country is initially in the hands of the top 5%. If mating is random, most of the children of the top 5% marry people with no wealth and the degree of inequality tends to fall over time. In practice, however, it seems unlikely that the pattern of marriage should be random in this way – a child from a family in the top 5% is much more likely to marry another child from the top 5% than is someone from a family with no wealth. The rich tend to marry the rich because they have the same social background and are quite simply more likely to meet each other. In the extreme case where the top 5% intermarry completely and no new blood enters their ranks, their share of the total wealth will not be reduced at all, even though estates are equally divided among all children. The pattern of marriage is similarly important in the case of primogeniture, where a woman may inherit if there is no male heir. This gives rise to the wealthy heiress who figures in so many novels and whose marriage to a wealthy young man may lead to the consolidation of two substantial fortunes.

Evidence about patterns of marriage is hard to obtain. In Table 13 are summarized the results concerning the pattern of marriage obtained in the 1949 social mobility study by the London School

Table 13: Degree of Assortative Mating in Britain in 1949

Social group of origin of husbands	Percentage marrying wives from social group:			
	I	II	III	IV
I. Professional and managerial	37	36	21	6
II. Supervisory and other non-manual	6	34	41	18
III. Skilled manual	3	20	54	24
IV. Unskilled and semi-skilled	1	15	43	41
All groups	6	24	46	25

Source: Glass (1954), p. 331.

of Economics. It shows the proportion of men from a particular social group marrying wives from different social groups. If the process were purely random, we should expect all rows to be identical (and equal to the last line). However, they are clearly not the same, and there is a definite tendency for numbers near the diagonal to be larger, and those off the diagonal smaller, than would be expected if the process were random. On a random basis, one would have expected, for example, only 30% of those in Group I to marry wives from Groups I and II, but in fact nearly three quarters did.

These results relate to the population as a whole, whereas we are primarily interested in the group of top wealth-holders, who make up only a small part of Group I. At the other extreme of generality, Table 14 relates to the sons and daughters of English dukes over the period 1330–1934, showing the numbers marrying members of the peerage, commoners and foreigners. Over the period as a whole about half the marriages of sons of dukes were with members of the peerage, which is clearly not consistent with the hypothesis of random marriage. There was a trend over the period towards increased marriage with commoners, but even in the last hundred years nearly as many married within the peerage as married commoners (whereas on a random basis an overwhelming majority would have married commoners). Bearing in mind the fact that the foreigners were often German princesses (or more recently American heiresses), this suggests that marriage among the aristocracy may have been a very effective way of maintaining the concentration of wealth.

Table 14: Marriages of Children of Dukes 1330–1934

| Born | Sons of dukes marrying: | | |
	Peerage	Commoners	Foreigners
1330–1679	72	29	19
1680–1829	121	97	20
1830–1934	62	67	26
All years	255	193	65

| Born | Daughters of dukes marrying: | | |
	Peerage	Commoners	Foreigners
1330–1679	109	35	17
1680–1829	159	81	19
1830–1934	81	69	22
All years	349	185	58

Source: Hollingsworth (1957), p. 24.

The final factor to be considered is that of family size. In the hypothetical example described above, it was assumed that the rich had the same number of children as the rest of the population. However, where estates are equally divided, differential fertility may have an important influence on the evolution of wealth-holding. If the wealthy tend to have larger families than the poor (and wealth is equally divided) the distribution will become more equal. In the population as a whole, family size has tended to be smaller for the higher social status groups: in 1961 that for employers and managers of large enterprises was 1·86 children, whereas for skilled manual workers it was 2·55, and for unskilled manual workers 3·1. Again it has to be remembered that the very rich form only a small part of the upper status groups, and they may well have larger families than others in the group of 'employers and managers of large enterprises'.* However, it seems unlikely that the differences are sufficient today for this to be a particularly powerful equalizing force. Moreover, it may not be right to assume that equal division is equally probable regardless of family size: in large families primogeniture is much more likely to be practised.

The Quantitative Importance of Inheritance

It is indicative of the current lack of interest in the subject of inheritance that much of the limited empirical evidence relates to conditions before the Second World War. The only recent study is that carried out by C. D. Harbury, on whose work I have drawn heavily. Harbury has examined in particular the relationship between the estates left by top wealth-holders and the estates left by their fathers, and on the basis of this information we can form some idea of how far the large estates of the sons could be explained by inherited wealth and how far by the fact that they were self-made men.

The basis for Harbury's investigation was a sample of large estates left in the years 1956 and 1957 (all those over £100,000 were included and a sample of those between £50,000 and £100,000). From the information provided about the date of death, the death certificate, which gave the age at death, could be traced at Somerset House. From this it was possible to calculate the approximate date of birth and to search in the Register of Births for the father's name. Where this was found, a search was then made for the estate of the father in the Probate Calendars.† This piece of detective work was a lengthy operation, and it is a tribute to the care taken in the investigation that there were only 14 complete failures out of the original 685 estates.

The results of Harbury's study are set out in Figure 3, which

*Although in the ducal families studied by Hollingsworth (1957) the average number of children per family over the period 1830–1934 was only 2·6.

†It was not always possible to find a single unambiguous entry in the Register of Births or to trace the father's will. In these cases, Harbury resorted to correspondence with relatives, solicitors and executors.

relates to estates over £100,000. It shows on the vertical axis the proportion of those leaving large estates in 1956–7 whose fathers' estates exceeded the figure shown on the horizontal axis. If the relationship between the wealth of the father and that of the son

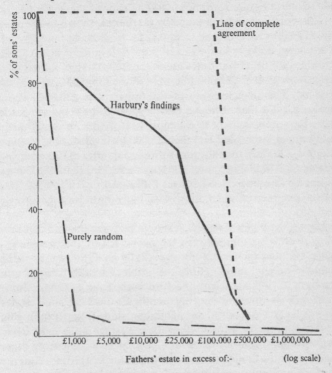

Figure 3: Relationship between Estates of Fathers and Sons
Source: derived from Harbury (1962), Figure 1 and text.

were a purely random one, the distribution of the fathers' estates would be the same as that for the fathers of any randomly selected sample of men dying in 1956–7, and we would have the situation shown by the dashed line in Figure 3 (the line marked 'purely random'). On a random basis, only 5% of the sons would have had fathers leaving more than £1,000 and fewer than 0·25% would have had fathers leaving more than £25,000. If, at the other extreme, the distribution of the fathers' estates had been exactly the same as that of the sons (i.e. wealthy sons had correspondingly wealthy fathers), this would have given the situation shown by the dotted line in Figure 3 (the line marked 'complete agreement').

The actual relationship found by Harbury is shown by the solid line in Figure 3. As can be seen, it is far from being random and, if anything, is closer to the line of 'complete agreement'. Around two thirds of the rich sons (estates over £100,000) had fathers who left estates of over £25,000 (i.e. were in the top 0·25% of wealth-holders). The median estate of the fathers was £50,000. These figures suggest that although there appear to be some self-made men, they are definitely in a minority. If we define as self-made those whose fathers left less than £5,000 (equivalent now to some £15,000–£20,000), they account for only a quarter of those leaving estates of £100,000 or more. Harbury concluded that 'the chance of leaving an estate valued at over £100,000, or even £50,000, was outstandingly enhanced if one's father had been at least moderately well off'.

In considering these results, it should be borne in mind that they show the relationship between the *estates* left by the two genera-tions, and that estates are not necessarily good indicators of the total wealth transmitted (since they exclude wealth passed on in the form of gifts *inter vivos* or settled in the form of trusts). Some of those sons whose fathers apparently died leaving small estates may in fact have received substantial amounts from them in gifts or settled property. Moreover, while the father is the most likely person to have transmitted wealth, it may have come from other members of the family, such as a childless uncle. Harbury cites the case of Lord Dulverton (of the Wills tobacco family) who died in 1956 leaving over £4 million. His father had left £3 million, but eight other members of the Wills family who had died since 1900 left over £2 million each.

Harbury's study was modelled closely on an earlier investigation for the years 1924–6 by Josiah Wedgwood, and it is interesting to compare their results. There are a number of reasons for expecting the importance of inheritance to have declined over the thirty years, and Wedgwood himself wrote in 1938:

I should expect to see the proportion of inherited wealth somewhat reduced, because . . . war, unsettled economic conditions, and especially inflation, combined with the relatively high rates of Estate Duty during the past twenty years, must reduce the economic influence of inheritance. [1939, p. 8]

(although he goes on to say that it would not alter his conclusions that 'unequal inheritances remain a most important factor in shaping the distribution of wealth'.) Harbury's results suggest, however, that Wedgwood's prediction has not been borne out. The curves corresponding to the results of the two studies are

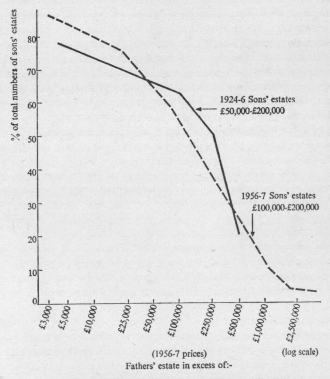

Figure 4: Estates of Fathers and Sons in 1924–6 and 1956–7
Source: Harbury (1962), Figure 3.

shown in Figure 4 (the estate size having been adjusted to allow for the rise in prices). These show no marked change in the import-ance of inheritance in the creation of the fortunes of the top wealth-leavers between the mid 1920s and the mid 1950s. The curves are close together and intersect twice. In both periods, around two thirds of the fathers left more than £25,000 (in 1956–7 prices). This suggests that there has been no clear decline in the importance of inheritance during the first part of this century.

In his study, Wedgwood went rather further and tried to esti-mate what proportion of the father's estate had in fact been passed on to the son on the basis of an investigation of the father's will. He emphasized that the resulting figures were necessarily only very approximate, but they are nonetheless interesting. In the case of men leaving over £200,000, between 40% and 50% of the father's estate had been passed on to the son (either directly or with a life interest for the surviving spouse). Since the average number of surviving children was around five, this demonstrates that, as far as the very wealthiest groups were concerned, equal division of estates was not the rule. Wedgwood commented as follows:

frequently . . . the lion's share of the estate went to one particular son – usually, but not always, the eldest. This was not only due to the custom of primogeniture among the landed aristocracy . . . but also to the intel-ligible desire of wealthy businessmen to perpetuate their economic power by leaving a large property intact in the hands of a single descendant, particularly when a minor portion of the estate is sufficient to provide for the reasonable requirements of the other members of the family. [1939, pp. 164–5]

He cites the case of a chemical manufacturer, with close on a million pounds to distribute among nine children, who left £150,000 between eight of them and the whole residue to the remaining son. However, in the case of smaller estates, equal divi-sion turned out to be more common.

Further evidence of the importance of inheritance is provided by a survey of 2,750 agricultural estates carried out by the Depart-ment of Land Economy at Cambridge under D. R. Denman in the early 1950s. This classified estates according to the length of time they had been in the hands of a single family, distinguishing in particular those that had belonged to the same family since before

1900. The results showed that about a third of the estates had been in the same hands since before 1900, and that these accounted for two thirds of the total acreage. Among estates of more than 5,000 acres, over 80% had been owned by the same family since the turn of the century. As Denman remarked, the study 'gives evidence of survival power among the old and large inheritances unsuspected by many'.

The results of these investigations may be summarized as follows: there is strong evidence that inheritance plays an important role in the development of large wealth-holdings. Wedgwood concluded that:

about one third owe their fortunes almost entirely to inheritance (including gifts *inter vivos*), another third to a combination of ability and luck with a considerable inheritance of wealth and business opportunity, and the remaining third largely to their own activities. [1939, p. 179]

Moreover, there is no apparent tendency for the importance of inheritance to decline over the course of this century.

Inheritance in Three Families

To illustrate the role played by inheritance and marriage in the development of wealth-holding, I have traced very briefly the history of three different types of family: a 'political' family (the Cecils), an aristocratic landowning family (the Grosvenors), and the Wedgwoods, a family whose wealth derives from the Industrial Revolution.*

The Cecil Family – Marquesses of Salisbury

The political importance of the Cecil family began with William Cecil, first Lord Burghley, born in 1520. However, his family had already been accumulating wealth for at least two generations. His grandfather had received grants of office and land from the king, and his father had added to the inheritance (among other things, he was left £100 by Henry VIII, although in view of the extent of the King's debts he may not have benefited from this legacy!). Lord Burghley inherited this in turn, and added greatly to the

*It should be emphasized that these 'histories' are highly selective.

family estates. When he died in 1598, his wealth was considerable, including manors in the counties of Northamptonshire, Rutland, Lincoln, Essex, Yorkshire, Hertfordshire, Middlesex and Kent. The estate was divided between Thomas Cecil, first Earl of Exeter, and Robert Cecil, first Earl of Salisbury (it is on the Salisbury branch that attention is focused here). After Robert Cecil, the political talent of the family fell into abeyance and the succeeding generations were characterized by a general lack of ability. The second Earl was described as 'notoriously incompetent' and as 'my simple Lord Salisbury' by Pepys. The third Earl was described by Macaulay as 'foolish to a proverb', and the fifth Earl's only claim to fame was that he drove the Hatfield stage-coach. What is of interest is that, despite the apparent mediocrity of these genera- tions, the wealth of the Cecils remained very substantial, and it was clearly only the combination of inheritance and marriage that permitted the family to preserve its wealth in this way. (The bene- fits from judicious marriage are illustrated by the fact that when the second earl married the daughter of the Earl of Dirleton, she received a marriage portion of £18,000, which was a considerable amount at that time.) The family returned to politics in the late part of the eighteenth century. The third Marquess (ninth Earl) was the last member of the House of Lords to be Prime Minister. The fifth Marquess, who was a leading Conservative Party poli- tician, had substantial business interests in this country and South Africa, as well as his estates at Hatfield (which have been in the family since William Cecil) and elsewhere.

The Grosvenor Family – Dukes of Westminster

The development of the Grosvenor fortune can be traced back to Hugh Audley, who was a successful moneylender at the beginning of the sixteenth century. His wealth included the manors of Ebury, Belgravia and Pimlico, at that time undrained marshland on the outskirts of the City of London. One of the Grosvenors, then a Cheshire family with an estate at Eaton, married the daughter (and only child) of Audley's heir in 1677. It was the sons of this mar- riage who began to develop the London estates (one of the streets being named after their original founder), which within the next hundred years became the most valuable in the country. This wealth was preserved in the family, being passed from generation to generation (much of it in the form of settled property), and survived the profligacy of such members of the family as the first Earl Grosvenor (whose racing debts when he died were over £100,000). When the second Marquess died in 1869, his son (the first Duke) inherited £4 million in settled property and £750,000 in absolute ownership. The income from the London properties was then some £115,000 a year. By the time his grandson (the second Duke) died in 1953, the estate had grown many times larger and the Estate Duty was estimated at some £20 million. After two further deaths, the estate is now somewhat smaller, but the family are reported to retain a substantial part of their London estates (including 180 acres of Belgravia and 90 acres of Mayfair), investments worth several millions in Canada and 140,000 acres (including half the original estate at Eaton). Nor are the Grosvenors the only large aristocratic landowners left in London. The Portman estate was still 108 acres (including Portman, Bryanston, Montagu and Manchester Squares) after the payment of £7½ million estate duties in the early 1950s. Similarly, there are the London estates of the Duke of Bedford, and of the Cadogan and Howard de Walden families.

The Wedgwood Family

The Wedgwoods differ from the Cecils and the Grosvenors in that their wealth is of rather more recent origin, dating from the Industrial Revolution. (In tracing their history I have been helped by the account given by Josiah Wedgwood of the part played in their history by 'the luck of inheritance and marriage', in his book *The Economics of Inheritance*, to which I have already referred.) Although the Wedgwoods had been small-scale potters for generations, the originator of the family fortunes was undoubtedly Josiah Wedgwood (1730–95), who revolutionized the industry and built up the Wedgwood pottery firm to the prominence it still retains. His career has been described by N. McKendrick as follows: 'Born the thirteenth son of a mediocre potter with only the promise – and a promise never fulfilled – of a £20 inheritance, he died in 1795 worth £200,000 and the owner of the finest industrial concern in England.' After his death, the business passed to his sons, and then subsequently to succeeding generations of the family. Although partnerships with outsiders were formed from time to time, the family always retained an interest, and in 1915 the tenth generation entered the firm. There are currently two members of the family on the board of Wedgwood Ltd. The history of the family illustrates very well the distinction between accumulated and inherited wealth: whereas Josiah Wedgwood was undoubtedly the archetypal self-made man of chapter 3, there can be little doubt that without inheritance his successors would not have remained in control of the business. As the more recent Josiah Wedgwood has commented:

it is chiefly to his industry and ability that the most well-to-do section of the family still owes its prosperity. Those of his descendants who have children living at the present day [1928] have in each case, during four generations, left estates ranging from £20,000 to £100,000. With one possible exception, none of them dissipated their patrimony, but none greatly increased it . . . In the final result, of the living descendants of the elder son of the common ancestor, nine generations back, 75% remain in the middle and upper-middle classes, having participated in inheritances of over £1,000 from the last generation; and in the case of 45 per cent, the estates were not less than £20,000. [1939, p. 182]

Inherited Wealth – Conclusions

From this analysis of the role of inherited and accumulated wealth, it is clear that inheritance is a factor of great importance in giving rise to concentration in the distribution of wealth in Britain. The conclusions reached by Wedgwood remain valid today:

The evidence . . . supports the opinion that, in the great majority of cases, the large fortunes of one generation belong to the children of those who possessed the large fortunes of the preceding generation . . . the rich men who have sprung from parents with insignificant resources are almost certainly a minority of their class. The attention which that minority attracts seems to be due to the fact that those who compose it are exceptional phenomena rather than numerous. [1939, p. 179]

5. The Case for Greater Equality

A society in which every member holds an equal quantity of property needs no special justification; only a society in which property is unequal needs it. – *Sir Isaiah Berlin*

The evidence regarding wealth-holding in Britain discussed in chapter 1 demonstrated that there is an extreme degree of inequality in the distribution of wealth. On the basis of the estate duty statistics, the top 5% of wealth-holders appear to own over half the total personal wealth, and other estimates have placed their share as high as three quarters. There are some hundred people in Britain worth at least £2½ million each, and some are worth many times this amount. This degree of concentration is higher than that in other advanced industrial countries such as the United States. There has been some decline over the course of this century in the degree of inequality, but there are reasons for believing that this reflects the rearrangement of wealth within families rather than redistribution between rich and poor. Concentration of wealth-holding in turn generates inequality of incomes, which is accentuated by the fact that the very rich tend to hold their wealth in the form of company shares and real property yielding a higher return than the assets typically owned by small savers. The concentration of share ownership is even greater than that in the distribution of wealth as a whole, which is important since shares convey not only income but also rights of control, and even allowing for the increasing power of corporation managers these still remain of considerable significance.

In chapters 3 and 4 a distinction was drawn between the acquisition of wealth through accumulation and the receipt of wealth through inheritance or gifts, and it was argued that inherited wealth is a factor of great importance in leading to the observed concentration. A person can only become a millionaire from scratch in his lifetime if he is able to obtain a very high rate of return on the capital he acquires, and this is only possible for highly successful entrepreneurs. It is certainly not true that the observed inequality can be accounted for by the saving of the mass of the population for its old age: only a small part of the inequality can be explained by age differences. Strong evidence of concentration in the distribution of inherited wealth is provided by the estate duty statistics, which show a high degree of inequality among people of the same age, and by the findings of Harbury and Wedgwood that those who die leaving large estates are likely to have had wealthy parents. Of those dying in 1956–7 with estates of over £100,000, two thirds had fathers who died leaving over £25,000. The effects of inheritance are further reinforced by the tendency towards selective marriage and by the custom of primogeniture. To a considerable extent, therefore, the very wealthy are not self-made men, but have inherited estates built up over generations. Moreover, there is no reason to believe that the importance of inherited wealth is declining over time.

This evidence provides the background for the examination in this chapter of the case for greater equality in the distribution of wealth in Britain. What justification can be given for the continuation of such extremes in the distribution? What costs would be entailed in reducing the degree of inequality? The arguments against greater equality can be considered under two main headings: the arguments of those who hold that greater equality is intrinsically undesirable, and those of people who agree that greater equality would be beneficial but feel that the deleterious consequences of greater equality (for example, an adverse effect on the incentives to work and save) are sufficient to outweigh the intrinsic advantages. I discuss these two standpoints in turn.

Intrinsic Arguments Against Greater Equality

As W. von Leyden has remarked, the concept of equality has for many people: 'a particularly powerful aesthetic appeal, such as is exhibited, for instance, in the golden section of a line. One might say in this respect that the principle satisfies a deep-rooted demand in men's thoughts for symmetry, unity, or regularity.' (1963, p. 57.) The moral justification of equality is, however, a less straightforward question than its purely aesthetic appeal. Moreover it is a subject which has been much neglected in the past few years, as D. Donnison has recently pointed out:

Governments of this country are being compelled to formulate increasingly explicit policies about ... the distribution of this world's goods among our people. To do so they must decide where they stand on some very old questions. These questions – about liberty, equality and fraternity – were much discussed by our forbears, but are now obscured beneath the dust of a decaying liberal faith. [1970, p. 3]

The case *for* greater equality is basically one of social justice, and rests on (1) the acceptance of the basic principle that the distribution should be equal unless departures from equality can be justified according to what are considered relevant criteria, and (2) the demonstration that the existing extremes of inequality cannot be justified by appeal to such criteria. The first of these statements – the presumption in favour of equality – has been described by Sir Isaiah Berlin as follows:

If I have a cake and there are ten persons among whom I wish to divide it, then if I give exactly one tenth to each, this will not, at any rate automatically, call for justification; whereas if I depart from this principle of equal division I am expected to produce a special reason. [1961, p. 131]

This statement as it stands is not particularly strong, since its force turns on the definition of 'relevant' criteria. At the same time it is undoubtedly widely acceptable. It is hard to imagine a serious case being put forward to justify *quite arbitrary* inequalities in the distribution. As has been argued by von Leyden:

no one, even our thorough-going anti-egalitarian, would be prepared to tolerate *any* kind of unequal treatment of other people, or *a fortiori* of himself. Though he may say there is no equality, he cannot say that there need be no sufficient reasons for unequal treatment and that these might all be irrelevant, that is, based on arbitrary decisions or other purely irrational factors.* [1963, p. 60]

---

*At the same time people may of course favour (otherwise arbitrary) inequalities which are to their benefit. Implicit in the justification of the basic principle of equality is the assumption that people judge the distribution independently of their own position on the wealth scale. For further discussion of this point, see Sen (1970), ch. 9.

If this basic principle is accepted, the case *against* measures to bring about greater equality in the distribution of wealth must be made on the grounds that existing inequalities can be justified according to what are considered relevant principles. If such a justification is to be provided by the opponents of greater equality it is likely to be on the basis of one of three main criteria:

(1) merit or deserts,
(2) need,
(3) social benefit.

Of these, the third refers to cases where the adverse consequences of greater equality are held to offset its benefits, and discussion of this is postponed to the second part of the chapter. The other two criteria are discussed in turn.

In the case of incomes, distribution according to *merit or desert* is usually understood to justify paying a man more who works harder, or does a more unpleasant job, or who has spent time acquiring knowledge or skills. Transplanting this concept to the distribution of wealth, it can be used to justify a situation in which a person who has saved in the past has more wealth than someone who has not: it being argued that the person who saved while working 'deserves' by virtue of his abstinence to have more wealth than a person who spent everything. This view has some affinity with the 'natural right' concept of property, that a person has a right to capital accumulated through his own labour. This doctrine is associated particularly with Locke, who wrote that:

Though the earth and all inferior creatures be common to all men, yet every man has a 'property' in his own 'person'. This nobody has any right to but himself. The 'labour' of his body and the 'work' of his hands, we may say, are properly his. Whatsoever, then, he removes out of the state that nature hath provided and left it in, he hath mixed his labour with it, and joined to it something that is his own, and thereby makes it his property. It being by him removed from the common state Nature placed it in, hath by this labour something annexed to it that excludes the common right of other men. For this 'labour' being the unquestionable property of the labourer, no man but he can have a right to what this is once joined to, at least where there is enough, and as good left in common for others. [1694]

In considering the extent to which inequality can be justified in this way by reference to 'deserts', it is essential to distinguish between wealth which a person has saved for himself (which I have referred to as accumulated wealth) and wealth that has been transmitted to him in the form of gifts or inheritances (inherited wealth). Inequality in accumulated wealth may in some circumstances be justified on grounds of deserts, particularly where it emerges because of differences in age or attitudes towards saving. Suppose that two people have the same earnings, receive the same amount of inherited wealth, and obtain the same return on their savings. If one decides to save his inheritance until he retires, whereas the other spends it at once, they may later on have very different amounts of wealth. We should not, however, regard this as inequitable, since the first man 'deserves' to have more wealth by virtue of having foregone consumption earlier. Similarly, if people are identical apart from their age, older people are likely to have more wealth (since they will have saved for their old age), but again we should not regard this as inequitable. This is not to suggest that all inequality in accumulated wealth can be justified on grounds of desert (it would be hard to argue, for instance, that the large capital gains made by property developers were 'deserved' on account of saving), but the criterion has some application.

In the case of inherited wealth on the other hand, the justification of inequality by reference to 'deserts' can scarcely be applied. A person who has inherited £1 million has not foregone consumption earlier in his life to acquire it – he has not, to use Locke's phrase, 'mixed his labour with it'. As Tawney remarked, 'the transmission of more than a minimum of wealth from generation to generation has, in the conditions of today, little more to commend it than would have the right to travel in perpetuity in first-class coaches!' It is true that the person making the bequest has abstained from consumption, but there is no reason why the heir (rather than someone else) should benefit from this. Heirs cannot be said to inherit through any 'merit' of their own.

For justification of concentration in the distribution of inherited wealth, we have therefore to consider if any argument can be made on the ground of need. On the face of it, it is difficult to imagine that anyone 'needs' to inherit £1 million. Moreover, for such a case to be convincing, it would have to be demonstrated that those who inherit have special needs over and above those of others. One such argument, based on an interesting variant of the concept of 'relative deprivation', is that where a child has been brought up to expect a substantial inheritance, the disappointment of these expectations would cause more hardship than if they had not been entertained. A (perhaps extreme) statement of this view is that by Lord Henry Petty in 1806 when discussing the income tax:

> Of all the dangerous doctrines that could possibly be held out in a legislative assembly, there was not one that could be more mischievous in its tendency than that of equalising all ranks of society by reducing the higher orders to a level with those of a different class, and depriving them of every comfort which they had a right to expect from their exalted situation. [Quoted in Sabine, 1966, p. 5]

As a defence of inheritance, this argument is clearly fallacious, since such expectations are only held *because of* the present laws permitting inheritance, and if there were no inheritance the expectations would not be held.* A more weighty argument for allowing unequal inheritance is that based on the right to support of the close family of the deceased. Since the husband would have continued to maintain his wife and children had he lived, it can be argued that they have a claim to support after his death. Since in many cases the succeeding children are not infant orphans but grown men in their fifties, this justification can only be applied to a minority of cases; and in any case it can only be used to justify an 'adequate' provision for their needs, not the vast bequests that are made at present. Moreover, as usually put, the argument totally ignores the needs of those families where the father was too poor to leave enough to support them; and the obvious solution seems to be that of providing improved social security benefits for all rather than relying on the institution of inheritance.

So far we have considered the justification of inequality in inherited wealth from the standpoint of the recipient. From the

---

*Although it could be argued that in the short run there should be transitional provisions with any reform to prevent hardship to those whose expectations were formed before the reform was announced.

position of the donor, it could be argued that limitation of inheritance (or gifts) would infringe the 'right' of individuals to spend their income as they see fit and that it would be 'unreasonable' to stop someone who wants to give his money to his children (performing his 'proper parental duty') rather than spend it on riotous living. In reply to this three points can be made. Firstly, as I have emphasized in chapter 2, the right to convey property is in no sense an absolute one, and it is subject to any restrictions that society chooses to impose. Secondly, whether or not such gifts could be considered 'reasonable' depends on the sums involved. If there had not previously been large inequality in inherited wealth and the amounts involved were moderate, then the argument might be acceptable. But where a person's ability to leave money to his children derives from substantial inheritance, it is much less so; and the transmission of estates of £1 million can scarcely be justified on the ground that it is a 'proper parental duty'. This was the view of John Stuart Mill, who favoured restricting:

what anyone should be permitted to acquire by bequest or inheritance. Each person should have power to dispose by will of his whole property; but not to lavish it in enriching some one individual, beyond a certain maximum, which should be fixed sufficiently high to afford the means of comfortable independence ... I see nothing objectionable in fixing a limit to what any one may acquire by the mere favour of others, without any exercise of his faculties, and in requiring that if he deserves any further accession of fortune, he shall work for it. [1891, p. 161]

Similarly, President Franklin Roosevelt felt that:

The transmission from generation to generation of vast fortunes by will, inheritance and gift is not consistent with the ideals and sentiments of the American people. The desire to provide security for one's self and one's family is natural and wholesome, but it is adequately served by a reasonable inheritance. Great accumulations of wealth cannot be justified on the basis of personal and family security. [Quoted in Kisker, 1964]

Finally, if an absolute limit on inheritance were felt to be undesirable, virtually the same effect could be achieved through appropriate taxation, in which case money 'spent' on gifts and bequests would be treated in the same way as money spent on tobacco, alcohol or other taxed goods.

In the preceding analysis, the case for greater equality has been based on an appeal to notions of social justice. The case has of course been argued on rather different lines by earlier writers. There are, for example, the arguments based on the desire for 'fraternity' which Donnison has traced from Tawney:

> What a community requires, as the word itself suggests, is a common culture, because, without it, it is not a community at all ... But a common culture cannot be created merely by desiring it. It rests upon economic foundations ... It involves, in short, a large measure of economic equality. [1964, p. 41]

through to Lord Balogh's recent tract on incomes policy: 'without greater equality in consumption, that consensus of opinion will never be reached which is needed to safeguard the steady progress of this country'. (1970, p. 61.) However, these arguments are open to objections. As Donnison has pointed out, it is fallacious to suppose that equality will necessarily achieve the aim that is desired. As he says, 'societies that grow more equal may prove to be not more, but much less fraternal – at least for a time'.

Alternatively, there are the 'economic' applications of utilitarian thought, illustrated by the following passage from Dalton (1925):

> the case against large inequalities of income is that the less urgent needs of the rich are satisfied, while the more urgent needs of the poor are left unsatisfied ... This is merely an application of the economists' law of diminishing marginal utility, which states that, other things being equal as the quantity of ... purchasing power increases, its total utility increases, but its marginal utility diminishes. An unequal distribution of a given amount of purchasing power among a given number of people is, therefore, likely to be a wasteful distribution from the point of view of economic welfare.

The problems inherent in this approach are clear. There is no necessary reason why the utility from a given income should be assumed to be equal for all persons or that it should be assumed to diminish as income increases. This difficulty can be avoided if we understand by 'utility' the value *attached by society* to a given income received by a given person, since it then seems quite defensible to assume that the valuation of a certain income should be the same whoever receives it and that the valuation of an extra £1 should fall as income rises. But such a translation of the approach considerably reduces its force, and effectively means that greater equality has become an ultimate rather than an intermediate goal.

This 'economic welfare' argument for greater equality has also been criticized by C. A. R. Crosland, who claimed (particularly with reference to incomes) that: 'we have now reached the point where further redistribution would make little difference to the standard of living of the masses; to make the rich less rich would not make the poor significantly less poor'. (1964, p. 123.) In the context of the distribution of wealth, this is clearly not true. At present the top 5% own more wealth than the remaining 95%, so that a more equal sharing of total wealth could double the wealth of the majority of the population. We have seen in chapter 2 that if all wealth were equally distributed it would provide every married couple with an income of over £9 a week. In this respect the distribution of wealth is quite different from the distribution of income; not only can inequality in the latter be more readily justified by appeal to deserts, but also the gap between those at the top and those at the bottom of the distribution of wealth is very much wider than is the case with income distribution.

The Standard of Equity

From this analysis, we can conclude that the existing degree of inequality in the amounts of wealth transmitted from generation to generation can be justified neither in terms of deserts nor in terms of need. In the case of accumulated wealth, such definite conclusions cannot be drawn, since inequality may be defensible on grounds of desert (although this justification applies only to certain types of accumulated wealth). These conclusions suggest that the major standard of equity to be adopted in assessing the desirability of different reforms should be that of greater equality of inherited wealth.

We should therefore judge the distributional consequences of reforms primarily in terms of their effect on the total inherited wealth received by a person over his life (the grand total when he dies of the gifts and bequests received). Two aspects of this standard of equity are of great importance – the *assessment over a person's lifetime* taken as a whole, and the restriction to *inherited wealth* – and these distinguish this approach to equity from that commonly adopted. In much of the discussion of inequality in wealth-holding, it is assumed that we are concerned with the current distribution of wealth among all persons alive at a particular moment (as considered in chapter 1). However, our discussion of the justification of equality suggests that this conventional approach, which draws no distinction between accumulated and inherited wealth, may be less relevant than one based on the distribution of inherited wealth alone. The treatment that a person should receive will be judged primarily in what follows on the basis of his having received (say) bequests worth £15,000 over his lifetime rather than on the fact that at some particular date his wealth totalled £25,000. The lifetime aspect is also important: by considering the distribution of inherited wealth, we are treating a person's lifetime as a whole rather than regarding each year in isolation. In this way, we avoid the problems which arise from people being at different stages of the life-cycle, unlike the conventional approach which treats young men of 18 in the same way as those on the verge of retirement.

The reason for adopting inherited wealth as the standard to be applied in assessing the distributional consequences of reforms is that inequality of accumulated wealth may in certain circumstances be held to be justified on grounds of deserts. This is not, however, true of all accumulated wealth and we should not therefore completely disregard the current distribution of wealth as a standard of equity. This is particularly important when we consider the question of control over capital resources, where it is immaterial whether the wealth was acquired through accumulation or inheritance. But in that case we have seen that it is not the current distribution of total wealth that is relevant so much as the distribution of ownership of particular types of assets, especially company shares. The criterion to be applied in assessing the inequality of control should therefore be the concentration of holdings of these assets. Inequality in this respect is hard to justify on grounds of either needs or deserts, although it may be defensible on the ground that society as a whole benefits from there being people with high levels of ability or experience in positions of authority. This and other 'consequential' justifications of inequality are discussed below.

Before leaving the subject of equity, I should refer to a further principle that is often introduced – that of 'horizontal equity'. This principle requires that any measure should treat equally people who were in the same circumstances before the measure was introduced, which in the present context would mean that two people with the same inherited wealth should receive the same treatment: they should pay the same amount of tax and receive the same benefits. In a sense this principle is nothing but a special case of the general argument given earlier – the rejection of unequal treatment based on 'irrelevant' considerations – and it is implied in acceptance of the case for equality: if a reform were to bring about complete equality of inheritance it would necessarily involve equal treatment for two people who had the same inherited wealth before the reform was introduced. However, in practice we are likely to be concerned with measures which, while reducing inequality, do not bring about complete equality. In this case it would be quite possible for two people with the same inherited wealth to receive unequal treatment. Suppose, for example, that we were to consider introducing an inheritance tax that fell only on financial assets and not on real property (the possibility of taxing *all* assets not being open). This would tend to reduce inequality between the rich and the poor, but would offend against the principle of horizontal equity in that Smith with the same total inheritance as Jones might pay more tax just because his inheritance was in the form of shares rather than old masters and Bugattis (it being assumed that the form in which wealth is transmitted is not regarded as a 'relevant' consideration for assessing equity). One interpretation of the principle of horizontal equity would assert that such unequal treatment of equals in fact imposes a 'cost' and that if the gain from the reduction of inequality between rich and poor were small, it would be a reason for rejecting the measure. As a distributional principle this is open to question on the grounds that it attaches undue weight to the before-tax distribution – a distribution which we have seen cannot in any sense be justified. However, as a statement about political attitudes it may be realistic: measures involving grave horizontal inequities are unlikely to attract support. Moreover, the existence of horizontal inequity is an indicator of our failure to satisfactorily close the gap between rich and poor. I shall therefore examine how far measures which have been proposed to secure redistribution do satisfy the principle of horizontal equity.

Consequential Arguments Against Greater Equality

Consequential objections to greater equality are based on what may be called the 'cake and shares' argument that the introduction of measures designed to bring about greater equality would so reduce the total available that everyone – even those whose shares had increased – would be worse off. To quote Sidgwick: 'the objection to Socialism is not that it would divide the produce of industry badly but that it would have so much less to divide'. (Quoted in Wedgwood, 1939, p. 32.) Let us therefore look at the most important ways in which the size of the cake might be reduced by measures designed to bring about greater equality in the distribution of inherited wealth. In doing so, we can distinguish between those effects inherent in the reduction of inequality and those associated with particular methods of achieving redistribution. In the latter case, the magnitude of the effect can only be assessed in the context of a specific proposal, and my purpose here is simply to outline the main factors to be considered.

Effect on Savings

The single most frequent objection to a redistribution of wealth is that it would lead to a reduction in the level of personal savings. This objection assumes both that personal savings would inevitably decrease, and that such a decrease would have adverse consequences. As far as the first of these assumptions is concerned, there is unfortunately little that can be said about the long-run effects. While it is widely believed that a more equal distribution of wealth would necessarily entail a reduction in the level of personal saving, we have seen in chapter 4 that very little is in fact known about the way in which savings behaviour is related to inherited wealth (or indeed to the current distribution of wealth). There is therefore little basis for this presumption, and Alfred Marshall expressed the view that: 'the causes which control the accumulation of wealth differ widely in different countries at different times and high savings may not be associated with inequality'. (Quoted in Lampman, 1957.) In the short run we may be able to predict more confidently the effect of greater equality, but this will depend sensitively on the means adopted to secure redistribution, and cannot usefully be discussed at this juncture.

Rather more can be said about the second assumption that undesirable consequences for the economy would follow if the redistribution of wealth in fact led to a reduction in personal saving. We can distinguish a number of reasons for concern about the level of saving. The first of these relates to the effect on the level of aggregate demand in the economy. In designing his economic policy, the Chancellor of the Exchequer will be trying to balance the overall supply of output (home production plus imports) with the overall demand (consumption plus investment plus exports plus government expenditure). If such a balance is not achieved, either unemployment will rise or there will be an excess demand for output affecting the balance of payments and possibly leading to inflation.* In considering a measure for redistribution (which for simplicity is referred to as a tax), the Chancellor will be concerned with its effect on the level of demand and in particular on consumption (the most likely component to be affected). Suppose, for example, that the tax raises a revenue of £100 million and that this leads to a reduction in consumption of £80 million. To maintain the same level of aggregate demand, the government will have to cut other taxes in such a way as to stimulate demand by £80 million or else increase government expenditure. Since tax reductions are obviously welcome, this causes no problem – even though personal savings have fallen by £20 million. If the tax were to lead

*Throughout the book it is assumed that the economy is at some 'desired' level of employment determined by the government of the day. At the time of writing (spring 1971) there are clear grounds for questioning the desirability of the choice made by the current government, but it is best to keep separate the issue of 'reflating the economy'.

to increased consumption (i.e. personal savings fell by more than the revenue), other taxes would have to be increased to maintain demand at the same level, and this might be less welcome. Whichever happens, however, it is clear that as far as the effect on the level of demand is concerned, it is the impact of the redistributive measure on *consumption* that is relevant and not the effect on savings as such, and that by appropriate action the government can offset the effect of the tax.

Although the effect on the level of aggregate demand will be the Chancellor's chief preoccupation in the short run, he may also be concerned about the composition of total demand and, in particular, the balance between consumption and investment. Many commentators on Britain's current economic position have argued the need for a shift of resources away from consumption towards investment. If we accept the (debatable) implication that faster economic growth is a desirable goal to pursue, we have then to examine whether redistributive measures would affect the rate of investment. In large part, this depends on the 'animal spirits' of investors (to use Keynes's felicitous phrase), an aspect which is discussed further below, but it may also be influenced by the cost of borrowing, which in turn reflects the availability of savings. In considering this question it is important to remember however that personal savings account for less than half of total saving, the remainder being made up from company savings and public savings (excess of government current revenue over current expenditure). If redistribution leads to a fall in personal savings, this can be offset by an increase in public savings. Similarly, public capital formation may be substituted for private investment, if the latter is adversely affected. In the past much of the investment undertaken by the public sector has tended to be complementary to rather than a substitute for private investment, but this could be changed, and in any event direct participation by the government is not necessarily involved, since the same effect could be achieved through investment incentives.

Finally, a reduction in personal savings might take the form of a capital flight from the country, which would have adverse effects on the balance of payments. If redistributive measures led rich people to leave the country (with their wealth), as might happen if higher taxes on capital in Britain made residence in the Bahamas more attractive to millionaires, the balance of payments would suffer. In the context of the European Economic Community careful consideration would need to be given to the steps being taken by the Community towards the removal of restrictions on capital movements, which mean that capital outflows would be potentially more serious than at present.

A reduction in personal savings consequent on the redistribution of wealth is important therefore in so far as it has implications for the level of aggregate demand, for the rate of investment and for the balance of payments. In the case of each proposal we need therefore to examine whether such adverse consequences are likely to follow and whether they can be offset by other policy measures (such as an increase in public saving).

Effect on Work Incentives

A second objection to measures to bring about redistribution is that they would have an adverse effect on the incentive to work. This objection may be interpreted in two different ways. Firstly, it could be held that work in itself is socially desirable, and any reduction therefore undesirable, with no account being taken of the fact that people may actually enjoy the extra leisure. (On this view, the consequences of people's taking an extra day's holiday at Christmas are seen solely in terms of the lost production, with no allowance for the pleasure they derived from sitting by the fireside with their families.) A more sophisticated objection is that the means of redistribution (say a tax on wealth) may distort the choice that people are making between work and leisure, and hence reduce the amount of work done to below the socially optimal level. In this case, the cost to society is not the total of working hours lost but simply the difference between the social value of the working and the leisure hours.

The concept of 'work effort' has a number of different dimensions. As usually interpreted, it refers to the number of hours worked or to the amount of effort made (e.g. on piece-work). However, it also concerns decisions whether or not to enter the labour force (e.g. the decisions of housewives who could go back to work, or of people considering whether or not to retire), whether to work in this country or to emigrate, and what kind of work to do. These aspects are often forgotten, but in quantitative terms are likely to be more important. We need, therefore, to examine the ways in which measures to achieve greater equality may affect these decisions. In some cases, such as that of the married woman deciding whether to go back to work, the decision may be made in much the same way as that of a person deciding whether to work an extra hour's overtime. In other cases it may be quite different. A decision about retirement, for instance, will depend on the resources available if the person stops work: if as a result of (say) a wealth tax he can save less, his pension will be lower and he may be less likely to retire at the minimum retirement age. In considering specific proposals these different dimensions have to be borne in mind. As in the case of savings, there is no presumption that the effect of redistribution would necessarily be adverse. In the case of inherited wealth it seems quite possible that greater equality would *encourage* people to enter the labour force. Dr Johnson, for example, defended primogeniture (rather than equal division of estates) on the grounds that 'it makes but one fool in the family'.

Enterprise and Risk-Taking

Closely allied to the effects on savings and work effort is the objection that redistribution would adversely affect enterprise – or the willingness of businessmen to take risks by investing in new techniques or new products. In other words, redistribution may dampen the 'animal spirits' of investors, and consequently cause the economy to grow less rapidly and render it less flexible in the face of changing conditions.

Whether the redistribution of wealth is in fact likely to have this effect on enterprise depends on two main considerations: the motivation of businessmen, and the opportunity for potential entrepreneurs to obtain access to capital. The first of these factors is clearly important, although it takes us largely outside the field of economics. The second factor – access to capital – depends on the funds which incipient entrepreneurs themselves possess (for example, inherited wealth) and on the availability of funds which can be borrowed for risky investment. As was suggested in chapter 3, the first of these may be of considerable importance, in that a moderate bequest has in many cases facilitated entry into business. The extent to which funds may be borrowed depends in turn on the attitudes of savers to risky types of investment. Lending money to a would-be Lord Nuffield is a dangerous undertaking, which may give a high return, but which is much more likely to lose the lender his capital. In considering the effect of different reforms, we should examine whether they would make savers more or less likely to take such risks with their money.

Under the heading of 'enterprise' we should also consider the argument that greater equality of control over production would have an adverse effect on managerial performance, since there could be no guarantee that the most able people would be in positions of authority. This raises two issues. The first concerns the effect of a more equal distribution of control on the method of selecting managers and the constraints that would be placed on their activities. This depends, of course, on the precise proposal under consideration and cannot usefully be discussed in the abstract. Secondly, there is the empirical question as to how far ability is at present the criterion for the selection of managers. If, as some writers have suggested, inherited wealth is as important a factor as ability in some sectors of the economy, there is no guarantee that the best-equipped people are in authority today. In his *Essays in Persuasion*, Keynes wrote that 'The hereditary principle in the transmission of wealth and the control of business is the reason why the leadership of the Capitalist Cause is weak and stupid. It is too much dominated by third-generation men.' More recently, this appeared in *The Economist*:

> The dynamic firms in Britain – as in Germany and Hong Kong and Japan – are more usually those built up from scratch by impecunious newcomers than those inherited as part of the family birthright. It is management consultants and foreign bankers, more even than socialist doctrinaires, who nowadays can be heard to bewail the effects of Britain's encrusted social structure. [20 March 1965]

Costs of Administration

A further objection to measures designed to redistribute wealth is that they would require administrative resources, and consequently impose a cost on society. In the case of fiscal measures, this applies particularly to the staff required by the tax authorities, and in the immediate future the overloading of the Inland Revenue might be a major argument against any new form of taxation. It also applies to the costs to individual taxpayers in providing the necessary information: a wealth tax, for example, would require individuals to make additional returns giving details of their assets. When we turn to non-fiscal measures there would also be costs of administration. This is true, for example, of schemes to give incentives for small savers (the cost of the advertising campaign for Save As You Earn). In many cases, the costs involved may be very difficult to assess, but wherever possible an attempt is made to do so.

Effect on the 'Quality of Life'

Finally, we should consider a rather different type of objection to the redistribution of wealth: that it would adversely affect the transmission of culture, and hence the 'quality of life'. This objection is based on the view that the great achievements of art and scholarship have been generated under the patronage of a cultured élite, and that this élite depends on the persistence of families enjoying a position of leisured affluence. This view has a long history. Burke argued in his *Reflections on the Revolution in France* that: 'the power of perpetuating our property in our families is one of the most valuable and interesting circumstances belonging to it and that which tends most to the perpetuation of society itself . . . the possessors of family wealth . . . are the natural securities for this transmission.' More recently, it has been put forward particularly by B. de Jouvenel in his *The Ethics of Redistribution*, and by T. S. Eliot, who argued in *Notes towards the Definition of Culture*:

If we agree that the primary vehicle for the transmission of culture is the family, and if we agree that in a more highly civilised society there must be different levels of culture, then it follows that to ensure the transmission of culture of these different levels there must be groups of families persisting, from generation to generation, each in the same way of life. [1948, ch. 2]

As C. A. R. Crosland has pointed out, 'these are seductive arguments, especially to socialists, always neurotically afraid of being thought analphabetic vulgarians'. However, we should note they rest on two crucial assumptions. Firstly, they assume that the élite of cultural patrons is best selected on the basis of inherited wealth. It is far from clear that this is so. Clive Bell in his essay *Civilization* argued the need for such an élite, but dismissed the present method of selection:

At present it [the leisured class] is chosen by inheritance, a grossly extravagant system. There is no reason for supposing that the children of rich parents will be exceptionally intelligent and sensitive; and, in effect, the proportion of the existing leisured class which could be described as 'highly civilized' is absurdly small. [1938, pp. 131–2]

Secondly, there is the assumption that the abolition of a leisured élite would necessarily entail a cultural loss, and that this could not be offset by patronage from the state and from the classes that would gain from the redistribution. There are good reasons for believing that private patronage by the wealthy was historically important. G. M. Trevelyan describes how:

feudal society divided up the surplus product of the labour of the rural serf among barons and knights, bishops and abbots. By stereotyping and regularising the inequality of incomes derived from the land, it enabled wealth to accumulate in the hands of Lords and Prelates and so stimulated the richman's demand for luxuries, whence grew the trade and the higher arts and crafts of the merchant cities ... The arts of civilized life were being forced into medieval England by the unequal distribution of wealth under the feudal and manorial system. [1943, p. 133]

It is not obvious, however, that this situation prevails today – or indeed has done so in recent centuries. The role of Lords and Prelates has at least in part been taken over by public bodies, and as Crosland has argued:

No doubt public patronage has as patchy a historical record as private patronage ... But it performs at least tolerably well in Britain at the moment. The Arts Council, Covent Garden, the art galleries, the British Museum, the Edinburgh Festival, much of the serious theatre, ancient monuments, many historic mansions, and to a growing extent even the Universities, all subsist on, or are aided by, public funds; and the State has not shown itself notably Philistine or unduly interfering as a patron. [1964, p. 175]

These views may appear unduly optimistic at a time when public expenditure is being cut, paintings are being exported to the United States to pay death duties, and there are serious doubts about the independence of bodies dependent on public funds. If, however, in conjunction with its redistributive programme, a government introduced measures to extend public patronage and guarantee the independence of bodies which it supports, there is no reason to believe that this could not replace the lost private patronage. This is not to deny the importance of careful planning of such measures, or the need for increased expenditure (it would require, for example, a much greater willingness on the part of the Treasury to help galleries keep paintings in this country), but the difficulties do not appear insuperable.

The Case for Greater Equality – Conclusions

In this chapter I have examined the arguments that can be made against measures to bring about greater equality. I have suggested in particular that no convincing justification can be given for the persistence of the present extreme inequality of inherited wealth. While it may be possible to defend the transmission of modest amounts of wealth from generation to generation (passing on, for example, the family silver), no justification can be given for one man inheriting £1 million and a hundred inheriting nothing. Inherited wealth at present is quite divorced from considerations of needs or deserts.

Objections to measures to reduce the extreme concentration of inherited wealth must rest, therefore, on the adverse consequences that greater equality might entail. These adverse consequences could take the form of a reduction in savings (which would have implications for the level of aggregate demand, for the rate of growth, and for the balance of payments), in work effort, or in enterprise and risk-taking. There may also be costs of administering the measures required to bring about greater equality. In the analysis of proposed reforms, I shall therefore assess their effectiveness in reducing inequality in the distribution of inherited wealth, and in each case examine whether there are associated adverse consequences of the type outlined, which cannot be offset by appropriate government policy.

Part II
The Reform of Wealth Taxation

If no convincing justification can be given for the persistence of extreme inequality in the distribution of inherited wealth, what can be done to bring about less inequality? There are two principal answers. Firstly, the tax system can be used to reduce the wealth of those at the top of the scale and to induce them to spread it more widely when they die. In Britain this means changes in the existing taxes on wealth (estate duty, capital gains tax and income tax) so as to make them more effective, or the introduction of new taxes. Secondly, there are reforms designed to increase the wealth of the great majority, who at present own virtually nothing. This can be achieved through an extension of the social ownership of wealth or through measures to increase individual wealth-holding.

In this part of the book we focus on the first group of measures – the reform of wealth taxation. Chapter 6 begins by examining the theoretical possibilities – what kinds of tax could be employed – and then describes the taxes that are in force in other countries (some of whom seem to have been more successful in reducing inequality). In chapter 7 we turn to the present tax system in Britain. What effect does it have on the distribution of wealth? How far is it true that death duties are a 'voluntary' tax? The next two chapters look at possible new taxes. Chapter 8 is concerned with proposals for introducing an annual wealth tax in Britain, outlining the principal effects of such a tax and examining the arguments for and against its introduction. Chapter 9 focuses on taxes on the transfer of wealth, and particularly on the possibility of introducing an integrated tax on all gifts and inheritances received by a person over the course of his life – a lifetime capital receipts tax.

6. Wealth Taxes –
An Introduction

The economist does not make new difficulties. He merely brings into prominence some that are latent in everyday discourse. The trouble of examining them in good light is worth what it costs; for it saves constant confusion of thought. – *Alfred Marshall*

Types of Taxes on Wealth

In analysing the effect of taxation on the distribution of wealth it is important to distinguish between three different types of tax:

(1) annual taxes on the income from wealth;
(2) annual taxes on the value of wealth;
(3) taxes on the transfer of wealth.

Exactly what these taxes entail requires some explanation.

Taxes on the income from wealth are levied by most industrial countries in the form of a general income tax: the income from interest, rent or dividends is mostly taxed in the same way as other income. In some respects, however, the income from wealth may receive special treatment. In Britain investment income is effectively taxed more heavily than earnings through the operation of the earned income relief (to be replaced by an investment surcharge under the plans announced in the 1971 Budget). On the other hand, the return to wealth accruing in the form of capital gains is subject to a lower effective rate of tax than other forms of income (and before 1965 long-term gains were completely tax free). In considering the case of a person holding assets which appreciate in value, we have to examine the effective rate on total income – including capital gains – to get an accurate picture of the weight of taxation on the income from wealth.

A tax on the value of wealth would be levied not on the income produced but on the net value of a person's wealth at some specified date in the tax year. With a proportional tax of 2½% on wealth, a man with wealth of £100,000 would be liable for tax of

£2,500 a year.* At first sight it might seem that this is in practice little different from a tax on the income from wealth: if a man's wealth yielded an annual income of 5%, then a 2½% wealth tax would give rise to the same tax liability as a tax on investment income at the rate of 50%. However, the important difference is that the wealth tax liability *would not be affected by the way in which the wealth is invested* or the income it yields. If the same man rearranged his portfolio so that the return rose to 6%, his liability under an investment income tax would increase, but under a wealth tax it would be unaffected. A man whose wealth was all in a form which did not yield any money income, such as old masters, yachts or even pound notes under the bed, would not be liable for any tax under an investment income tax, but would pay just as much wealth tax as the man who had invested the same amount in shares. This leads people to argue that a wealth tax in Britain would be more effective as a redistributive measure (since it would reach those who held their wealth in the form of old masters and yachts) and would not discourage people from holding their wealth in the form of high-yielding assets. These arguments are examined at length in chapter 8. Wealth taxes are in fact in use in a number of countries, including West Germany, the Netherlands, Switzerland and Sweden, and they are discussed later in this chapter.

Taxes on the transfer of wealth differ from the other two types of tax in that they are levied not annually but only when wealth is transferred from one person to another in the form of a bequest or gift: it is not the possession of wealth that is taxed but its transfer. This represents a quite different principle, and the choice between wealth transfer taxes and taxes on wealth (or investment income) is one of the major decisions that has to be made in deciding a strategy for wealth tax reform.

Within the category of wealth transfer taxes, there are a number of distinctions that should be clarified. First, the tax may be based on the *donor* or on the *recipient*. This refers not to the person liable

*In general the tax schedules proposed for a wealth tax have not been proportional but *progressive*: i.e. the proportion of wealth paid in tax would *rise* with the level of wealth. The simplest example of a progressive tax is one where all wealth below a certain level is exempt, and wealth above this level is taxed at a constant rate.

to hand the money over to the Inland Revenue, but to the basis for determining the tax due. If a tax is based on the donor, the rate is determined according to the *total transferred* by a person. This is the case with the present estate duty, where the tax rate is based on a person's total estate regardless of how it is divided between the beneficiaries. If, on the other hand, the tax is levied on the recipient, the rate is based on the *amount received* by each person. An example would be an inheritance tax levied according to the size of each individual bequest. The importance of this distinction depends on the degree of progression of the tax schedule (if the tax were proportional, the same percentage would be paid in tax whichever basis were adopted). Under estate duty, tax of £746,500 would be paid on an estate of £1 million however it was divided. If, however, estate duty were to be applied to individual bequests, and the estate was shared among ten people, then much less tax would be paid (£465,000). (The switch from a donor basis to a recipient basis would clearly encourage the division of estates, and this point is discussed at greater length in chapter 9.)

Secondly, wealth transfer taxes may be classified according to the degree of integration, that is, the extent to which transfers are cumulated when assessing the tax due. The different possibilities can be illustrated with reference to the case of a donor-based tax. At one extreme, we could have a completely integrated tax on all gifts made by a person during his life and on his estate at death, the tax due being assessed on the basis of the cumulated total of gifts plus the estate.* The other extreme is a tax like the present estate duty falling primarily on estates and only including gifts made within a certain period before death (gifts made earlier in life being completely exempt). Between these two extremes come intermediate cases where both gifts and estate are subject to tax, but they are not aggregated when determining the tax due. A number of countries operate separate estate and gifts taxes, where the latter is levied each year on the gifts made in that tax year. Closer to the completely integrated tax is the system in the United

---

*This does not mean that no tax would be paid until the person died. Under such a tax there would no doubt be an equivalent system to Pay As You Earn (Pay As You Donate?) with tax being levied at the appropriate rate on each gift, the rate rising progressively as the cumulative total increased.

States, where estates and gifts are taxed separately, but the gifts tax is based on the cumulated total of gifts made by a person during his life. In the case of recipient-based taxes, similar distinctions can be made, with the possibilities ranging from a tax treating all bequests and gifts separately, through a tax on the total received in each tax year, to a tax based on the cumulative total of gifts and bequests received by an individual over the course of his lifetime. The significance of the degree of integration – over different types of transfer and over time – depends again on the progressiveness of the tax schedule. Under a scheme of proportional taxation, it would make no difference whether the tax was assessed annually or over a lifetime; but with a progressive schedule the tax paid on a series of gifts could be very much smaller with an annual assessment period than with a lifetime assessment. Similarly, where estates and gifts are subject to separate, progressive taxes, a judicious pattern of gifts may allow the wealthy donor to reduce his tax liability very substantially, whereas this would not be possible with an integrated estate and gifts tax.

This number of possible variations may well be confusing, so a guide to the different types of wealth transfer tax is shown in Figure 5. This does not exhaust the conceivable permutations but gives some idea of the field, both with respect to those actually in force in different countries and those that might be introduced.

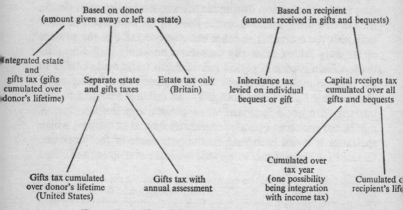

Figure 5: A Classification of Wealth Transfer Taxes

I have outlined above the three main types of tax on wealth to be considered in this part of the book (a fourth possibility – that of a capital levy – is discussed in Part III), and the distinction between them will play an important role in the analysis which follows. At the same time, it should be emphasized that reform of the system of wealth taxation must be seen as a whole, and the relationship between the different types of taxation must be carefully considered. Changes in one type of tax are likely to have repercussions on other forms of taxation, and one cannot propose reforms without regard to these consequences. For example, the effects of introducing a wealth tax would depend on whether the wealth tax paid could be deducted from gross income before income tax is assessed. Suppose that a man earns 8% on his wealth and is paying income tax and surtax at a rate of 75%, so that he receives 2% after tax. If a wealth tax of 2% is introduced and no allowance is made when assessing income tax or surtax, his net return is reduced to nothing; but if the wealth tax could be set against income tax and surtax, his net income would only be reduced to $1\frac{1}{2}$%. Such inter-relationships require careful consideration when we discuss specific proposals for reform.

Redistributive Effect of Taxation – Appearances and Reality

The central purpose of reforming wealth taxation in Britain is to achieve greater equality in the distribution of wealth, and particularly in the distribution of inherited wealth. One of the chief aims of the analysis is, therefore, to assess the contribution made by the present tax system to redistributing wealth, and the extent to which greater redistribution could be achieved through the reform of wealth taxation. This section is concerned with some of the problems which arise in trying to make such an assessment.

The first point to be stressed is the importance of distinguishing between the *formal* (*or nominal*) *incidence* of a tax and its *effective incidence*. 'Formal incidence' concerns the person who nominally pays the tax and on whom the legal liability to hand over the money is imposed. In the case of a wealth tax this is the individual wealth-holder, just as with income tax it is the income receiver, and with corporation tax it is the company. The question of effective incidence, on the other hand, is concerned with the person who *actually bears the burden* of the tax after allowing for adjustments made in response to its introduction: i.e. after allowing for the ways in which the person on whom the tax is formally levied may alter his behaviour and therefore shift part (or all) of the burden on to others. There is no reason to suppose that the effective and nominal incidences of a tax will necessarily coincide. As it was put by an early mathematical economist, Fleeming Jenkin, 'it is well known that many taxes do not fall ultimately on the person from whom they are in the first instance levied'. We have therefore to compare the entire economic situation before and after the tax is introduced, as described by Lady Hicks in her textbook on public finance:

In order to discover the full economic consequences of a tax we have to draw and compare two pictures – one of the economic set-up . . . as it is with the tax in question in operation; the other of a similar economic set-up, but without the tax. It is convenient to call the difference between these two pictures the *Effective Incidence* of the tax. It will be seen that it must often be a very complicated picture; and moreover, since both situations cannot exist together, one of the pictures must be hypothetically established by reasoning and not by observation. [1968, p. 140]

The dangers of not making a distinction between nominal and effective incidence can be illustrated by an example taken from outside the field of wealth taxation – that of the tobacco duty. The nominal incidence of the tax falls on the cigarette manufacturer, who pays the duty on the tobacco leaf as he withdraws it from bond. It seems very unlikely, however, that the full impact of the tax falls on the profits of the cigarette manufacturers; each time the duty is increased, they raise the price to the consumer (or make equivalent adjustments to the quality), and a large part of the *effective* burden falls on the smoker. It is not necessarily the case that the effective incidence differs from the formal incidence, and after examining the likely effects of the tax, we may conclude that the burden is not going to be shifted on to anyone else. Indeed, in the case of wealth taxation this has been the conclusion reached by a number of authors. The important point is that we should be aware that it is possible for the actual effect of a tax to be rather different from that expected from its formal incidence.

The second problem to be considered in assessing the distributional consequences of a tax reform is that a tax may appear to have a substantial redistributive effect, but be rendered ineffective by loopholes which allow avoidance or evasion. An example would be where, for administrative reasons, certain types of asset (for example, woodlands) are excluded from the scope of a wealth tax. We should then have to examine how far this type of asset was owned by the rich, and the extent to which they would be likely to rearrange their portfolios to include more woodlands. It has in fact often been alleged that because of the wide opportunities for avoidance the present estate duty is largely ineffective. In the next chapter I discuss how far this view is in fact correct (and the extent to which the situation has been changed by the last Labour government's Budgets). Avoidance is relevant not only to the assessment of the degree of redistribution between the wealthy and the less wealthy but also to the considerations of the political acceptability of tax reform. It would be likely to detract seriously from its public acceptability if we were to propose a tax such that, as a result of avoidance, the well-informed (and possibly less scrupulous) members of the community could pay much less than others with the same wealth. As it has been put by G. S. A. Wheatcroft, 'our social stability depends to a considerable extent on our taxes not being thought too unfair. The tax-gatherer may be regarded as a beast but, like the old schoolmaster, he should be a just beast.' (1969(b), p. 15.)

The problems outlined above of distinguishing nominal and effective incidence and of allowing for tax avoidance should be considered not only when analysing the consequences of tax reforms but also in the design of the reforms themselves. In the *Wealth of Nations* Adam Smith included as one of his canons of taxation that 'the tax which each individual is bound to pay ought to be certain and not arbitrary'. He was referring to certainty for the individual, but certainty is as important for society as it is for the individual taxpayer. In my view, an important aim of the reform of wealth taxation should be to make the effective incidence as transparent as possible. In designing new taxes we should attempt to make it quite clear just how much (or how little) redistribution is taking place.

Basis for Comparing Taxes

Chapters 8 and 9 are concerned with possible changes in the tax system entailing the introduction of new taxes or the modification of existing taxes. It may be useful at this juncture to discuss the general basis for an examination of the effect of changes in taxation. Such changes could take one of three main forms:

(1) the introduction of a new tax and the abolition of an existing tax (or a reduction in its rates);
(2) the introduction of a new tax and the use of the revenue to increase wealth-holding at the lower end of the scale;
(3) the introduction of a new tax as a net addition to taxation.

Suppose first that the government were to introduce a new tax and reduce (or abolish) an existing tax. On what basis would it decide by how much the existing tax could be reduced? One possibility would be to reduce the tax by an amount such that the revenue to the government remained the same, leaving the Budget balance unaffected. If a wealth tax raised £300 million revenue, then another tax could be reduced by an amount yielding the same revenue. However, if the government were to do this there would be no guarantee that the level of aggregate demand would be unaffected. As argued in the previous chapter, the effect on the level of demand is likely to be a primary concern of the Chancellor of the Exchequer. Suppose, for instance, that he was considering the introduction of a wealth tax yielding £300 million and reducing income tax by 2½% (which would cost about the same in revenue terms). Since a substantial part of the wealth tax would be paid out of savings (a question discussed in detail in chapter 8), whereas the cut in income tax would lead to a large rise in consumption, the net effect would be inflationary. As such the package would scarcely be acceptable to the Chancellor (assuming that he was otherwise following a stable demand policy) and he would argue that income tax could only be reduced by an amount which kept the level of demand unchanged. In considering tax 'swaps', we have therefore to base the comparison on tax rates which would have the same effect on aggregate demand. This means that we must predict the effect of the proposed change on the level of consumption, investment and other components of final demand. Such projections are not easy to make, and in the case of wealth taxation are rendered more difficult by the long period of time over which the effects are likely to operate. For this reason, the figures used later are only very approximate, and chiefly relate to the immediate effects of tax changes. The important point, however, is that we should not blithely use revenue as a basis for comparison and assume that balancing the budget is all that matters.

The second type of change is one in which the revenue from the introduction of a new tax would be used by the government to encourage wealth-holding at the lower end of the scale. There is, however, little difference in substance between this and the previous case. If, for example, the government introduced tax remissions for saving it would simply be equivalent to reducing taxation, and any subsidy of this kind can be seen simply as a negative tax. Again, therefore, the basis for analysis that we should adopt is one where the level of aggregate demand would be left unchanged: if we are considering using the proceeds from a wealth tax to finance a capital element in the National Insurance retirement pension, the amount that could be handed out would depend on the amount by which the recipients increased their consumption.

Thirdly, there is the possibility of introducing a new tax as a net addition to taxation – if for example the government brought in a wealth tax with no other adjustment in its budget. This could, however, only have a neutral effect on aggregate demand in the rather special case where consumption is completely unaffected (the tax being paid entirely from a reduction in personal saving). If the tax were to be deflationary – if consumption were in fact decreased – then to maintain the same pressure of demand the Chancellor would have to reduce another tax (or increase government expenditure). If the wealth tax were actually to be inflationary, with consumption increasing, then the Chancellor would have the more unpleasant task of raising other taxes (or cutting expenditure). In this sense, the third possibility does not represent a valid basis for comparison, and the introduction of a new tax is likely to involve some compensating adjustment elsewhere.

The effect on the level of aggregate demand is undoubtedly the primary consideration for the Chancellor, but the revenue raised by a tax has some effects which should be taken into account. In the case of the introduction of a wealth tax and a reduction in income tax, we saw that the revenue from the wealth tax would probably be larger than that from the income tax reduction (allowed on the basis of maintaining demand at the same level). This means that the government's budget surplus would be increased (or its deficit decreased). In other words, it could use the revenue to reduce the National Debt by buying up government stock that is outstanding or by reducing the new issues that it had planned to float. This reduction in the National Debt would itself have implications for the distribution of income and wealth. Since interest would no longer have to be paid, there could be a reduction in taxation, which might in turn affect the accumulation of wealth. We should therefore look not only at the direct effect of a new tax on the distribution of wealth, but also at the indirect effect of a reduction in the National Debt. It is important to bear this consideration in mind when reading chapters 8 and 9, where I focus solely on the direct effects; discussion of the effect that increased revenue may have in reducing the National Debt is postponed to chapter 10.

Taxes on Wealth in Other Countries

Before embarking on this brief survey of taxes in other countries, I should enter two qualifications. First, it is important to consider a particular tax in relation to the fiscal system of the country as a whole: the effect of a wealth tax for example is difficult to assess unless something is known about the treatment of income from capital. In the space of this short survey, it is not, however, possible to give a full description of the fiscal systems of the countries concerned. Secondly, the information given below is not guaranteed to be up to date. My purpose is not to provide a current tax guide but simply to illustrate the taxes which are (or have been) employed.

Annual Wealth Taxes

Wealth taxes are employed in a number of Western European countries, where they have had a long history (some Swiss cantons having had continuous experience with wealth taxation since the thirteenth century). Annual wealth taxes have also been adopted in the past two decades by a number of Latin American and Asian countries including Ceylon, India, Pakistan, Colombia and Uruguay.

Some of the most important features of the wealth taxes in force in these countries are described briefly below:

Tax Base. In most cases, the tax is in theory levied on the total net wealth of the person (or family), but for administrative and other reasons there are usually a number of exemptions. Sweden, for example, exempts household effects, life insurance policies, pension rights and works of art.

Exemption Level. The level at which a person becomes liable for the wealth tax affects both the redistributive effect of the tax and the administrative problems. The figures below show the exemption levels in a number of European countries:

		£ (approximate)
Luxembourg	100,000 Fr	850
Switzerland	10,000 SwF	1,000
Norway	30,000 Kr	1,750
West Germany	20,000 DM	2,400
Netherlands	40,000 Fl	4,700
Denmark	90,000 DKr	5,000
Sweden	100,000 Kr	8,000

There is a wide range, with a low exemption level in Luxembourg and Switzerland and a much higher level in Sweden. The rates shown apply to a single person and in a number of countries the exemption is higher for a married couple. In certain countries there are also higher exemption levels for old people.

Tax Rates. The rates of tax above the exemption level differ between countries (in some cases the rate increases with the level of wealth):

Switzerland	0·2–0·6%
Netherlands	0·5%
Luxembourg	0·5%
Norway	0·5–1·75%
Sweden	0·8–1·8%
West Germany	1·0%
Denmark	1·2–2·3%

Tax Ceiling. In a number of countries, the wealth tax and the income tax are linked in such a way as to ensure that the total rate of taxation does not exceed a certain ceiling. In the Netherlands the total tax (income tax plus wealth tax) cannot exceed 80% of the taxpayer's income, and Sweden has a similar provision. In West Germany, the wealth tax is allowed as a deduction against taxable income, so that the total tax cannot exceed the income from the capital, unless this by itself is less than the rate of wealth tax.

Administration. The administration of the wealth tax is commonly linked to that of the income tax. In Sweden it is included on the same tax return, and the P.A.Y.E. system is designed to cover the wealth tax liability as well as that under income tax.

Wealth Transfer Taxes

Taxes on wealth transfers are used in a large number of countries. In some countries, such as the United Kingdom, the United States, Italy, Canada and Japan, they are the principal means of taxing wealth; however, many countries with an annual wealth tax also impose these duties, including Sweden, Norway, Denmark, Germany, Netherlands, Colombia and India.

In considering the different taxes employed, I follow the classification suggested earlier in the chapter:

Donor-based taxes with complete integration. Taxes with complete integration are virtually unknown, but there are two countries which approach it quite closely. In Colombia a person is taxed at death on the total of all gifts made during his lifetime plus his estate. However, since no credit is allowed for the separate gifts tax paid, this does not represent complete integration. In Italy, there are separate gifts and estate taxes, but the value of *inter vivos* gifts made by the decedent to his heirs must be added to the value of his estate in determining the rate of estate duty payable.

Donor-based taxes with incomplete integration. Britain represents an extreme case as far as integration is concerned in that it does not tax gifts at all (apart from those made within seven years of death). In between Britain and the case of complete integration come countries, such as the United States, which tax gifts at a lower rate than bequests. Under the United States Federal tax system, the gifts tax rate is only three quarters of that on estates, and there are additional lifetime exclusions and annual exemptions for gifts to any one person. A person who gives away $500,000 during his life pays considerably less tax than if he leaves it as an estate at his death, the effective rate being some 20% rather than 35% (although gifts deemed to have been made 'in contemplation of death' are in fact taxed as part of the estate). The degree of integration under the United States system is greater than that which was used in Canada, where the gifts made by a person were not cumulated over his lifetime but were taxed on an annual basis. In this way, twelve annual gifts of $10,000 only bore tax at a rate of 10%, whereas the annual rate on a gift of $120,000 was over 20%.

Recipient-based taxes. These have likewise been adopted with differing degrees of integration. A number of countries tax the share received by a person from a given estate together with gifts received from the decedent during his life. Such taxes have been (or are) in force in France, Belgium, the Netherlands, West Germany and Norway.* However, these taxes fall a long way short of a completely integrated tax on capital receipts, where the rates of taxation would be progressive with respect to the total value of

*With this type of taxation, it is common for the rate of tax to depend not only on the size of the gift but also on the relationship between the donor and the recipient. In France, the rate of inheritance tax for property passing from father to son or husband to wife varies between 5% and 15%, whereas for property passed between uncle and nephew the rate is 50%, and the rate for total strangers is 60%. The British Legacy Duty (abolished in 1949) depended similarly on the degree of consanguinity.

bequests and gifts received by a person during his lifetime. The only country to have had a complete lifetime accessions tax of this type is Japan, where it was introduced in 1950 as a result of the Shoup Report on Japanese Taxation (although the tax was subsequently modified). Under the Shoup proposals, there was to be a progressive tax on lifetime accessions, with rates ranging from 20–75%. Where a gift or bequest was received, it was to be added to the amount received to date and the tax computed on the resulting total. The current tax liability was then to be computed by subtracting the tax paid to date.

Integration of receipts tax with income taxation. A proposal not so far discussed is that gifts and bequests should be regarded in the same way as income and should be taxed under the ordinary income tax. This scheme was in fact enacted in the United States income tax of 1894 (which was declared unconstitutional). Although it did not appear in subsequent legislation, the idea was later advocated by H. Simons of the University of Chicago, and more recently it has been taken up by the Canadian Royal Commission on Taxation (the Carter Commission). In its report in 1966, the Commission recommended that gifts and bequests be taxed as income to the recipient on the same basis as earnings, dividends, etc. The estate and gift taxes would then be repealed, leaving the income tax as the sole vehicle of taxation on wealth transfers. Although it is unlikely to be enacted, this proposal is an interesting one, and is considered in chapter 9.

7. The Impact of the Present Tax System

We know that the astuteness of lawyers and the vigila ι care for personal interests continually are at work to defeat and escape the operation of the law – and this with such extraordinary success that, although there has been an immense increase in the personal property of the country, such an increase is scarcely traceable in the tables of your Legacy Duty. – *W. E. Gladstone, 1853*

The principal tax on wealth in Britain today is the estate duty, and the first part of this chapter examines its effectiveness in bringing about greater equality in the distribution of wealth. The second part of the chapter is concerned with the taxation of investment income and its impact on the accumulation and transmission of wealth.

Estate Duty

Death duties have a long history, and there is evidence of their having been paid in Egypt in the second century B.C. on the registration of property devolving by reason of death. In Britain, they have their origins in the Anglo-Saxon *heriot* rendered to the feudal lord on the death of a tenant and in the fees paid to ecclesiastical courts for issuing grants of representation. The British government's use of taxes on the transfer of property at death began with the Probate Duty enacted in 1694, a duty based on the stamp duties introduced in the States of Holland a number of years earlier. The circumstances of their introduction in Holland may be of interest to a modern Chancellor:

The States of Holland, finding the impositions laid upon merchandise to be very heavy, and yet that they were not enough neither for defraying the charges which daily grew upon them, by a public edict invited any of the subjects to make their proposals, with the promise of a large reward to such as should find a way of raising taxes that might be less burdensome to the people, and more useful to the government. [Soward and Willun, 1919]

Today no reward seems necessary to induce people to enter the competition!

The English Probate Duty was a fixed amount independent of the sum transferred and it was not until 1779 under Lord North that the first attempt was made to vary the tax paid according to the value of the property. Lord North was also responsible for the introduction of Legacy Duty, which varied with the amount received by each beneficiary. This was extended by Pitt in 1796, although it applied only to personal and not landed property (a Bill to include the latter was passed only by the casting vote of the Speaker and was consequently withdrawn). The exemption of landed property from Legacy Duty was a source of considerable discontent, and in 1853 Gladstone introduced a corresponding tax (Succession Duty) on real and settled property. Gladstone was also responsible for the modification of Probate Duty in 1881. In 1889, Mr Goschen introduced for the first time an element of progression into the schedule with his Temporary Estate Duty, and this paved the way for the introduction of the modern estate duty by Sir William Harcourt in his Budget of 1894 (in the place of Probate Duty and the Temporary Estate Duty). The 1894 estate duty applied to all property passing at death, with a progressive schedule of rates rising to 8% on estates over £1 million. The Legacy and Succession Duties remained until 1949, when they were abolished by Sir Stafford Cripps.

The present estate duty retains basically the same form as that enacted in 1894, although there has been a long series of amendments covering detailed provisions. Duty is charged on the capital value of property 'deemed to pass on death', by which is broadly understood all property over which the deceased had disposition, all property in which he had a life interest (such as a trust fund) and all gifts made within the preceding seven years. There are a number of special provisions, including reduced rates of duty on agricultural property, business assets owned directly and gifts made more than four years before death. Certain types of property (for example, growing timber) do not need to be aggregated with the rest of the estate, and therefore effectively bear a lower rate of duty. Some property is exempt altogether, including property settled on a surviving spouse which bore estate duty on the first death, certain gifts (up to £5,000 in consideration of marriage), property left to charities (up to £50,000) and objects of national, scientific or artistic interest (under certain conditions). There is also a 'quick succession' relief, under which property passing on two successive deaths within a five-year period is taxed on a reduced scale on the second death.

The Rates of Estate Duty

The scale of duties introduced by Harcourt in 1894 was described by its opponents as 'perfectly monstrous', and the maximum rate of 8% was said by one speaker in the House of Commons to 'throw into shade everything that had ever been done in the way of highway robbery'. What he would have thought of the current rates is hard to imagine! The rates at present in force (March 1973) are shown below:

Size of estate	No property surviving spouse	Whole property surviving spouse
£	%	%
15,000	0	0
25,000	11	0
50,000	24	12
100,000	37	29
200,000	50	45
1,000,000	69	67
2,500,000	73	77

The principal changes in the estate duty rates between 1894 and the present day are illustrated in Table 15, which shows the exemption level and the duty payable on representative estates.

For estates of £10,000 the rate of duty has fallen, but above this level there has been a steady rise in the rates over the period, and the duty on large estates has risen very sharply. Moreover, when allowance is made for the effects of inflation, the effective rate of tax can be seen to have risen even more: £100,000 in 1894 would be worth very much more in purchasing power today. The figures given in brackets in the last line of the table show the rate of duty payable in 1972 on an estate of the same real value as in 1894. On

Table 15: Changes in Estate Duty 1894–1972

	Budget*	Exemption level £	Duty payable (%) on estate: £10,000	£100,000	£1,000,000
Harcourt	1894	100	3	5½	7½
Lloyd George	1909	100	4	8	14
A. Chamberlain	1919	100	4	14	28
Churchill	1925	100	4	19	29
Snowden	1930	100	4	19	38
Simon	1939	100	4	23	46
Dalton	1946	2,000	4	30	65
Cripps	1949	2,000	4	45	75
Jenkins	1969	10,000	0	47	75
Barber†	1972	15,000	0 (30)	37 (65)	69 (75)

*Only those budgets are included in which there were major changes in the rates.

†Assuming no property left to a surviving spouse.

Source: annual reports of the Inland Revenue, various years.

this basis, the duty on an estate of £100,000 has risen from 5½% to 65%. On the other hand, even allowing for inflation, the exemption limit is now considerably higher than in 1894, so that the burden on the smallest estates has been lightened. The combined effect of budgets and inflation has been, therefore, to make the estate duty more progressive at both the top and the bottom of the scale.

It is widely believed that the British death duties are much fiercer than comparable taxes in other industrial countries. According to one textbook, 'the U.K. estate duty is probably the highest in the world for any country of comparable social and economic structure' (Sandford, 1969). This conclusion is usually based on a comparison of the top rates, and in particular of the 75% rate in Britain, with the lower top rates in the United States, Australia, Canada and other countries. But it is not only the maximum rate that is relevant, and to make a proper comparison we should examine the whole tax schedule. The argument that comparable estates pay more tax in Britain than elsewhere requires a definition of what is meant by 'comparability'. One basis for comparison would be to take estates of the same value, using the exchange rate to convert from one currency to another, so that an estate of £100,000 would be compared with one in the United States of $240,000. However, this approach takes no account of the differences in average wealth between countries – a person with wealth of £100,000 in Britain has something like 40 times the wealth of the average person in Britain, whereas a man worth $240,000 in the United States has only about ten times the average. For a comparison of the tax paid by people in the same position in the wealth scale, it seems more reasonable to take not the exchange rate, but the ratio of average wealth in the countries concerned as the basis for comparison. In the case of Britain and the United States (Federal Estate Tax), this gives a conversion rate of about $10 to £1, and the following results:

Estate		Tax rate (%)	
£ in U.K.	$ in U.S.	in U.K.	in U.S.
10,000	100,000	0	5
25,000	250,000	11	19
50,000	500,000	24	25
100,000	1,000,000	37	30
200,000	2,000,000	50	36
1,000,000	10,000,000	69	60
2,500,000	25,000,000	75	70

It appears from this comparison that for smaller estates the tax rates are rather lower in Britain. The minimum exemption is more generous and the British rate does not catch up with that in the United States until the estate reaches some £60,000. The rate on large estates is higher, although the gap tends to narrow for estates above £1 million. These figures relate to the basic tax schedule and make no allowance for any special provisions (e.g. where the property is left to a surviving spouse). For any individual estate, the tax paid may therefore be rather different from that shown. In particular, the United States law has a more generous treatment of property left to a surviving spouse, which may effectively halve the rate of duty. On the other hand in Britain the reduced rates for agricultural property and business assets, the non-aggregation provisions and the special treatment of settled property may have the same effect.

Finally, it may be helpful to give some idea of the overall importance of estate duty in relation to total government revenue and total personal wealth. The revenue from estate duty in 1970–71 was £360 million. As such, it accounts for about 3% of government revenue, so that its fiscal importance is relatively small. The contribution of death duties to total tax revenue has in fact fallen steadily over the century. In 1909, when Lloyd George described them as a 'revenue-producing machine of very high efficiency', they accounted for about 12% of total revenue. The revenue from estate duty also represents a small proportion of total personal wealth – 0·3% – or less than one tenth of the annual *increase*.

Impact of Estate Duty on the Distribution of Wealth

Although death duties had their origins in this country in the need to raise revenue, the modern estate duty has been seen by many as a means to achieve a more equitable distribution of wealth. When Dalton in his 1946 Budget raised the duty on large estates and lowered that on small estates, he argued that these measures would reduce 'from both ends, the gap which separates the standard of living of the great mass of our fellow citizens from that of a small privileged minority'. How successful has estate duty been in achieving this aim?

In chapter 1 we saw that over the course of this century there has been a decline in the degree of inequality in the distribution of wealth, the share of the top 1% having fallen from 69% in 1911–13 to about 40% in 1960. This might appear to suggest that death duties have been effective in bringing about redistribution, but there are two reasons why this conclusion does not necessarily follow. Firstly, as was argued in chapter 1, the fall in the share of the top 1% may simply reflect the rearrangement of wealth-holdings within families, as the rich pass their wealth on earlier to avoid estate duty. This argument was supported by the finding that, while the share of the top 1% had fallen, that of the next 4% had increased substantially. To the extent that this 4% includes the sons of the very rich, the redistribution has been very much a 'family affair'. Estate duty may have been responsible for this development but it cannot be claimed as a genuine redistribution of inherited wealth.

Secondly, there is the methodological problem arising from our not knowing what would have happened had estate duty not been in force. It is possible that there were in any event forces at work leading towards greater equality of wealth-holding, and that estate duty only had a minor influence (or perhaps no influence at all) in accelerating this trend. On the other hand, the distribution of wealth might have become considerably more unequal had it not been for estate duty. Sir Hubert Henderson, for example, argued in 1926 that 'had it not been for the death duties Britain would have become by now a Paradise of the Idle Rich in a degree far greater than is actually the case'. Closely related to this point is the possibility that the burden of estate duty may not be fully borne by those on whom it is nominally levied. The effective incidence of the tax may not be the same as its formal incidence. If, for example, estate duty has reduced the supply of savings (particularly the savings available for investment in risky undertakings), it may have caused the return to capital to be higher than it would otherwise have been. The impact of estate duty would therefore have been partly offset by the increased income accruing to wealth-holders. Unfortunately we have no real way of testing whether or not this has in fact happened.

It is difficult, therefore, to draw any firm conclusions about the effectiveness of estate duty. It may, however, be useful to get some idea of the *maximum* effect that estate duty could have on the assumption that the effective incidence coincides with the nominal incidence (and that there is no room for avoidance – an assumption which is discussed later). For this purpose, let us consider a hypothetical family living off the income from their wealth, and examine the effect of estate duty on the wealth transmitted from generation to generation (assuming an average generation length of 33 years). The first generation of the family is assumed to have died just as Harcourt's 1894 Budget took effect, leaving an estate of £500,000 (equivalent to some £4 million today). This would have been subject to duty of 7%, and the son would have received £465,000.* Let us assume for the moment that the amount which he saved out of the income was just enough to maintain the real

*No account is taken in these calculations of the Legacy and Succession Duty payable, but this would have made little difference.

value of his capital, so that when he died in 1927 he left a gross estate of some £925,000. The duty on this estate would have been £268,250. The grandson would in turn have lived until 1960; and if he too had just maintained the real value of his inheritance his estate would have been £1,700,000 and the estate duty £1,360,000. On this basis, the (after tax) inherited wealth of the current generation would have been 68% of the estate left by his great-grandfather. In real terms, however, it would have been less than 15%, which suggests that death duties would have had a powerful equalizing effect. While not exactly 'riches to rags', the fall of the family fortunes in real terms would have been quite dramatic. Moreover, only one of the deaths in this hypothetical family was at a time when the present very high rates of estate duty were in force.

In this example, we have assumed that the family did not attempt to build up the estate to its previous level – there was no additional saving to offset the inroads of estate duty. In chapter 3 we have seen that by investing in a selection of 'respectable' equities, they should in the past have been able to earn a return of 6%, allowing for income tax and inflation. (In view of the amount of wealth they are assumed to own, they would also have been subject to surtax, although this would not have applied to that part of the return which was in the form of capital gains.) If they had saved a quarter of this income the accumulation would have done much to offset the effect of estate duty. Notwithstanding the tax paid in 1894, 1927 and 1960, the present representative of the family would still leave an amount equivalent to £2 million today. This shows that the effectiveness of estate duty in reducing the transfer of wealth between generations depends sensitively on the way in which the rich react. It is of course true that the extra accumulation necessary to offset estate duty reduces the consumption of the wealthy, and in this sense the tax is a burden, but it does not bring about the more equitable distribution of inherited wealth with which we are concerned.

Avoidance of Estate Duty

In assessing the redistributive effect of estate duty, it is clearly very important to examine how far the effective rate of tax is reduced through avoidance. As the quotation at the beginning of the chapter demonstrates, concern with the avoidance of death duties is not simply the result of the high rates of duty in recent years: it appears that the wealthy were anxious to avoid tax when the rates were 10% or less. However, the current high rates of duty have undoubtedly increased the incentive to avoid (or evade) death duties and the problem is without question more serious than in 1853. Every day *The Times* typically carries several advertisements of the following type:

GREAT NEWS for the AFFLUENT UNDER 60s! At last your Estate Duty problem can be solved without disturbing the composition of your existing assets in any way.

Heirs . . . or estate duty? *Choose* while you still have a choice. If you let it, Estate Duty will make a mockery of your life's work!

There are, of course, both *avoidance* and *evasion*, the former being a legal readjustment of one's position to reduce the duty payable and the latter being illegal (such as failing to declare all the assets of the deceased). Evasion is probably unimportant, if only because avoidance is so easy, and it is on avoidance that I shall concentrate here.

Estate duty avoidance is a highly specialized subject, and it is beyond the scope of this book to do more than sketch a few of the main avenues (it must also be remembered that these change over time as both poacher and gamekeeper become more sophisticated; for example, some of the most celebrated loopholes were closed in the Labour Budgets of the 1960s, but further methods of avoidance have been developed in response):

Gifts. The most obvious way to avoid estate duty is by the transfer of wealth before death by gifts *inter vivos*. The estate duty would, of course, be unworkable if all gifts made before death were exempt, since everyone who died in his bed could make a gift of his whole estate just before he expired. The law has always been that gifts made within a certain period of death were treated as passing at death and aggregated with the estate. Initially this period was three months, but since then it has been extended and is currently (since the 1968 Budget) seven years. This means that gifts are only a successful means of avoidance if they are made with sufficient foresight. There are, however, reduced rates of duty for gifts made more than four years before death, and there are special provisions for particular types of gift. Gifts up to £500 are exempt; gifts made 'in consideration of marriage' are exempt if less than £1,000 (£5,000 for parents and grandparents). For a gift to escape duty, it must be given outright with no right of use or other benefit retained by the giver. In so far, therefore, as the spectre of King Lear pursues would-be estate duty avoiders, the use of trusts (which are discussed later) rather than direct gifts may be more attractive.

Assets which bear lower rates of duty. There are two classes of assets on which reduced rates of estate duty are payable – agricultural land and private business assets – and in both cases the duty charged is reduced by 45%. The first of these concessions stemmed from the feeling that land carried certain responsibilities which other forms of property did not. Queen Victoria, for example, wrote to Harcourt at the time of his 1894 Budget that 'The Queen is much concerned about the provisions made in the Budget regarding death duties which, in her opinion, cannot fail to cripple all landowners. Many properties are now only kept afloat at considerable loss to the proprietors.' The second concession was introduced more recently (1954) when there was concern that death duties were leading to the break-up of family businesses, since the assets had in some cases to be liquidated to meet the duty. Holding wealth in the form of these specially treated assets undoubtedly forms one avenue of avoidance, although the amount involved is fairly small.

Assets not aggregated with the rest of the estate. The general rule is that all property in the possession of the deceased or in which he had an interest is aggregated, and the aggregate value determines the duty payable. In some cases, however, property is not aggregated and is treated as a separate estate, which leads to a reduction in the total duty payable (the duty payable on two estates of £25,000, for instance, is about half that payable on one estate of £50,000). One example of this which used to apply before the 1969 Budget was property of artistic, national, scientific or historic interest. Although no longer relevant, this is an interesting example of the devices that can be contrived. Under the estate duty rules, no duty is liable on property of this type (e.g. old masters) so long as they are kept or eventually sold to a national or local museum. If they are sold to a private buyer, duty has to be paid; however, under the pre-1969 rules, the duty payable was at the rate applicable to the rest of the estate. So if a millionaire died in 1968 leaving his son £1 million of pictures and £4,999 in other wealth, no duty would be payable even if the son sold all the paintings at once to an American collector – for the rate of duty on the rest of the estate (£4,999) was nil and this was the rate applied to the pictures! A case where the non-aggregation provisions still operate is growing timber, and this enjoys the further concession that the duty is not payable until the timber is sold.

Trusts. When discussing gifts *inter vivos*, it was pointed out that a person may wish to retain some control over his wealth rather than give it away outright. For this reason, he may prefer to leave his money in the form of a trust, where the beneficiary does not have control over the capital; and this device was commonly used in the past to ensure that profligate heirs did not dissipate their inheritance. However, it was also used in medieval times as a means of avoiding the feudal dues payable to the lord of the manor when land was transferred to a minor, and today trusts are often used in the same way as a means of avoiding estate duty. In general, an interest in a trust fund attracts estate duty when the recipient dies: it counts as part of his estate. There are, however, two exceptions to this rule which provide means of avoiding (or reducing) estate duty. The first is where property is settled on a surviving spouse. In that case, duty is payable when the first spouse dies, but not when the survivor dies. The second is where the trust takes the form of a *discretionary trust*. The essence of this form of trust is that the beneficiaries are not entitled to any interest in the fund and have no enforceable claim on any part of the income or capital. The settlor provides the trustees with a list of beneficiaries, but how the income and capital is shared out between them is completely at the discretion of the trustees (in practice of course, they are likely to take into account the settlor's wishes). Providing that the beneficiaries did not include the settlor or his wife, that there was more than one surviving beneficiary, and that the seven-year period applying to gifts elapsed before the settlor died, then – before the 1969 Budget – the trust did not attract estate duty on anyone's death. No duty was payable when a beneficiary died since he had no *right* to any part of the fund, and nothing could be said to pass on his death. In this way, estate duty could be avoided for a number of generations, and this factor undoubtedly accounts for the increase in popularity of such trusts in recent years. G. S. A. Wheatcroft, for example, expressed the view a few years ago that 'in Great Britain it is probably true to say that 95% of all discretionary and accumulation trusts are created solely for tax-saving reasons'. Since the 1969 Budget, however, the position has changed, and a person who has received income or capital from a discretionary trust over the seven years before his death becomes subject to estate duty. The proportion of the trust fund included in his estate is broadly equal to the proportion of the income of the fund which he has received over that seven years. This reform will undoubtedly reduce the effectiveness of discretionary trusts as a means of avoidance, but it will still be open to trustees to allocate the income in such a way that little (or no) estate duty is paid.

Emigration. The most extreme form of estate duty avoidance is for a person to leave the country, taking his capital with him. In order to avoid duty in this way, he has to establish domicile in a foreign country and prove that he has permanently severed connection with this country. Apart from the possible disadvantages of separation from his family, this manoeuvre has to be carried out with some care (and he has also to choose his tax haven with circumspection). Emigration, therefore, represents a quite drastic rearrangement of a person's affairs, and is not really in the same class as the other measures.

This brief survey shows that there remain a number of ways in which estate duty liability can be reduced or avoided altogether. The situation has been well described by the chairman of one City firm as follows:

We cannot take our assets with us but we do have the option of leaving most of them either to our family or to the estate duty office.

Apart from those with very modest means, anyone who takes specialist advice – preferably in good time, but if necessary at the eleventh hour – will be able to reduce the Inland Revenue's share and so benefit his family. [*The Times*, 23 September 1970]

The avoidance of estate duty does in general involve some re-arrangement of assets or loss of control over their use; however, the gains are likely to outweigh these disadvantages. The ease of avoidance is in fact such that: 'whenever a particularly large estate is reported in the press with the duty paid representing between 60% and 80% of the value of the estate, the deceased is regarded as an eccentric.' (Revell, 1967, p. 110.) It is not of course true that every rich man seeks to avoid estate duty – it is clear from the estate duty returns that many do not. Some people do not do so because they lack the necessary information or advice; others because they are unwilling to contemplate the prospect of death and to make provision for it; some people believe that avoidance, while legal, is morally or socially unacceptable. At the same time, there are undoubtedly many who have the advice and are undeterred by moral doubts or the unwillingness to contemplate death, as is illustrated by Lord Montagu's very explicit account of the way in which he set about avoiding estate duty:

As the prosperity of the estate and Company grew, so I turned my thoughts in the direction of how to avoid the break-up of the estate, and perhaps of the Motor Museum, upon my death. In other words, how to pass them on intact to my heirs and successors. I was advised, like the Duke of Norfolk, to make an application to the Court for the rearrange-ment of the Trust set up by the terms of my father's Will to release to me absolutely a proportion of the estate and to resettle the remainder on my son, Ralph, and his heirs and successors on the same terms as the present Trust, subject to certain provisions which avoid Estate Duty in the event of his premature death before attaining the age of twenty-one. I first had to obtain the approval of other members of my family who are beneficiaries. The proportions for the partition of the estate were calculated to provide the maximum saving of Estate Duty bearing in mind my expectation of life and Ralph's. Later to reinforce this measure and further to safeguard the future, I have in mind to make over to my son a further share of the estate. [1969]

Avoidance and Estate Duty Revenue

One of the striking features of estate duty is the failure of the revenue to rise in line with the increases in the rates of duty, a fact which, as we have seen, worried Gladstone 120 years ago. Table 16 shows the receipts of death duties as a percentage of total personal wealth at different dates in this century. In 1911–13, the duties represented 0·25% of total personal wealth; by 1966 this had increased to 0·39% – a very much smaller increase than one would have expected in view of the rise in the rates of duty. In 1911–13, the highest rate was 15% estate duty (plus possibly 10% Legacy and

Table 16: Revenue from Death Duties as a Percentage of Total Personal Wealth

1912	0·25
1927	0·42
1933	0·45
1937	0·46
1948	0·59
1954	0·47
1960	0·46
1966	0·39

Source: see Notes on Sources.

Succession Duty). An estate of £1 million passing in direct line would have attracted duty at the rate of 11%, whereas the rate today would be 75%. We can estimate that had the 1966 rates of duty been in force in 1911 (with the exemption level and the tax brackets the same percentage of average wealth), the revenue payable would have been 1·5% of total personal wealth. This is nearly four times the actual percentage collected in 1966, and would have implied a revenue in 1966 of some £1,200 million rather than the actual revenue of £300 million.

The failure of the revenue from estate duty to increase in line with the rising rates of duty might simply reflect greater equality in the distribution of wealth, with a larger part of total wealth being held by those in lower estate duty brackets. However, there are grounds for suspecting that a considerable part can be explained by avoidance. It is, of course, difficult to estimate the amount of avoidance that takes place, but we can make some attempt to do so in the case of gifts *inter vivos* and discretionary trusts. An approximate way of estimating the extent of avoidance through gifts (suggested by A. A. Tait) is to take the gifts which failed to escape (because the donor died before the qualifying period was up) and use 'mortality multipliers' to blow this figure up to cover the whole population. Using this approach, we obtain estimates that the gifts avoiding estate duty in 1966 amounted to £350 million, which is about a quarter of the value of the estates subject to duty in that year, and the estate duty payable would have been some £100 million.

Secondly, there are discretionary trusts. J. R. S. Revell has estimated that in 1961 discretionary trusts amounted to £200 million, but he himself said that 'many people who have practical experience of settled property would claim that the figure . . . is far too low'. He also suspected that an assessment 'taken today [1966] would yield a much larger figure because corporate trustees all report a great increase in this form of trust placed under their control'. Suppose, therefore, that we take a figure of £1,200 million for 1966, and that we assume (1) that the trusts have been set up to avoid estate duty expected on average in 10 years' time, and (2) that duty would have been payable at an average rate of 50% (if the rate were much lower, the saving on estate duty would not cover the cost of setting up and administering the trust). The annual loss of estate duty revenue on these assumptions could be some £60 million. This estimate is extremely crude, but individual cases coming before the courts (seeking powers to vary the terms of a trust) confirm that the savings on estate duty (at least before the 1969 Budget) could be very large. For example, on 23 March 1966, *The Times* reported the case of the trusts set up by the Duke of Norfolk, covering estates worth £3 million. Under the re-arrangement of the trust approved by the High Court, the son (then aged 10) of General Fitzalan Howard would inherit £1,246,000, or some £900,000 more than if the original trust had continued and estate duty had been paid.

Some further evidence is provided by the survey conducted by D. R. Denman into agricultural estates in Britain. This showed that 17% of the estates which had been in the possession of the same family since the beginning of the century had not been subject to estate duty: i.e. no estate duty at all had been paid in a period of 55 years. For the estates as a whole, the frequency of estate duty worked out at once every 51 years. As the author points out, 'the frequency of the occasion of estate duty levy will depend upon the ages of the successive owners and heirs and also upon the ability of the estate to avoid the imposition of the levy'. Whatever the ages of the owner and the heir, it seems very unlikely that the average generation length would work out at 51 years, and avoidance must have been important.

Implications of Estate Duty Avoidance

We have seen that the present estate duty allows a number of avenues of avoidance and that there are grounds for believing that the amounts involved are appreciable. Those families willing to make the necessary arrangements may be able to preserve their family fortune for many generations. The effectiveness of estate duty as a means for achieving a more equal distribution of inherited wealth is, therefore, significantly less than is suggested by the nominal rates of tax. There is the appearance of high taxation but not the substance. As Henry Simons said of the American tax system:

The whole procedure involves a subtle kind of moral and political dishonesty. One senses here a grand scheme of deception whereby enormous surtaxes are voted in exchange for promises that they will not be made effective. Thus the politicians may point with pride to the rates, while quietly reminding their wealthy constituents of the loopholes. [1938, p. 219]

Whatever one's views about the desirability of redistribution, this kind of deception cannot be regarded as an equitable basis for our system of wealth taxation. As I have stressed in the previous chapter, it is essential that the taxes being paid, and the extent of redistribution, should be clear to all – in taxation, as in the courts, justice should be seen to be done. Where those with good tax advisers – and perhaps fewer scruples – can pay little tax while others pay tax at rates up to 75%, there can be little respect for the equity of taxation.

Taxation of Income from Wealth

Under the British system of income taxation, the income from wealth is taxed as a progressive rate. In 1973 a single person with an investment income of £3,000 (and no earned income) paid some 30% in tax; at £10,000 a year the rate reached some 50% and for the 100 or so people whose investment incomes exceeded £100,000 the average rate was 85%. The tax system discriminates against investment income through the investment income surcharge, a discrimination which has been described by *The Economist* as 'the hidden wealth tax' (5 October 1968). In 1973 a single person with an investment income of £6,000 a year pays £600 more tax than a person with the same amount of earned income; so that if the investment income corresponded to wealth of £60,000 (implying a return of 10%), we can say that there was an extra tax on wealth of 1%.

The claim that the differentiation between earned and unearned income represents a 'hidden wealth tax' is in some respects misleading. Firstly, in that it falls on the *income* from wealth not the *value* of wealth, it does not represent a tax on wealth so much as a tax on investment income. Secondly, the claim overlooks the consideration that one of the chief reasons for the discrimination is that earnings involve certain costs which are not present with investment income. These may be monetary costs which cannot be deducted as expenses (such as the cost of travel to work) or non-monetary costs in the form of effort, irksomeness and the sacrifice of leisure. In part therefore the lower rate of tax on earned income represents an allowance for these costs (which should be subtracted in arriving at 'net' income), and to this extent the provision cannot be seen as discrimination against investment income.

In seeking discriminatory treatment of investment income, *The Economist* would have been better advised to have focused on the effect of inflation, since the tax treatment of the real capital losses due to inflation clearly involves discrimination against the income from wealth. Suppose that a person has wealth of £20,000 invested in an asset which yields 10% per annum and has a fixed money value. He would pay the same tax as a person earning £2,000. However, if prices (and earnings) have risen by 5% during the year, the real value of his wealth has fallen, and to arrive at his real income we should subtract a real capital loss of 5% × £20,000 = £1,000. On this basis he should pay the same tax not as a person earning £2,000 but as a person earning half that amount. In terms of the rate of tax on *real* incomes, there is therefore discriminatory treatment against investment income of this type in an inflationary world, and this may mean that there is a considerable 'hidden wealth tax'. A man with investment income of £20,000 pays over £12,000 in tax. If the rate of inflation equals half the return, the real income is only £10,000 and the effective rate of tax is over 100%.

Investment income appears on this basis to be discriminated against quite heavily. However, no allowance has been made so far for *capital gains*. Suppose first that capital gains were completely free from tax. If the value of a person's assets rose by exactly the amount required to offset the real capital loss due to inflation, no discriminatory treatment would be involved: the person's real income would equal the amount received in interest or dividends. There is, however, no reason at all why the capital gains on all assets should be exactly this amount. On some assets there are no capital gains. On others the capital gains exceed the rate of inflation. In the case of assets such as company shares (where in the long run there are likely to be real capital gains) a person would receive part of his real income in a tax-free form, thus reducing the overall effective tax rate. For example, if the dividend is 9% and the capital gain 6%, where dividends are taxed at a rate of 45% and capital gains are tax-free, the effective rate of tax is only 27%.

It is sometimes suggested that the exemption of capital gains from taxation would compensate for the discriminatory treatment due to inflation. It is clear, however, from the preceding analysis that this would only be the case where the capital gains were exactly equal to the rate of price increase. Since the rate of capital gain varies on different assets, the exemption of capital gains would introduce discrimination between different types of investment income (and assets providing real gains could in fact be taxed less heavily than earned income – the discrimination would be reversed). Horizontal equity requires that all investment income should be treated in the same way for tax purposes, and on this basis the only fully equitable form of taxation is one where capital gains are taxed equally with other investment income. If allowance is to be made for the effects of inflation, it has to be done for all investment income and not just for assets giving rise to capital gains. As it was put by the Minority Report of the Royal Commission on the Taxation of Profits and Income:

> If a man regularly saves up a part of his earnings by adding to his savings deposits or paying premiums on a life assurance, it may equally happen that as a result of inflation the real value of his accumulated savings is constantly shrinking. He is in no different position from another man who attains the same increase in the money value of his capital as a result of capital appreciation. The fact that in times of inflation money appreciation will not mean a corresponding real appreciation may be regarded as an argument against the taxation of saving as such. It is not an argument for the differential treatment of capital appreciation as against other forms of saving. [Para. 37]

As far as equity is concerned, therefore, capital gains should be taxed in just the same way as other investment income. In Britain, however, this is not the case. Although the Long Term Capital Gains Tax introduced by Mr Callaghan in 1965 represented an important step in that direction, capital gains are still taxed at a considerably lower rate than other investment income, and for high incomes the rate of tax can be lower than that on earned income.* There are two main reasons for this. Firstly, the nominal rate of tax is lower than that on other investment income. The basic rate is a flat 30 % on all gains (or half the standard rate of income tax where this is to the taxpayer's advantage). This means that the rate is less than the standard rate of income tax, and for the surtax payer it may be much lower than the rate he pays on other investment income. Secondly, the tax is only payable when

---

*As introduced in 1965, gains realized within twelve months of purchase were taxed under the ordinary income tax and surtax, and the Long Term Capital Gains Tax applied to gains realized more than twelve months after purchase. Since in 1971 Budget all capital gains are taxed under the Long Term Tax.

the asset is sold (when the gain is realized), so that there may be a long period between the accrual of the gain and the tax's being paid to the Inland Revenue. This delay is important, since it means that the interest on the tax due accrues to the taxpayer rather than to the Exchequer. This may be quite valuable to the taxpayer: a ten-year postponement can reduce the effective rate of tax from 30% to around 20%. The present system of capital gains

Table 17: Effective Rate of Tax on Different Types of Income

| Level of real income | Rate of tax for a single person as a percentage | | |
	Income earned	Income all dividends*	Income* 1/5 dividend 4/5 capital gains†
2,000	25	61	21
5,000	30	85	28
10,000	36	87	32
20,000	51	109	35
50,000	65	125	41
100,000	70	130	46

Notes: The income tax rates relate to 1973–4.

*It is assumed that inflation represents $\frac{1}{3}$ of the gross return in the case of investment income.

†In the case of capital gains, a ten-year holding period is assumed.

Source: own calculations.

taxation falls therefore considerably short of the goal of taxing capital gains in the same way as other investment income. The consequences of this are illustrated in Table 17, which shows the effective rate of tax on real income accruing largely as capital gains compared with that on investment income derived solely from dividends and that on earned income. As we have seen earlier, the tax on real investment income is considerably greater than that on the corresponding earned income and can be over 100%. The effective rate of tax on investment incomes accruing largely as capital gains, however, is substantially lower, and in this example is even lower than that on earnings. The tax appears to be much less progressive when we allow for capital gains (and becomes still less so when allowance is made for the increasing importance of capital gains as we go up the income scale). Again we have a situation where tax rates are believed to be high, but in fact this can be quite illusory.*

Taxation of income serves to bring about greater equality of the distribution of income; it can however be suggested that in conjunction with easily avoided taxes on the transfer of wealth they tend to preserve inequality in the distribution of wealth. O. Stutchbury, for example, has argued that: 'The British system of direct taxation on individuals is mercilessly severe on the *Creator*, but, providing relatively painless estate duty avoidance procedures are set in train, the system exacts very little indeed from the *Conserver*.' (1968, p. 1.) Similarly, Joan Robinson has said that inequality 'perpetuates itself, for one finds it easy to make money if one has some, and next to impossible if one has not'.

As far as the taxation of investment income is concerned, we have seen in chapter 3 that the present combination of income taxation and a high rate of inflation means that even if a small saver accumulates all the after-tax income from his capital, he is unlikely to build up a substantial amount over his lifetime.† When we consider those at the top of the wealth distribution, it is true that the average rates of tax on real investment income are high (and may be over 100%). However, we have seen that the wealth of the rich is heavily concentrated in those assets which yield capital gains and that the effective rate of tax may therefore be no greater (or even less) than that for people with much smaller holdings of wealth. This is further reinforced by the fact that the very wealthy may be able to postpone realization of their gains for long periods, and thus postpone the tax payment.‡ The effective tax

---

*There are a number of other ways not discussed here in which investment income receives favourable tax treatment: the exemption of the imputed return to owner-occupied houses and other real assets (such as old masters), the special provisions for pension schemes, the concessions for growing timber, etc.

† The treatment of the first slice of investment income as earned income for tax purposes will help in this respect.

‡ The scope for this has widened as a result of the abolition in the 1971 Budget of the charge to capital gains tax of property passing at death. Previously death had been regarded as a 'realization', but it is now in theory possible for an asset to be passed on for several generations without paying

burden may not be as progressive in its incidence as appears at
first sight: the millionaire with his money in growth stocks may
pay much the same percentage in tax as the man with £500 in the
bank. In these circumstances the distribution of wealth tends to
become frozen: the tax rate is high enough on small savers to make
it difficult for them to accumulate substantial wealth, and not
sufficiently high on the rich to prevent them from preserving their
wealth intact.

Finally, there is the impact of high rates of taxation on *earned*
income, which may prevent people from accumulating wealth
through saving out of their earnings. We have seen that the
present tax system does provide some limited discrimination in
favour of earned income, but it seems unlikely that this discrimination can be extended much further. If the differential between
the tax on earned and unearned income were to be widened, the
tax on unearned income would have to rise (to maintain the same
level of aggregate demand), but since the present marginal rates of
tax on unearned income are close to 100% at the top of the scale,
this scarcely seems feasible. Marginal tax rates of over 100% on
income can be ruled out on the grounds that people would then
allocate their wealth so as to *minimize* the return and there would
be no demand for income-yielding assets.* The same effect, however, could be achieved by introducing a tax on the *value of* rather
than on the *income from* wealth. This may be illustrated by a
simple example. Suppose that the return to shares is 8%, then a
tax on investment income of 75% plus a wealth tax of 3% would
be equivalent in its distributional effect to a tax on investment
income of 112·5% – but there would still be an incentive for the
person to allocate his wealth to the most profitable use (since he
keeps 25% of any extra income he gets). It is to the possibility of
introducing an annual wealth tax that I turn in the next chapter.

---

capital gains tax. At the same time, the charge imposed every fifteen years on
accrued gains on assets held by discretionary trusts was also abolished, so that
property held in this form can escape capital gains tax for long periods (as well
as providing a means for reducing Estate Duty liability).

*It should be noted that although inflation may cause the *average* tax rate
to be over 100%, it does not affect the *marginal* tax rate, so that this is less than
100% at present even in terms of real income.

8. A Wealth Tax for Britain?

If earned incomes are to be relieved, new ways of raising public revenue must be found. We therefore propose to look again at the possibilities of taxing wealth. We recognize the need to maintain a high level of savings, and see no reason why a tax should bear on modest sums of capital. But large accumulations of unearned wealth must make their contribution to a fair society. – *Labour Party mid-term manifesto, 1968*

The idea of introducing a wealth tax in Britain similar to those operated in Scandinavia and elsewhere has attracted considerable attention. In this chapter, I first describe what such a tax would involve, and then examine the case for its introduction. This case has been argued in a number of different ways, and I begin by considering the proposal that the wealth tax should be a replacement for surtax (or the top rates of income tax from 1973–4). The arguments for this proposal are based on the desirability of a shift in taxation from earned to unearned income and on the view that a wealth tax would encourage risk-taking and work effort. Secondly, I consider the wealth tax as an essentially redistributive measure, where the revenue is used in part to finance a capital element in the state pension. Finally, I discuss the reform of capital gains taxation as an alternative to the introduction of a wealth tax.

A Wealth Tax in Britain

The design of a wealth tax involves a number of points of principle, and many points of detail, and the tax could take a wide variety of forms. In what follows I describe the most important elements and the likely structure for such a tax if it were to be introduced in Britain.

The basis for the tax would be a person's *net* worth: i.e. the total value of his assets less his liabilities. In theory it would cover all forms of wealth, but there would undoubtedly be a number of exemptions, as is the case with all European wealth taxes. There would be strong pressure to exclude owner-occupied houses (as under the capital gains tax), household effects, rights to pension funds and life insurance policies (as in Sweden). Arguments have also been made for exempting agricultural land. Most proposals for a wealth tax plan to include property held in trust, although this would give rise to considerable administrative problems. The tax would be payable by all persons domiciled in Britain, and would cover all wealth owned by them abroad. It would not be paid by companies, since persons holding shares in companies would then effectively be taxed twice. The tax paid under the wealth tax would not be deducted when assessing income tax. The tax could be levied on the basis of the individual (as with estate duty) or on the basis of the income unit (as under income tax). Most of the concrete proposals for a wealth tax assume that the former basis would be adopted, but if our concern is with the distribution of wealth between *families* rather than individuals, there are good grounds for aggregating the wealth of husband and wife (and possibly dependent children).

In the various proposals for a wealth tax, a number of different rates of taxation have been suggested. Where the wealth tax has been considered as an alternative to surtax, the proposed rates of tax have been fairly low. A. T. Peacock, for example, suggested in 1963 two possible schedules with an exemption level of £25,000 and rates of between 0·75% and 1·5%, and *The Economist* made similar proposals (22 January 1966). Where the wealth tax has been viewed as a basically redistributive measure, the schedule has been more progressive, with a higher exemption level and higher marginal rates of tax. O. Stutchbury has proposed a wealth tax with an exemption level of £50,000 and marginal rates reaching 4% at levels above £200,000. In 1969, a Labour study group suggested a similar schedule, with rates reaching 5% on wealth above £400,000.

As a basis for discussion, I consider two possible schedules of rates of taxation. Under the first, which is similar to Peacock's schemes, all wealth above £25,000 would be taxed at a rate of 1%. The implications of this schedule for people with different levels of wealth are shown in the second column of Table 18. With the second schedule (based on that proposed by Stutchbury), the exemption level would be higher and the rates more progressive:

		Marginal rate of tax (%)
Wealth below	£50,000	0
Wealth between	£50,000 and £100,000	1%
,, ,,	£100,000 and £150,000	2%
,, ,,	£150,000 and £200,000	3%
Wealth above	£200,000	4%

This means that a person with wealth of £100,000 would pay £500 a year (nothing on the first £50,000 and 1% on the second £50,000) and a person worth £200,000 would pay £3,000 a year – see the third column of Table 18. From Table 18 it is clear that the first schedule would tax those in the range of £25,000–£100,000 more heavily but would have much lower rates at the very top than the

Table 18: Rates of Wealth Tax

	Total tax payable as a percentage of wealth*	
Wealth (£)	First schedule	More progressive schedule
£25,000	0	0
£50,000	0·5%	0
£100,000	0·75%	0·5%
£150,000	0·8%	1·0%
£200,000	0·9%	1·5%
£500,000	1·0%	3·0%
£1 million	1·0%	3·5%
£2 million	1·0%	3·8%

*Percentages rounded.
Source: own calculations.

second, more progressive schedule. If we compare these schedules with those in force in the European countries that have a wealth tax, we can see that both the exemption level and the marginal rates of tax are higher – the British tax would be more progressive (particularly if the Stutchbury proposal were adopted).

Even with the lower exemption limit of £25,000 only a small number of people would be liable for the wealth tax. On the basis of the estimates of the distribution of wealth prepared by the Inland Revenue, it can be calculated that some 500,000 *individuals* had wealth in excess of £25,000 in 1968, although the number of *income units* above this level would have been rather higher.* If the exemption level were £50,000, the number of individuals liable for the tax would fall to 180,000, which is under half the number of surtax payers. From the same source, we can estimate that the yield of the wealth tax in 1968 with the first schedule of rates would have been some £210 million, and that from the more progressive schedule £280 million.† These estimates are based on the assumption that the tax would be levied on an individual basis; if it were based on the combined wealth of husband and wife the revenue would be significantly higher. The revenue from the wealth tax (under either schedule) would probably be rather larger, therefore, than that from surtax, which was £225 million in 1968–9.

In order to administer the wealth tax, the Inland Revenue would require information about the net worth of all taxpayers. For the bulk of the population, it would simply need to assure itself that they were below the exemption level; but for the half million or more people above or close to the exemption level, it would have to obtain an accurate valuation of their total net worth (excluding any exempted assets). Where the assets are readily marketable, valuation would not involve any major problems (for example, government bonds and quoted company shares have a readily ascertainable price at a given date), but in other cases special valuation procedures would be required – a difficulty which is discussed further below.

Effect on Aggregate Demand

As we have seen earlier, one of the Chancellor's main concerns when considering changes in taxation is the effect which they

*A man and wife each owning £20,000, for example, would not be liable for the tax on an individual basis, but would be liable if the tax were assessed on their combined wealth.

†These figures represent the gross increase in revenue, and we have to allow for the reduction in the revenue from other taxes. Since it is assumed that the wealth tax could not be set against income tax, there would be no direct loss of revenue from this source, but there would be an indirect effect in that total property income would become more equally distributed (leading also to a reduction in Estate Duty revenue).

would have on the level of aggregate demand. If a wealth tax were introduced, it would have to be accompanied by compensating adjustments in other taxes to maintain the desired level of demand, and indeed one of the justifications given for the tax is that it would allow taxes on earned income to be reduced. It has however been suggested by the Confederation of British Industry (C.B.I.) that a wealth tax would actually be *inflationary*, which would mean that other taxes would have to be *raised* to maintain the same pressure of demand:

Firstly there will probably be a fall in the rate of saving out of income. Secondly, owners of wealth are likely to consume some of their wealth to avoid tax liability and preserve their standard of living . . . It follows that a wealth tax could lead to increased inflationary pressures unless the Government compensates for these effects by introducing restrictions on the level of consumers' expenditure either through increased taxation or through cuts in public expenditure. [From report referred to in *The Times*, 22 August 1969]

There are a number of reasons why this argument is not convincing. Firstly, as I have argued in chapter 6, to justify the claim that a tax would be inflationary, it has to be demonstrated that *consumption is actually increased*. It is not sufficient to argue that people seek to 'preserve their standard of living'; this would simply mean that all the tax was paid out of reduced personal saving and there would be no impact on aggregate demand. For the tax to be inflationary, consumption has to be increased or savings reduced by more than the tax paid. It is possible that consumption might in fact be increased if the primary motivation for saving stemmed from the return offered (since the return to wealth would be reduced by the tax). As we have seen, however, there are likely to be other motives influencing a person's savings behaviour, in particular the desire to provide wealth on which he can draw in old age or which he can pass on to his heirs. If in the face of the wealth tax he were to maintain his level of consumption, it would mean that the amount he could accumulate for these purposes would be considerably reduced. If he were actually to increase his consumption, then the amount accumulated would be even further diminished. This reaction to the imposition of a wealth tax would only occur therefore where a person was willing to accept a quite appreciable fall in the amount saved for old age or for transmission to the next generation, and for this reason it seems unlikely that an increase in consumption would be widespread. I have already referred in chapter 4 to the pressures on the wealthy to maintain intact their family wealth, a factor which is likely to be particularly important in the case of landed property. Similarly, a person saving to provide his heirs with what he feels to be a 'comfortable' amount would have to save more under a wealth tax to achieve his aim. Those with a weaker desire to pass on wealth might well not increase their savings, but it seems unlikely that they would actually reduce their saving by more than the amount of the tax, since this would produce a very large reduction in the net bequest.

Secondly, the C.B.I. look simply at the reactions of those who would currently be paying the tax, and quite ignore the impact on the consumption of the heirs. They argue that:

Wealth in the United Kingdom is concentrated in the upper age groups . . . These people are likely to want to preserve their standard of living in consumption terms and are unlikely to protect and preserve the transfer of wealth in total to their heirs.

If, however, those in the upper age-groups preserved their standard of consumption unchanged, the wealth tax would fall effectively on the transfer of wealth to their heirs. This in turn would be likely to influence their consumption behaviour, their reduced 'expectations' leading them to consume less. This means that even if the older wealth-holders preserve their standard of consumption, that of the next generation would be reduced. It might be thought that this argument assumes too great a degree of calculation in people's behaviour. It should, however, be borne in mind that the person subject to the tax would not be the typical man in the street or even the typical professional man. It is only the very wealthy who are assumed to be making this kind of calculation, and they appear at present to devote considerable care to avoiding estate duty.

From this analysis it appears, therefore, that the C.B.I. have not substantiated their claim that the wealth tax would be inflationary. It is not sufficient to argue, as they do, that savings would be reduced as a result of the tax. It has to be shown that savings would be reduced by more than the tax revenue, and they give no convincing reasons for expecting this to be the case. On the other hand, it seems likely that any reduction in consumption would be small and that the tax would largely be paid out of savings: all the effects referred to above involve fairly minor adjustments of consumption plans. The broad conclusion is therefore that the most likely outcome would be a small reduction in consumption, with most of the tax being paid out of reduced saving.*

This means that the introduction of a wealth tax *would* allow some (limited) reduction in taxation or increase in expenditure. In what follows, I consider two main possibilities. The first is the abolition of surtax (or – if Mr Barber's proposals are enacted – the top rates of income tax).

The present revenue from this source is rather less than the amount which would be raised by the wealth tax, but there are reasons for expecting the deflationary effect of surtax to be rather larger per £ of revenue than with the wealth tax. Those with large earned incomes would tend to gain from the switch and their marginal propensity to consume is probably higher than that of people with substantial wealth, and insofar as the wealth tax would have higher administrative costs (discussed below), these would represent a claim on real resources, thus adding to demand. In view of this, the wealth tax with the first schedule of rates (and based on the income tax unit rather than on the individual) may be regarded as a reasonable 'swap' for surtax from the point of view of aggregate demand. Secondly, when considering the scope for a 'redistributive' wealth tax, I assume that the compensating adjustment would take the form of a capital element to be included in the state pension (the details of such a scheme are described in chapter 11). The amount involved would be small: if the wealth tax reduced consumption by only £50 million, and we assume that

*This conclusion relates to the immediate effect of introducing a wealth tax. If the wealth tax were to encourage risk-taking and enterprise (a possibility discussed later), there might in the longer run be an increase in investment, thus raising the level of demand.

the pensioners would spend all the capital payment during their retirement, then the amount per person would only be some £75.*
It is clearly absurd to suggest – as some Labour M.P.s have done – that *all* the revenue from a wealth tax could be used to pay higher pensions. This would lead to a very substantial increase in consumption and would therefore be inflationary. Finally, we should note that in both cases the revenue from the wealth tax would exceed the revenue lost from the reduction of other taxes (or the increase in expenditure). To this extent the wealth tax would contribute towards the reduction of the National Debt – a subject discussed in chapter 10.

A Wealth Tax to Replace Surtax?

In this section, I examine the arguments for the introduction of a wealth tax with the first of the two schedules of rates outlined above to replace surtax (or the higher rates of tax now that the unified tax system has been introduced).

The distributional effects of such a change depend first on the effective incidence of the wealth tax and whether it is possible for the rich to shift part of the burden on to others (through an increase in the return which they receive on their wealth). Such shifting of the burden would be most likely to occur if the tax led to a decrease in total savings or if it reduced the willingness of the rich to invest in risky assets. The former effect was discussed above, where it was agreed that there would be a fall in personal savings; however, there would be a corresponding increase in public saving. In that the government would run a smaller budget deficit, there would be less need for government borrowing and hence more funds available for other purposes. As far as risk-taking is concerned, it has in fact been argued that a wealth tax would have the reverse effect and actually *encourage* investment in risky undertakings. Although, as we shall see below, there are doubts about this argument, it seems unlikely that there would be a significant disincentive effect. It seems reasonable to conclude, therefore, that the effective incidence of a wealth tax would be likely to coincide

* This figure makes an allowance for the administrative costs.

with its nominal incidence – that there would be little shifting of the burden of the tax. This is indeed the view expressed by most writers on this subject, including A. T. Peacock and J. F. Due. The latter, for example, concluded that 'on the whole it would appear difficult for persons to pass off the burden of the tax onto others'. (1960, p. 313.)

The consequences of replacing surtax by the wealth tax for people with different levels and types of income are illustrated for 1973 in Table 19. There would be two principal distributional

Table 19: Effect of Replacing Surtax by a Wealth Tax

Income (£ per year)	Gain to a single person	
	If income all earned	If income (£ per year) all unearned*
2,500	—	—250
4,000	—	—550
5,000	—	—750
7,000	+160	—990
10,000	800	—950
20,000	+4,360	+610
30,000	+8,830	+3,080
50,000	+17,830	8,080

*Assuming a (taxable) return of 5%. The wealth tax is assumed to replace the higher rates of income tax in force in 1973–4.

Note: figures are rounded.

Source: own calculations.

effects: the shift in the burden of taxation from earned to unearned income, and the change in the relative treatment of people with different amounts and types of investment income. Those with earned incomes would clearly gain from the replacement of surtax by a wealth tax; however, in view of the earnings allowance against surtax, this benefit would not be felt until quite high earnings levels: a single person does not begin paying higher rate tax until his earnings reach some £5,600 a year, and for married men the limit is higher. This means that even though the change might benefit some people with little wealth, the redistribution would be of a very special kind. In order to benefit, a person would have to be in the top 1% of earners, so that even if he had not been born with inherited wealth, he would not have done too badly since! For those people with investment income, the substitution of this particular version of a wealth tax would have two main consequences. Firstly, it would affect the relative treatment of different types of investment income. One of the chief arguments for a wealth tax is that it would fall on all wealth, including that yielding a return in non-pecuniary form (such as yachts or old masters) or in a monetary form not subject to tax at the same rate as other income (*capital gains*). To this extent, the change would ensure greater horizontal equity between people who receive their investment incomes in different forms. Moreover, insofar as it is the very rich who tend to hold their wealth in a form that yields non-taxable income, the change would have a progressive effect on the overall distribution of wealth. This redistributive effect may, however, be offset by the second factor: the fact that those with very large (taxable) investment incomes would tend to gain from the substitution of a wealth tax for the higher rates of tax. As can be seen from Table 19, it is not the very wealthy but those in the middle wealth-ranges who would lose from the change. This can hardly be regarded as equitable, and a wealth tax with this schedule of rates would scarcely contribute to a levelling of the distribution of wealth. (With a more progressive schedule, this would not necessarily happen.)

The case for introducing a wealth tax of the type considered to replace the higher rates of income tax is not, therefore, especially compelling as far as the redistribution of wealth is concerned. this has been recognized by many of those who have argued for such a reform, and they have laid most stress on other aspects – particularly the possible benefits for the *growth* of the economy. This is illustrated by a passage from the National Economic Development Committee's report *Conditions Favourable to Faster Growth*, where it asked:

whether it might not help growth to tax the dimension of personal wealth and to place less emphasis on the differential taxation of the income produced by wealth. A wealth tax in one form or another exists in a good many countries. The introduction of a wealth tax here would be a controversial step but it may have a useful role in any major review of taxation related to a programme for growth. [Para. 170]

The most important ways in which a wealth tax might stimulate growth are through its effects on risk-taking and on work effort, and these are discussed in turn.

The Wealth Tax and Risk-Taking

The proponents of a wealth tax argue that it would encourage risk-taking among investors, and hence stimulate the growth of the economy. The basic argument is that at present surtax penalizes those who invest in risky assets,* whereas under a wealth tax the liability would be the same regardless of the form in which the wealth was held. The argument may be illustrated by a simple example (where we take a simplified version of the present taxes on investment income with a tax rate of 50%). Let us assume that a man can invest in shares with a yield of 8% or alternatively in old masters yielding no money income. With a tax on investment income of 50%, the additional amount he gets from investing in the risky asset (shares) is 4%, whereas with a wealth tax of (say) 3% he would get the full 8% difference:

| | After tax yield (%) | |
	Old masters	Shares
Investment income tax at 50%	0	4%
Wealth tax at 3%	−3%	5%

There would be a much larger inducement to invest in shares under the wealth tax and so, it is argued, the wealth tax would favour risk-taking.

However, while the argument that a wealth tax would encourage risk-taking is widely accepted, it is not necessarily correct. In particular, it overlooks the effect of the tax on the riskiness of different assets, which is likely to be an important factor influencing investment decisions. In fact a tax on investment income *reduces* the risk involved, whereas this is not the case with the wealth tax. In the example given in the previous paragraph, let us suppose that

*By 'risk' is meant the risk in money, not real, terms.

the return on shares was made up of a 50% chance of a return of 3% and a 50% chance of making 13%. The investment income tax reduces the range of after-tax returns (which can be taken as a measure of risk) to $1\frac{1}{2}$–$6\frac{1}{2}$%; the wealth tax, on the other hand, leaves the range unchanged at 0–10%. So that while the average return on shares is higher relative to that on old masters under a wealth tax, the range of possible outcomes (or the risk involved) is greater. Under the wealth tax, the investor could end up with nothing, which could not happen with the investment income tax. With an investment income tax, the government is in effect sharing part of the risk with the investor (since the revenue depends on whether the investment turns out well or not) and the combined risk-taking by the government and the investor may be higher than with a wealth tax.*

In theory, therefore, there is no presumption that the introduction of a wealth tax in place of surtax would increase the willingness to invest in risky assets. Whether or not it could be expected to do so can only be determined by empirical evidence, and in the absence of such evidence, there are grounds for remaining agnostic about the benefits to be derived.

The Incentive to Work

The second principal argument for introducing a wealth tax in place of surtax is that it would improve the incentive to work. People in the surtax range would no longer face high marginal rates of taxation and this, it is argued, would lead them to increase their work effort.

This also is a questionable argument. At an *a priori* level, there is no presumption that a reduction in the tax on earned income would necessarily discourage work effort, since it gives rise to two effects operating in opposite directions. The first effect – and the one on which attention is normally focused – is that a reduction in

*Doubts about the beneficial effects on risk-taking are further reinforced when we consider the fact that much of the return to risky investments comes in the form of capital gains which are not taxed under surtax anyway. Even if the risk-taking argument were correct in principle, the abolition of surtax would not have much effect on the differential between risky and safe assets. Indeed, insofar as the risky assets give a lower taxable income than safe assets, it would have the reverse effect.

income tax would mean that a person kept more of each extra pound earned, and on this account he would be likely to decide to work more. There is, however, a second, less noticeable effect: that a reduction in income tax would raise the net income he got for working a given number of hours, so that he might well feel able to 'afford' more leisure. To this extent, a reduction in taxation would tend to *discourage* work effort, and if this effect were sufficiently powerful, it might outweigh that operating via the increased take-home earnings at the margin. Overall, it is quite possible therefore that a reduction in income taxation might cause people to work less hard than before. As a (rather extreme) example of this possibility, let us suppose that a person plans to retire when he has saved enough to buy a country cottage. If surtax was reduced he would be able to buy the cottage sooner and retire earlier, thus reducing his work effort.

If we turn to the empirical evidence, we find that those studies which have been made are limited both in number and in their scope, and have produced no definite results. In a recent survey of the evidence, C. V. Brown and D. A. Dawson asked:

Can the studies reviewed above provide a clear-cut answer to the question 'do direct taxes have a disincentive effect?' The only intellectually honest answer is NO . . . if we want an answer to this question further research is essential. Until such research is forthcoming the only safe line is one of agnosticism. [1969, p. 66]

It must, however, be remembered that we are concerned here not with a general cut in income tax but with a cut which will affect only those in the very top earnings range – typically top managers and professional people. The motivation of the members of this group, and consequently their reaction to tax changes, may be rather different from that of the rest of the labour force. One might expect the intrinsic interest of their work to be a more important factor, reducing the importance of pecuniary factors; at the same time they may enjoy greater freedom to vary their hours of work and intensity of effort, so that taxation might have more effect. An empirical study relevant to this group is that carried out in 1956 by G. Break, who interviewed 306 solicitors and accountants, many of whom were paying surtax. The results showed that income taxation was in some cases a disincentive to work effort, and that its importance tended to increase with the level of income; however, the numbers involved were small, and there were almost as many cases where it acted as an incentive.* Break himself concluded that 'It can be stated with considerable certainty ... that this net effect, be it disincentive or incentive, is not large enough to be of great economic or sociological significance.' We may also draw on recent work on the motivation of senior salaried personnel in industry, which has distinguished two broad factors of importance. The first, associated with *job context* (salary, physical conditions of work, pensions, etc.), provides a necessary condition for effective work, but does not act as a positive incentive. The positive motivation to perform well in a particular job is associated with *job content*: intrinsic interest, scope for achievement, responsibility, etc. Without these a person is likely to adopt a wholly instrumental attitude to work. The conclusion drawn by W. W. Daniel as regards the effect of taxation was that it has no effect on the positive motivators (job content) and that it has little impact on job context, which is based primarily on a comparison of gross salary with that of colleagues and other reference groups. He concluded that 'in order to argue that the level of taxation influences the effectiveness of people on the job, it becomes necessary to claim that a high level of taxation produces such a degree of dissatisfaction in the work situation that it reduces effectiveness, that it produces a malaise which pervades a whole section of society'. (1968, p. 236.)

In the absence of evidence that surtax payers are suffering from this degree of malaise and that it is adversely affecting their work effort, there seems little ground for believing that the replacement of surtax by a wealth tax would lead to a substantial increase in work effort; and A. T. Peacock was probably correct to conclude that 'it seems doubtful whether a changeover from surtax to a net

*In that these conclusions are based on the respondents' interpretations of their own behaviour, they must be treated with caution. Since taxation provides a socially acceptable rationalization of behaviour, one might expect such a study to overstate the significance of disincentives. Break did, however, eliminate some of the implausible cases – including that of an Irishman who claimed that taxation was a disincentive and yet worked 80 hours a week!

wealth tax would increase the supply of effort to any marked extent'. (1963, p. 396.)

Conclusions

The substitution of a wealth tax for surtax would make a very limited contribution towards achieving greater equality in the distribution of wealth. There is no guarantee that it would have the beneficial effects on risk-taking and work incentives which have been claimed, so that it cannot be regarded as a promising means for stimulating the growth of the economy. The case for this type of wealth tax is not therefore very convincing.

A Redistributive Wealth Tax

In this section I examine the case for introducing a wealth tax as a net addition to taxation as has been proposed by (among others) a Labour Party study group and the T.U.C., with the revenue being used to pay a capital element in the state pension and to reduce the National Debt (in such a combination as to ensure an unchanged level of aggregate demand). It is assumed that the tax schedule would be the more progressive of the two outlined at the beginning of this chapter (with the rate of tax reaching 4% on wealth over £200,000).

The impact of the wealth tax on holdings of different sizes is shown in Table 20. As a measure of its effect on the distribution of wealth, I have also shown the rate of growth of capital that would be possible if all the income from wealth were saved (the growth being expressed in real terms allowing for inflation of 5%; as before it is assumed that the burden of the wealth tax would not be shifted through an increase in the return on wealth). The figures show that the wealth tax would represent a very substantial proportion of the income remaining after income tax and surtax, and there would be a negative net return in real terms on holdings above about £175,000. Those at the top of the wealth scale would find it impossible to maintain the real value of their wealth (even holding it in a form generating considerable capital gains) and there would undoubtedly be a narrowing of the differential between the top and the bottom of the wealth distribution. This would be reinforced by

Table 20: Impact of the Redistributive Wealth Tax

Wealth	Gross income*	Net income† (in money terms)	With wealth tax	
			Wealth tax payable	Maximum growth (in real terms)
(£)	(£)	(£)	(£)	(£)
50,000	5,000	3,700	0	+2·4
100,000	10,000	6,600	500	+1·1
200,000	20,000	11,800	3,000	−0·6
500,000	50,000	25,500	15,000	−2·9
1 million	100,000	47,500	35,000	−3·8

*Assuming a dividend of 5% and capital gains at the rate of 5%.
†For a single person with no earned income. The income tax rates relate to 1970–71 and those for surtax to 1969–70. Capital gains tax is taken into account (with an assumed holding period of 10 years).
Source: own calculations. All amounts rounded to nearest £100.

the uniform increase in the wealth of those over retirement age as a result of the capital payment as part of the National Insurance pension.

The introduction of a wealth tax in this form would undoubtedly contribute towards bringing about greater equality in the distribution of current wealth. The gap between the very rich and the rest of the population would be narrowed, albeit gradually, and this would lead to greater equality of incomes and of economic power. We have to remember, however, that we are concerned not only with the *current* distribution of wealth, but also with the distribution of inherited wealth, and it does not necessarily follow that the effects would be the same.

The impact of the wealth tax on the distribution of inherited wealth would depend on the relationship between current wealth and inherited wealth, and on the way in which the tax influenced the transmission of wealth between generations. In the case of those who had already inherited when the tax was introduced, the larger their inheritance the larger would tend to be their current wealth – and hence their liability under the wealth tax. The average person who inherited very little or nothing at all would not be affected by a tax with an exemption level of £50,000 (as well as exemptions for owner-occupied houses, life insurance, etc.), so that the tax would largely be paid by those who had received substanstantial gifts or bequests or who were beneficiaries from trusts. However, the correspondence between current wealth and inherited wealth is not perfect. Those people who did save more than £50,000 during their lifetimes would be liable for the tax even though they had not benefited from any transmitted wealth. Moreover, for those who had inherited wealth, the amount of wealth tax payable would depend on the way in which they allocated their consumption over their lives. A person who inherited £100,000 and then spent it all within five years would pay much less tax than someone who received the same amount but saved it for later in his life. In the extreme case where a person put it all on a losing horse the day he inherited, no tax would be payable under a wealth tax! Similarly, we might have two people each inheriting £40,000, one of whom had saved £15,000 out of his earnings. This person would be subject to the wealth tax, whereas the less thrifty heir would not be liable. The wealth tax paid would not, therefore, necessarily be related to the amounts inherited and the tax could give rise to serious horizontal inequity between people with the same inherited wealth.

The effect of the wealth tax on the amount of wealth transmitted between generations would depend on the way in which a family reacted to the tax. It might preserve its planned consumption level and pay the tax out of its savings, in which case the amount passed on to the next generation would be reduced. Alternatively, the present generation might reduce its own consumption, so that the tax would not be fully paid out of savings, in which event the amount passed on to the next generation would be less reduced. For the amount passed on actually to increase, however, the present generation would have to cut its consumption by more than the amount of the tax, which seems unlikely. As we have seen, the wealth tax may make it quite impossible for top wealthholders to preserve the real value of their capital out of the income it provides. The probable effect of the wealth tax would therefore be to reduce the amount passed on by wealthy families, and hence to narrow the differences in inherited wealth. This narrowing would, however, take place more slowly than with a tax on the transfer of wealth: the size of the effect would depend on how much wealth tax had been paid, and this would only build up slowly. The immediate effect on the transmission of wealth is in fact likely to be insignificant.

To sum up this analysis, the imposition of an annual tax on wealth would contribute to reducing inequality in the distribution of inherited wealth through a reduction in the amount transmitted from one generation to the next, although it would work more slowly than a tax on the transfer of wealth. Its direct effect would be more haphazard. It would tend to tax more heavily those with substantial inherited wealth, but the correspondence would not be perfect and there would be serious horizontal inequities. More-over, levying the wealth tax on current rather than inherited wealth means that it does not serve to make clear that redistribu-tion is primarily concerned with the latter. I have earlier stressed the importance of making transparent the purpose and extent of redistribution, and this also has tactical advantages. A wealth tax can easily be opposed on the grounds that it would catch the life savings of a 'small saver' as well as large inherited estates, and indeed the purpose of *The Times* editorial on life-cycle savings (quoted in chapter 3) was to rebut the Labour Party's proposals. The wealth tax may not, therefore, be the ideal instrument for achieving greater equality of inherited wealth.

Effect of a Wealth Tax on Savings and Work Effort

The most common objection to a redistributive wealth tax of the type considered here is that it would have an adverse effect on the level of savings, and this was recognized in the quotation from the Labour Party manifesto given at the beginning of this chapter. In large part this objection has already been taken into account in the construction of the specific proposal considered, the capital pay-ment to pensioners being determined on such a basis that the level of aggregate demand remained unchanged. (If the wealth tax were to cause consumption actually to rise, other taxes would have to be increased, but we have seen that this is unlikely.)

We should, however, consider the possibility of a 'capital flight' – that the wealth tax would lead people to take their wealth out of the country on a large scale. If the tax applied to wealth held overseas by British residents (as with estate duty), leaving the country would not by itself be enough to avoid the tax, and it would be necessary to change domicile. This would be a major step, and the costs (personal and other) of such a rearrangement of a person's affairs might prevent this happening on a large scale.* Moreover, a number of European countries have introduced wealth taxes without any apparent serious outflow of capital. The combined effect of a wealth tax and surtax would, however, be more severe than taxation in other countries. The C.B.I. pointed to the ceiling that many countries operate. The Netherlands, for example, limit the total tax liability to 80% of the income from wealth, but with the tax considered here, the total income tax and wealth-tax liability for a millionaire would be 155% of the income assessed for income tax.† If a capital flight appeared at all probable, it might be possible for it to be limited by exchange controls of the type that have been in operation at various periods. A more attractive possibility is that of subjecting to estate duty capital transferred abroad permanently: for this purpose, crossing the Atlantic would be regarded in the same way as crossing the Styx. It is not clear that this would be administratively feasible, but the suggestion certainly warrants further examination.

The second objection commonly raised to a redistributive wealth tax is that it would adversely affect work incentives. This involves rather different considerations from those discussed earlier in this chapter, since its validity rests on there being a relation between taxes on *unearned* income and work effort. The C.B.I. have argued that this operates through the incentive to save: 'We believe a probable consequence of the introduction of a wealth tax to be a reduction in the incentive to save; since the accumulation of savings is an important motive for working, we are convinced that the incentive to work would be reduced.' This

---

*Allowance has also to be made for the growing political risk that present tax havens may become less favourably disposed towards foreign capital.

†In terms of Table 20, his income assessed for income tax (dividends) would be £50,000 and the income tax and surtax about 85%. To this we have to add the wealth tax, amounting to 70% of the dividend income. It should be noted that in this example the tax paid is less than 100% of *total* money income (including capital gains).

argument suffers from two drawbacks. Firstly, a wealth tax would not necessarily discourage saving, and might have the reverse effect. Secondly, it ignores the effect on the heirs of those subject to the wealth tax. If because of the tax less wealth was passed on in the form of bequests and gifts, there would be good reasons for expecting the heirs to work harder. Their 'reduced expectations' would mean that they would have to work more to achieve a certain standard of living: there would be an 'income effect' in the direction of increased work effort.

It is not, therefore, at all clear that a wealth tax would be a disincentive to work effort. In any event, it seems likely that the effect would be small, since only a small number of people would be liable for the tax at any stage in their lives. In this connection it is worth noting that a survey by A. J. Merrett of the wealth of salaried managers (a group which many people consider to be the most important when considering work incentives) showed that only a quarter had assets above £50,000, so that when we allow for the exempted wealth only a few would have been subject to the wealth tax.

Administrative Problems of a Wealth Tax

The third objection (which applies to a wealth tax of any form) concerns the problems of administration. One of the main reasons for Mr Callaghan's not introducing a wealth tax in 1964 (the sensitivities of foreign bankers apart) was undoubtedly the administrative difficulty involved. The principal problem of administration would be that of valuation: the physical assets of private businesses, buildings, unquoted shares, jewellery, pictures, etc., would all give rise to serious problems. In some cases these could be avoided by the exclusion of certain types of asset, such as personal effects and owner-occuped houses, but clearly not all the difficulties could be dealt with in this way. Closely related to the question of valuation would be that of evasion, which in the case of easily portable assets such as jewellery might be quite important.

The problems of valuation and ensuring compliance mean that the administrative costs of the tax would be substantial. According to the estimates given earlier, with an exemption level of £50,000 some 180,000 people would have been liable for the tax in 1968. If we add those below the line who would still have to be checked, it means that the Inland Revenue would have to deal with some 200,000 wealth-tax returns a year. This is over double the number of estates paying estate duty each year and the wealth involved would be over twelve times as much. The administration would in some ways be easier than with estate duty: there would be some savings from being able to check the wealth-tax returns against those for income tax, and it would not be necessary to start afresh each year. The cost of administration would depend partly on the number of cases and partly on their complexity, which would probably increase with the amount of wealth involved. In view of this, it may be reasonable to estimate the cost of administering a wealth tax as four times that for estate duty, which in 1968 would have amounted to some £15 million. If one assumes that the cost to the taxpayer (the time required to fill out the tax return and the cost of obtaining advice from accountants or lawyers) is about the same, the total cost of administration would be £30 million – or some 10% of the revenue.* This is a very much higher figure than that for other taxes, the comparable figure for income tax being 2·9% of the revenue. So that even if a wealth tax were administratively feasible at present (a question which can only be answered in consultation with the Inland Revenue), it would be very expensive to operate.

To overcome the high costs of administration, it has been suggested by advocates of the wealth tax that we should adopt a system of self-assessment similar to that used in Sweden, where taxpayers complete their own assessment of wealth and a random check is carried out by the authorities. They point out that under-assessment is often revealed by comparing the income tax and wealth-tax returns (and that where there is a capital gains tax with the person's own valuation being used as the base for calculating the gain, any understatement of his wealth will increase the capital gains tax due). Other safeguards have also been suggested – such as

*This estimate is rather lower than that reached by G. S. A. Wheatcroft (1963). The difference arises partly from the fact that the tax discussed here has a higher exemption level, and partly from Wheatcroft's having assumed that the private costs would be 2½ times those of the Inland Revenue, which in the present case would give a total cost of over £50 million.

providing the Inland Revenue with the right to purchase any asset at some percentage above the taxpayer's own valuation. However, while self-assessment would undoubtedly reduce the Inland Revenue's costs, the saving is partly illusory, since the taxpayer in his own defence would have to ensure that his assets were properly valued and the cost of valuation would simply be transferred from the Revenue to the taxpayer.

In addition to the problems of valuation, the wealth-tax legislation would have to cover such aspects as the treatment of trusts and closely controlled companies. The proponents of the wealth tax have intended that it should include wealth held in trust, but as we have seen in chapter 7, trusts have caused serious problems for estate duty legislation and the same would undoubtedly be true of the wealth tax. G. S. A. Wheatcroft has outlined some of the possibilities for dealing with discretionary trusts and other cases where no simple allocation is possible. He says, however, that it is 'doubtful whether any rules will be other than arbitrary'. The position of closely controlled companies would give rise to similar problems of allocation and special rules of the type applied for estate duty and surtax would no doubt have to be devised. In view of these and other complications, Wheatcroft concluded that 'there is little doubt that on balance there would be a substantial increase in the complexity of our tax laws'.

A Redistributive Wealth Tax – Conclusions

Our principal objective as far as redistribution is concerned is the achievement of greater equality of inherited wealth. We have seen, however, that the annual wealth tax is not an ideal instrument for this purpose and might involve serious horizontal inequity between people with the same inherited wealth. For this reason, I feel that we should look instead to the reform of wealth transfer taxation as a means for reducing the concentration of inherited wealth, and this is discussed in the next chapter.

The wealth tax would lead to greater equality in the *current* distribution of wealth, and hence in the distribution of income and economic power. To the extent that we are concerned about the control associated with large holdings of wealth, there may still therefore be a case for a wealth tax. However, the introduction and operation of the wealth tax would involve a very considerable administrative burden on the Inland Revenue and might well not at present be feasible. In view of this, I consider in the last part of this chapter the possibility of achieving the same effect without such severe administrative difficulties through a reform of capital gains taxation. We have seen in earlier chapters that the scope for accumulating substantial wealth has in many cases rested on the generous tax treatment of capital gains. Moreover, despite the Capital Gains Tax introduced in 1965, capital gains still receive preferential treatment and the effective rate of tax may be significantly lower than on other investment income.

Reform of Capital Gains Taxation

It has earlier been argued that capital gains should be regarded as income in the same way as wages or dividends and that there is no justification for separate tax treatment. Moreover, gains represent income at the date they *accrue*, and assessment should not be postponed to the date when the holder chooses to *realize* them by selling the asset in question. Ideally, therefore, we should aim to tax capital gains by subjecting them to income tax and surtax at the date of accrual: at the end of each tax year, the gains made during that year would form part of taxable income. Taxation of accrued gains means, however, that we should require valuation of a person's chargeable assets at some date in each tax year, and the information collected would be little different from that required under a wealth tax (only assets such as cash, bank deposits, and building society deposits would not have to be valued). The Minority Report of the Royal Commission on the Taxation of Profits and Income, while arguing strongly for capital gains taxation, felt that the valuation problems of an accrual-based tax would be insuperable. This view is open to question, but it is clear that a reform of capital gains taxation which adopted an accrual basis would not offer any significant advantages over a wealth tax as far as the problems of administration are concerned. In what follows, I consider therefore the reform of capital gains taxation while retaining taxation on a realization basis.

If the reformed capital gains tax has to be on a realization basis, it can be argued that the taxation of gains as other income would involve considerable inequity: gains accruing over a series of years would be taxed as a lump in the year the asset was sold and hence (with the present progressive income tax and surtax schedule) be subject to a higher rate of tax. A taxpayer who enjoyed a gain of £500 per year for ten years, and then sold the asset, would be taxed in the tenth year as though he had income of £5,000; and this would involve a much higher rate of tax than where the gain had been taxed each year at the rate appropriate to an income of £500. Such situations would be particularly important where the gains arose from a single, indivisible asset: such as, for instance, a man selling a business which he had built up gradually over a long period. This problem applies in exactly the same way, however, to other forms of income: a person who has high earnings in one year but little in the next (say a pop star or writer) pays more tax than a person whose income is spread more evenly. It is part of the general problem of the *averaging* of fluctuating incomes. At present the provisions for averaging under the British income tax are very limited, and there are good reasons for extending their scope. The tax year is simply an administrative unit, and little justification can be given for taxing people more heavily just because their incomes fluctuate.

The question of averaging for surtax purposes was discussed at length by the Millard Tucker Committee on the Taxation of Trading Profits. They recommended a scheme for averaging income over a five-year period, the effects of which on capital gains were described by the Inland Revenue as follows:

The net capital gains of any year ... would be treated as income of the following year for assessment to income tax and surtax. Any taxpayer could, however, elect at any time, but then once and for all, for averaging treatment. Then the surtax bill for the current year would be adjusted to what it would have been had the net capital gains of that and the preceding four years accrued evenly over those five years – any surtax actually paid being set off against the notional five years' bill. [Final Report of the Royal Commission on the Taxation of Profits and Income p. 438]

The Royal Commission on the Taxation of Profits and Income considered in its Final Report, published in 1955, whether these averaging provisions could be extended to income tax and concluded that 'a general scheme allowing averaging of income over a period of years is administratively impossible'. The principal objections were that records would have to be kept of the 20% of taxpayers who were relieved from tax by the allowances, since the five-year averaging provisions could apply if their income increased, and that the reduced rates of tax would make it worthwhile for many people with small incomes to elect to average. The situation today, however, is rather different in that the proportion relieved from tax by the allowances is less than 10% and that there are no reduced rates of tax. Averaging would, therefore, chiefly apply to those in the surtax ranges, and the amount of extra work involved would be considerably less than was envisaged by the Royal Commission.*

The specific proposal considered here, therefore, is the abolition of the 1965 Capital Gains Tax and the taxation of all realized gains as income, accompanied by the introduction of a five-year averaging period.† As was pointed out by the Inland Revenue in their evidence to the Royal Commission, the five-year period for averaging would not be perfect, since capital gains accruing over a longer period would still bear more tax than a regular income. It must, however, be remembered that the recipients of capital gains would still enjoy the advantage of delay in the tax payment from the date of accrual to the date of realization. The longer an asset was held, the more tax would be paid on account of the progression of the tax schedule (after five years); but the longer it was held, the larger the benefit from postponement of the tax payment. These two factors offset each other; and although they would not cancel out precisely, the long-term holder of capital gains would not in general be as heavily penalized as was suggested by the Inland Revenue (indeed he might well still pay less tax than on a comparable dividend income).

*In their memorandum to the Royal Commission, the Inland Revenue agreed that averaging for surtax only 'could, at some expense in staff, be made to work'.

†There is also a case for limiting some of the present exemptions of the gains from certain assets: for example, an upper limit could be placed on the value of the exemption for owner-occupied houses.

A further feature which should be discussed is the treatment of capital losses. Should capital losses be treated symmetrically with capital gains, so that a person could set losses against other income? If the tax was based on accrual, there would be no major objection to this liberal provision for losses. However, for a tax levied on realized gains only, serious difficulties would arise. As it was put by the Minority Report of the Royal Commission: 'it is always open to a taxpayer to turn a paper loss – at least in easily marketable securities – into a realized loss, and to cover himself (if he has no real desire to liquidate his investment) by repurchasing the security afterwards'. (Para. 65.) If losses could be set against any form of income, this would effectively allow the taxpayer to borrow money from the Exchequer. Similarly, if losses could be set against past gains:

the tax payer could so manipulate his realizations [by formally selling securities whenever the price happened to be low enough to show a loss] that in an extreme case he would avoid paying tax altogether during his lifetime even though he might enjoy a steady appreciation on the total of his assets.* [ibid.]

For these reasons, it is assumed that capital losses could only be set against gains realized in that tax year or else carried forward against future gains.

Consequences of Capital Gains Tax Reform

The distributional consequences of the reform of capital gains taxation outlined above should be clear from the earlier analysis. It would increase substantially the tax paid by those who hold their wealth in a form generating capital gains, and, as we have seen, these people tend to be the very wealthy. Instead of enjoying the present preferential treatment of capital gains, they would be subject to the full rates of income tax and surtax. This reform of capital gains taxation would make it much harder for those with inherited wealth to maintain their capital intact and the redistributive effect would not fall far short of that from an annual wealth tax.

*Although this problem would be less severe than with the present proportional rate, since the progressive rate would provide an incentive to 'even out' realizations.

It would also secure a much greater degree of horizontal equity between those holding their wealth in different forms. It is very difficult to estimate how much additional revenue would be raised. At the very least the reform would increase the tax payable from 30% to the standard rate of income tax on unearned income (at present 38·75%), and it seems reasonable to suppose that the average rate payable would be 45% or more, leading to a 50% increase in the revenue. On the basis of the projected revenue for the year 1971–2 this would mean an extra £80 million.

The principal objection raised against the taxation of capital gains is that it would adversely affect risk-taking. Even the authors of the Minority Report of the Royal Commission agreed that this was important, and therefore restricted their recommendations to the taxing of capital gains under income tax. Our discussion of this question earlier in this chapter showed, however, that there is no presumption that an increased tax on the income from risky investments would necessarily make them less attractive. The expected return would be lower, but so also would be the risk, since the government would be sharing both with the taxpayer.* In theory, therefore, there are no grounds for expecting that risk-taking would necessarily be discouraged, and the likelihood of this happening can only be established by empirical evidence. One reason for not expecting any major rearrangement of the port-folios of the rich is what has been called the 'locking in' effect of capital gains taxation. This refers to the fact that where the tax falls on realized gains, there would be an incentive for the taxpayer to delay realization as long as possible so as to postpone payment of the tax, with the result that people would be less willing to adjust their holdings in response to changed conditions.† Some writers have criticized this aspect of capital gains taxation as impairing the efficiency of the capital market, but this view is not shared by everyone. Keynes, for example, argued that excessive trading on the stock exchange tended to destabilize real investment, and that there might be grounds for making 'the purchase of an

*Although the extent to which the government is an equal partner in the risk-taking depends on how far the person can make use of the loss-offset provisions.

†Assuming that this was not outweighed by the loss of averaging facilities.

investment permanent and indissoluble, like marriage, except by reason of death or other grave cause'.

As far as saving and work incentives are concerned, there is little reason to expect the effects of a reform of the capital gains tax to be very different from those of a wealth tax. The administrative costs involved, however, would be considerably less. Under the scheme considered here, the only modification of the present procedure would be the introduction of the five-year averaging period. There would be no need to collect any information about the gains in addition to that obtained for the present tax. The operation of the averaging procedure would mean some increase in work for the Inland Revenue, since records would have to be kept for longer periods, but the additional administrative cost would be substantially less than that of a wealth tax.

Capital Gains Tax Reform – Conclusions

In his 1971 Budget, Mr Barber abolished the provisions under which capital gains realized within twelve months of purchase were taxed as other income. In this section I have examined the case for moving in the reverse direction and taxing all capital gains as income. This would contribute towards achieving a more equal distribution of current wealth and prevent very large accumulations of wealth through capital gains. Unlike the wealth tax it would not involve an annual valuation of wealth and the administrative problems would be considerably less serious. It appears to be a better way of achieving much the same objectives.

9. Taxing the Transfer of Wealth

When Augustus resolved to establish a permanent military force for the defence of his government against foreign and domestic enemies, he instituted a peculiar treasury for the pay of the soldiers . . . To supply the deficiency, the emperor suggested a new tax of five per cent on all legacies and inheritances . . . Such a tax . . . was most happily suited to the situation of the Romans. – *E. Gibbon*, The Decline and Fall of the Roman Empire

The analysis of the previous chapter showed that a wealth tax would not be the ideal method for achieving greater equality of inherited wealth. In this chapter I examine therefore the possibilities for a reform of wealth-transfer taxation, and in particular the taxation of gifts.

Strategy for Wealth-Transfer Taxation

Reform of wealth-transfer taxation could take a number of different directions. In chapter 6 we saw that such taxes differ in the basis of assessment, in the degree of integration, and in their relationship to the system of income taxation. In the first part of this chapter, I discuss the different strategies which might be adopted for reform, beginning with that closest in spirit to the present estate duty.

An Integrated Gifts and Estate Tax

Recent Chancellors of the Exchequer have made progress towards closing the loopholes in estate duty, and an important contribution was made in the 1968 Budget by the extension from five to seven years of the period for which gifts were assessed for estate duty. There is, however, a strong case for carrying this process further and subjecting all gifts to taxation whenever they are made. Britain must be almost alone among Western countries in its generous treatment of gifts *inter vivos*: for example, the United States has operated a gifts tax for a long time. A tax on gifts could take a number of different forms, of which the following three are the most important:

(1) a tax on gifts made in a given tax year, the rates being progressive with respect to the total in that year;
(2) a tax on the total gifts made by a person over his lifetime – a cumulative total being kept of all gifts made and the tax being charged progressively with respect to this total;
(3) an integrated gifts and estate tax, with the total of gifts being cumulated over a person's lifetime and his estate added as a 'final gift' (this is equivalent to an integration of (2) with the present estate duty).

The taxes in operation in other countries are in most cases of the first or second type. The tax which used to be operated in Canada, for example, had an annual assessment period (i.e. was of type (1)). This meant that a person could reduce his tax liability (or avoid tax altogether) by making a large number of small gifts in different tax years: for example, twelve annual gifts of $10,000 only bore tax at the rate of 10%, whereas the annual rate on a gift of $120,000 was over twice as great. Apart from convenience of administration, there is little rationale for adopting an annual assessment period rather than cumulating gifts over a person's lifetime. From the point of view of equity, our concern is with the total wealth transferred to the next generation, and the way in which the transfer is divided between different years of the donor's life is irrelevant. The first type of gifts tax appears, therefore, to be inferior to the second. This second procedure has been adopted in the United States, where the total value of gifts is cumulated and the tax based on the aggregate over a person's life. In any particular tax year his gifts made in that year are added to last year's cumulative total, the total tax liability is determined, and then the cumulative total of tax paid so far is subtracted to give the amount due in that year. The rates are three quarters of those of the estate tax on a corresponding estate, although there are a number of additional exemptions in the case of the gifts tax.

There has, however, recently been discussion in the United States about the possibility of integrating the gifts tax with the estate tax: i.e. of moving form type (2) to type (3). On equity grounds such an integration of the two taxes appears desirable, since there are no reasons for distinguishing between wealth transmitted in bequests and that transmitted in the form of gifts. The main argument that has been made against this integration is that the lower rates of tax on gifts are likely to increase lifetime giving, and that this is to be encouraged. A. R. Prest, for example, has argued that: 'lower rates [on gifts] are likely to encourage inter-vivos gifts relatively to transfers at death and this may well be an effective way of furthering the general aims of redistribution of wealth'. (1967, p. 316.) It is not clear, however, that this would be the case. If the tax on gifts was lower than that on estates, then presumably people would tend as at present to pass on wealth earlier in their lives, but there would be no incentive to pass it on to anyone other than the person who would have received it anyway. All that is likely to be involved is redistribution between different generations of the same family; and although this might make the current distribution more equal, it would do nothing to reduce the concentration of inherited wealth. The same people would inherit as before. Equity considerations point, therefore, in the direction of an integrated gift and estate tax; and this conclusion is further reinforced by administrative factors. If gifts were taxed at a lower rate, it would be necessary to exclude 'deathbed' gifts in order to prevent estate duty avoidance. The method used in the United States of treating gifts 'in contemplation of death' as part of a person's estate has been the cause of much litigation;* and the adoption of a seven-year rule would be essentially arbitrary. With an integrated gifts and estate tax these problems would be avoided.

An integrated gifts and estate tax would involve a record being kept of every gift made by a person during his lifetime. Each gift would be taxed at a rate which would increase progressively with the total given away to date, and at his death the donor's estate would be added and taxed accordingly. In order to avoid having

*All kinds of factors may be introduced as evidence of the donor's motive: age, health, state of mind. One American authority has commented that: 'Any tax provision becomes unduly pathetic when it gears the liability to such nonsense as the decedent's happy disposition, his practice of golfing once a week, or his entrenched habit of pottering about his garden.'

to keep a record of small gifts (e.g. Christmas presents), there would be an annual exemption for small gifts (say under £100) to a particular person. To see how the tax would work let us take the illustrative rate schedule shown in Table 21. The second column shows the marginal rate of tax (the rate applied to each £1 in that range); the third column shows the average rate payable at the lower end of the bracket (so that the average rate on a total of £200,000 would be 50%); and the fourth column gives the present estate duty rates for an *estate* of each size. The exemption level proposed for the integrated tax is £20,000, or higher than for the estate duty. As a result, the average rate of tax would be less at the lower wealth levels, although above £200,000 there would be little difference.

Table 21: Rate Schedule for an Integrated Gift and Estate Tax

Value of gifts plus estate (£)	Rates of tax (%)		Estate duty average*
	Integrated tax		
	marginal	average*	
£20,000 –	25	0	10
£30,000 –	40	8	17
£50,000 –	50	21	31
£100,000 –	65	36	47
£200,000 –	75	50	57
£500,000 and above	85†	65	67

*For amount at lower end of range and assuming no property left to a surviving spouse.

†With a ceiling of 80% overall.

Source: own calculations.

The introduction of a gifts tax integrated with the estate duty would close one of the most important avenues for avoidance, and would add greatly to the effectiveness of the British wealth transfer taxes as a means for redistributing inherited wealth. On the assumption that there would be no shifting of the burden of the tax, and that substantial avoidance would not be possible (a question discussed later in this chapter), the integrated transfer tax would make it much more difficult for a family to preserve a large fortune intact. The effect of the tax may be brought out by an example. Suppose that a man gives £100,000 to each of his three children when they reach the age of 21 and leaves an estate of £200,000 when he dies. The tax liable would be:

	Total gifts plus estate to date £	Tax payable £	Total tax paid to date £
Albert reaches age 21	100,000	35,500*	35,500
Bertha reaches age 21	200,000	65,000 (£100,000 at 65%)	100,500
Charles reaches age 21	300,000	75,000 (£100,000 at 75%)	175,000
Father dies	500,000	150,000 (£200,000 at 75%)	325,500

*£10,000 at 25%, £20,000 at 40%, £50,000 at 50%.

Comparing this with the estate duty payable at present (assuming that the father lives until Charles is 28) – £99,750 – we can see that the tax on large transfers of wealth would increase very substantially. The effective rate of tax would rise from 20% to 65% of the total amount transferred.

We have seen, however, in chapter 7 that the impact on the distribution of wealth may be offset by the ability of the family to carry out net capital accumulation. If it received an income of 6% in real terms after tax and saved a half of this income, it would preserve intact an estate of £400,000 even with integrated tax discussed here (assuming an average generation length of 33 years). The reform of capital gains taxation would reduce the after-tax return to large holdings, so that this rate of accumulation might be less attainable. Nonetheless, a real net accumulation of 2% would serve to maintain an estate of £150,000 under the integrated tax. The effect of the introduction of an integrated gifts and estate tax may, therefore, be smaller and slower-working than is thought desirable on equity grounds. Since the tax rates can scarcely be increased much further, we have to seek other means for increasing the effectiveness of transfer taxation; in particular we should examine the scope for including a positive incentive for donors to spread their wealth more widely. Under an integrated gifts and estate tax there would be no such incentive, for the same tax would be paid on £1 million given to one person as on £1 million spread among fifty people in gifts of £20,000 each. Yet from the point of view of achieving greater equality of inherited wealth, the latter would be much more desirable – and £10 each given to 100,000 people still more so! To incorporate an incentive to spread wealth widely, the tax paid has to be related to the amount received by each person rather than the total given away, and I turn now to consider the possibility of introducing a recipient-based transfer tax.

A Lifetime Capital Receipts Tax

The simplest form of wealth-transfer tax based on the recipient is that levied on individual bequests, so that each heir is taxed on his share of a given estate and the tax rate increases progressively with the size of this share. If, however, we treat gifts in the same way, we return to the problem that where wealth is passed on in small parcels to the same person very little tax may be paid. In view of this difficulty, most countries operating this type of tax cumulate gifts from one donor and add them to any bequest received. In other words, a record is kept of all gifts made by John Smith to Alfred Jones and the tax rate increases progressively with the cumulative total. When John Smith dies any bequest to Alfred Jones is added to the total of gifts and taxed accordingly. While this system provides an incentive for donors to spread their wealth widely, it does not, however, provide them with an inducement to give it to those who have received little from others. A bequest of £25,000 would bear the same tax in the hands of a man who had already inherited £1,000,000 from other sources as in the hands of someone who had inherited nothing.

To avoid this difficulty J. E. Meade has proposed that the tax liability be based not only on the individual gift or bequest from one person but also on the existing wealth of the recipient. He has suggested a scale such that the tax rate on a gift or legacy of £10,000 would range from zero if given to someone whose wealth was £1,000 to 80% if given to someone already worth £100,000. This would encourage people to pass on their wealth to those who own little, but it suffers from certain disadvantages. Meade's proposal effectively involves a tax based jointly on the amount transferred and the recipient's wealth: the more wealth the recipient possessed, the larger would be the tax due on any bequest he received. However, we have seen in the previous chapter that there are a number of reasons why the current distribution of wealth may not be the best basis for taxation, and from the point of view of bringing about greater equality in the distribution of inherited wealth, a tax which varies with the beneficiary's current wealth may not be the most appropriate. It means, for example, that the tax would be higher on gifts received by older people who had saved for their old age. Although the distribution of current wealth is clearly closely related to the distribution of inherited wealth, the correspondence is not perfect. In the extreme example given earlier of the person who used any gift or bequest received to back losing horses, no tax would be paid, since his current wealth would always be zero – even though the total received over the course of his life might be very substantial. Secondly, the adoption of such a tax would involve the valuation of the wealth of each beneficiary each time that a transfer was made, which would mean considerable administrative problems and expense.

A more promising approach is to take Meade's alternative proposal of relating the tax on gifts and bequests to the total that a person has received to date in bequests or gifts– a *lifetime capital receipts tax*. Similar proposals have been made by C. T. Sandford and O. Stutchbury (who refers to it as a 'Gratuitous Enrichment Tax' or G.E.T. for short). The way in which the tax would work has been described by Meade as follows:

> Every gift or legacy received by any one individual would be recorded in a register against his name for tax purposes. He would then be taxed when he received any gift or bequest . . . according to the size of the total amount which he had received over the whole of his life by way of gift or inheritance. The rate of tax would be on a progressive scale according to the total of gifts or bequests recorded against his name in the tax register. [1964, p. 57]

The main purpose of the tax would be to cover gifts and bequests, but other capital receipts could be included. Sandford would extend its scope to include winnings from gambling or the pools,

'golden handshakes' and lump-sum gratuities,* and Stutchbury
would include school fees – doubled for good measure! In what
follows it is assumed that the tax would only apply to gifts, bequests, and pools and gambling winnings. Charities would not be
liable to the tax. The framing of the legislation for a lifetime capital receipts tax would have to cover a number of detailed points,
such as the precise definition of the receipts falling within the scope
of the tax, the definition of the recipient unit, and the treatment of
trusts. These are discussed later in this chapter.

The rates proposed for the lifetime capital receipts tax have in
all cases been highly progressive. A possible tax schedule is shown
in Table 22, where the exemption level is £10,000.† A comparison
with the estate duty rates shows that the duty would be rather
higher, but it must be remembered that the tax would be levied on
the amount received, not on the total given away. If an estate of
£100,000 was divided between two heirs (neither of whom had any
other taxable receipts), the tax would be paid at an average rate of
34%, which is considerably less than the corresponding estate duty
rate. Only where estates were passed on as a whole, or left to those
who had already received substantial inheritances, would the tax
rate be higher than at present. This means that the revenue could
possibly be less than that from estate duty, although the inclusion
of gifts *inter vivos* now escaping tax and of gambling and other
winnings would tend to augment it, and on balance the net effect
would probably be a small increase. It should be emphasized, however, that even if the lifetime capital receipts tax did not generate
any additional revenue, it might still be a much more effective
means of securing redistribution. The amount of revenue is not
necessarily a good indicator of the extent of redistribution: if the

*Sandford also proposed that realized capital gains should be included in
the scope of the lifetime capital receipts tax (and the present tax abolished).
This would mean that gains were taxed progressively, and that there would be
no averaging difficulties. The possibility of setting realized capital losses
against inherited wealth may, however, allow the tax liability to be deferred for
considerable periods. It is also likely to increase the problems of correlating
the receipts tax and the income tax.

†This schedule is broadly similar to that suggested by Sandford (1971, Table
7.3), although the exemption level is rather higher than his (he suggests that
all receipts above £2,000 should be taxed).

lifetime receipts tax led the rich to give away their wealth in small parcels to people without much wealth the revenue might be very small, but the tax would have been highly effective.

Table 22: A Lifetime Capital Receipts Tax

Total lifetime receipts	Marginal rate (%)	Average rate* (%)	Estate duty rate* (%)
£10,000—	30	0	0
£20,000—	40	15	6
£30,000—	50	23	14
£50,000—	75	34	24
£100,000—	80	55	37
£200,000—	85†	67	50
£1,000,000—	85†	80	62

*For amount at lower end of the range and assuming no property left to a surviving spouse.

†With a ceiling of 80% overall.

The way in which the tax would work may be illustrated by a simple example:

Receipt	Cumulative total of receipts	Tax due on receipt	Total tax paid to date
Bequest of £20,000	20,000	3,000 (£10,000 at 30%)	3,000
Gift of £10,000	30,000	4,000 (£10,000 at 40%)	7,000
Wins £5,000	35,000	2,500 (£5,000 at 50%)	9,500
Bequest of £65,000	100,000	45,000 (£15,000 at 50%+ £50,000 at 75%)	54,500

At each point the total receipts are cumulated, and the tax due calculated. From this the total tax paid to date is subtracted to get the amount payable on the current receipt. When, for example, the bequest of £65,000 is received, the total tax due on the cumulative total would be £54,500; but £9,500 has already been paid, so that the current tax liability would be £45,000. (The tax liability can never exceed the amount currently received, since the marginal tax rate is always less than 100%.)

Taxing Wealth Transfers as Income

An alternative approach to the taxation of wealth transfers on a recipient basis is to regard all gifts and bequests received as income to the recipient, thus integrating the wealth transfer tax and the income tax. Such an approach has recently attracted attention on account of its adoption by the Carter Commission as part of its programme for reforming the Canadian tax system. Its proposals have been described as follows:

> The core of the Commission's recommendations concerning gifts and inheritances was that they should henceforth be taxed as income to the donee, on the same footing as such various receipts as wage and salary income, dividend payments, royalties, and other familiar components of taxable income, without allowing at the same time any deduction of the amounts transferred from the donor's taxable income. The federal estate and gift taxes would be repealed, leaving the income tax as the sole vehicle of transfer taxation. [Jantscher, 1969, p. 122]

In other words, a gift or inheritance received by a person would be added to his income for income tax purposes and taxed at the appropriate income tax rate: a person with earnings of £2,000 who received a gift of £5,000 would be taxed as though he had income of £7,000. The rate of tax on wealth transfers would depend, therefore, on the rates of personal income tax (it should be noted that the Commission recommended that the maximum rate of income tax should be 50% and that there should be extensive averaging provisions).

There are essentially two arguments for such an integration of wealth-transfer taxation with the income tax system. The first is based on the view that wealth transfers should be treated in exactly the same way as other receipts – such as earnings or dividends – for the purposes of assessing the equity of taxation. If, as in chapter 2, we define income in a given period as 'the amount that a person could have consumed while leaving the value of his wealth unchanged between the beginning and the end of the period', gifts and bequests should clearly be included. H. Simons commented that: 'To exclude gifts, inheritances, and bequests, would be to introduce additional arbitrary distinctions; it would be necessary to distinguish among an individual's receipts according to the intentions of second parties.' (1938, pp. 56–7.) However, while this argument may justify the inclusion of wealth transfers in an *ideal* income tax, it does not follow that wealth-transfer taxation should necessarily be integrated with the *existing* income tax. In particular, we have to bear in mind that the present income tax is based on an annual assessment period, whereas it has been argued above that the relevant assessment period in the case of gifts and bequests is the lifetime of the individual. There are, of course, strong reasons for adopting a lifetime assessment period for the income tax (this would be the logical extension of the averaging procedures discussed at the end of the last chapter); and if this were done, there would be no objection on this score to the integration of the wealth transfer tax and the income tax. It seems highly unlikely that such a radical change in the income tax system will take place in the foreseeable future, and it seems unrealistic to base the reform of wealth-transfer taxation on the assumption that lifetime averaging would be introduced for the income tax. The integration of wealth-transfer taxation with the income tax would be likely, therefore, to involve the acceptance of an annual assessment period (or a five-year averaging period if the arguments of the previous chapter were accepted).

The disadvantages involved in abandoning the lifetime assessment period were fully recognized by H. Simons:

... the treatment of gratuitous receipts as taxable income, while clearly preferable to inheritance taxation as it stands, would fail to capture some of the virtues of inheritance taxation – in its ideal form – i.e., in the form of the cumulative personal tax on beneficiaries. As against such a levy, our inclusive levy on annual income would impose relatively inadequate total taxes with respect to large transfers which were carried out very gradually. [1938, pp. 193–4]

He therefore proposed that a supplementary tax should be introduced on the receipts of wealth transfers cumulated over the beneficiary's lifetime, which would be in addition to the inclusion of these receipts in the income tax base (although credit would be allowed for the income tax paid). This would in effect mean a return to the lifetime capital receipts tax discussed in the previous section, and we should have gained nothing from the integration of wealth-transfer taxation with the income tax. There is, therefore, little from the point of view of equity to recommend the adoption of the Carter Commission's proposals in Britain in the context of the present income tax. To quote the assessment of one commentator who considered the relevance of the Carter recommendations to the United States: 'It is one thing to propose that income-inheritance tax as part of a newly reconstructed and equitable income tax, quite another to tack it on to a jerry-built structure that itself badly wants repair.' (Jantscher, 1969, p. 138.)

The second argument for integration is the more pragmatic consideration that if transfers and income are taxed at different rates, there is likely to be an incentive for the individual to transform one into the other. With the rates for a lifetime capital receipts tax outlined in Table 22, he might well prefer to receive gifts in the form of income: we should have a situation where people are actually keen to have their income taxed by the Inland Revenue! In order to reduce the scope for avoidance, the definition of gifts and the treatment of marginal transactions would clearly need more careful consideration. This would add to the complexity of the legislation and the difficulties of ensuring compliance. However, since there are at present provisions to prevent income from appearing as gifts, it should not be impossible to design the lifetime capital receipts tax so as to prevent the reverse from happening; and it seems unlikely that this is a sufficiently important problem to outweigh the equity advantages of the separate wealth-transfer tax.

Strategy for Wealth-Transfer Taxation – Summary

We have considered three principal ways of reforming the present system of wealth-transfer taxation: an integrated gifts and estate tax, a lifetime capital receipts tax, and the taxation of transfers under the income tax. All three measures would represent a major improvement over the present situation as far as achieving greater equality of inherited wealth is concerned, but the lifetime capital receipts tax has definite advantages over the other two proposals. It would be based directly on the total inherited wealth received by a person over his lifetime and thus would make clear the object of redistribution. It would provide a strong incentive for donors to spread their wealth widely, so that its impact would be greater than that of a donor-based tax such as the integrated gifts and estate duty. The lifetime capital receipts tax would be superior to the annual assessment period that would be implied by an integration of wealth-transfer taxation with the present income tax.

The Government Green Paper on Inheritance Taxation

In his 1972 Budget speech Mr Barber announced that the Government is undertaking a thoroughgoing review of the taxation of capital on death, and at the same time a Green Paper was published on *Taxation of Capital on Death: A Possible Inheritance Tax in place of Estate Duty* (Cmnd 4930).

The first part of the Green Paper outlines some of the criticisms which have been made of the present estate duty, including the following:

(1) the increasing burden through the effect of inflation on property values, leading to 'an excessive burden on property [which] can be held to discourage the creation and preservation of wealth'. The main argument advanced in this connection concerns the effect on small firms.

(2) 'the duty payable is not related to the size of the legacies [received by the beneficiaries] nor to their taxable capacity'. As a result, 'the duty does nothing to encourage the wider distribution of wealth'.

(3) 'the tax does not lend itself to variation of the burden by reference to the relationship of the deceased to the beneficiary'.

The Green Paper also refers to the criticism which was the principal concern of chapter 7 – the ease of avoidance – but does not appear to regard this as a serious matter:

These issues raise the question of how far anti-avoidance legislation should be taken. There is already a considerable body of such law, much of it passed in recent years, and in relation to gifts inter vivos the ambit of charge has been progressively widened. Indeed, the seven-year period for such gifts is itself criticized as being too severe.

It is far from clear what this passage means, and it certainly does not justify the neglect of the problem of avoidance in the subsequent analysis.

The latter part of the Green Paper considers the possibility of replacing estate duty by an inheritance tax: i.e. of moving from a donor to a recipient basis. It gives particular attention to two possible types of inheritance tax. The first (Variant I) involves the aggregation of all inheritances (including gifts within the relevant period) which a person received on the death of a single donor, but ignores any other circumstances of the beneficiary. This form of tax is the simplest to administer but is open, as the Green Paper recognises, to the objection that the same tax would be charged on a bequest of £20,000 to a person who had received no other inheritances as to a rich man who had inherited large amounts from other people. Moreover, the Green Paper points out that:

the tax burden could be artificially reduced if the members of a family in one generation agreed among themselves that each would divide his estate among the members of the family in the next generation. Each member of the next generation would thus get a number of modest inheritances (taxed at a low rate) from his father and his uncles instead of one large inheritance from his father (taxable at a higher rate).

In view of these objections to Variant I, they also put forward Variant II, under which all inheritances would be aggregated over a specified period of years (taken as ten years for the purposes of illustration). This would mean that when a person received an inheritance, the rate of tax payable would depend on the total received in the preceding ten years. The way in which this would work may be illustrated by one of the examples given in the Green Paper (which takes the estate duty rates for illustration):

A person inheriting (for the first time) in 1975 an amount of £80,000 would pay duty of £26,250. If in 1980 he inherits a further £295,000, the tax would be calculated as that due on £375,000 minus that due on the previous amount (£80,000):

	Duty on £375,000	£222,250
less	Duty on £80,000	£26,250
equals	Duty due in 1980	£196,000

Finally, suppose that in 1986 the person inherits a further £30,000. By that time the bequest received in 1975 would no longer be taken into account and the liability would be calculated as follows:

	Duty on £325,000	£187,250
less	Duty on £295,000	£166,250
equals	Duty due in 1986	£21,000

The Green Paper also discusses the differentiation of rates according to consanguinity (as with the legacy and succession duties abolished in 1949). The specific possibility examined is that there should be three separate scales for (1) surviving spouses and lineal issue, (2) other near relatives (brothers, sisters, nephews and nieces), and (3) remote relatives and strangers. The effect of differentiation would be that an inheritance of £100,000 would bear tax of £27,000 on the first scale and £46,000 if left to a stranger. The main argument for such differentiation is that a widow or other near member of the family is more likely to be dependent on the deceased. The issues raised are close to those discussed earlier in relation to the definition of the tax-paying unit, and the adoption of a family unit could be seen as an alternative to differentiation according to consanguinity. It has the advantage that it would benefit dependent children but not those who had left the family unit. As was pointed out in Chapter 6, in many cases the succeeding children are not infant orphans but grown men in their fifties.

The inheritance tax Variant II differs from the lifetime capital receipts tax discussed above in two important respects:

(1) *the assessment period* would be limited to a specified period rather than covering the individual's lifetime. The lifetime assessment period is considered in the Green Paper but dismissed on the grounds that:

'administratively it would represent a most formidable task ... Moreover it might be objected that a taxpayer ... could have his tax bill settled by reference to events of long ago which might have no bearing on his present taxable capacity'.

The first objection based on the administrative cost should clearly be taken seriously; however, the magnitude of the problem appears to have been exaggerated. If a ten-year period were to be adopted, it would still be necessary to refer to the records on the occasion of every gift or inheritance, whether or not any tax was due, and to agree a new cumulative total with the taxpayer. Moreover, if the cumulative total can be agreed on each occasion, there will be no need to maintain all old records, and the effective difference between the ten-year period and lifetime cumulation becomes rather small. The second objection is effectively a rejection of the lifetime concept of equity and the reason given is scarcely convincing.*

(2) the proposed tax would exclude *gifts inter vivos* (apart from those within a given period of death – the present seven-year rule). As we have already seen, the Green Paper gives little weight to the problem of avoidance through gifts. From the discussion it is unclear whether the government feels that nearly all gifts are now caught by the seven-year rule (and hence an extension of the tax base is unnecessary) or whether it considers that gifts should not in general be subject to tax. The former interpretation scarcely accords with the evidence presented in chapter 7; and the latter interpretation is quite inconsistent with the principles of equity developed in the preceding chapters.

The willingness of the government to consider reform of wealth-transfer taxation is to be welcomed; however, for the reform to have a significant equalizing effect on the distribution of wealth it is essential that the tax be extended to cover all gifts *inter vivos* and on equity grounds the assessment period should be the individual

---

*The adoption of a limited assessment period will also give rise to situations where the amount of duty may depend very critically on the date of transfer. If a person received an inheritance of £50,000 on 1 January 1976, and his father died on 31 December 1985 leaving him a further £15,000, he would pay duty on the second bequest of £7,000. If, however, his father lived a day longer, the son would pay nothing on the second bequest.

lifeline. The government should therefore go beyond the Green Paper and should replace estate duty by a lifetime capital receipts tax. It is with the implications of this more radical reform that the remainder of this chapter is concerned.

A Lifetime Capital Receipts Tax in More Detail

The chief features of the lifetime capital receipts tax were outlined earlier in the chapter, together with a suggested schedule of tax rates. There are, however, two further aspects which require discussion: the definition of the tax-paying unit and the treatment of trusts. We should also consider the scope for avoidance and the measures that could be taken to ensure compliance. (Those readers willing to take the details of the lifetime receipts tax for granted may prefer to omit this section and turn to the discussion of its implications on page 184.)

Definition of the Tax-Paying Unit

In the case of estate duty, the tax is assessed on an individual basis and there is no aggregation of the estates of married couples. If a man leaves his estate to his widow, and she leaves it in turn to their children, estate duty is payable twice (subject to the exemptions referred to in chapter 7). In the case of the lifetime capital receipts tax, such a procedure would scarcely be in accordance with the equity objectives of taxing the transfer of wealth between generations. Moreover, where gifts are subject to tax, this basis for taxation would involve serious problems of enforcement. All gifts between husband and wife would have to be taxed, and this would mean policing all inter-spousal transactions, which would be extremely difficult. Gifts to a married couple would have to be apportioned between them, and this apportionment would be essentially arbitrary. There are, therefore, strong grounds for regarding a married couple as a single unit for the purposes of the lifetime capital receipts tax (as for income tax), all inter-spousal gifts and bequests being ignored.

The application to a married couple of the lifetime capital receipts tax rates as they stand would involve their paying more tax than if they had remained single. The joining together in holy matrimony of two inheritances of £50,000 would increase the tax payable from £34,000 to £54,500, and this would provide a strong incentive for the wealthy to live in sin. It may therefore be felt (on grounds of equity rather than morality) that the tax rate payable by a married couple should be less than that for a single person. The most reasonable procedure would be for receipts of £x accruing to a couple to be taxed at the rate applicable to receipts of £$x/2$ for a single person: a married couple inheriting £100,000 would pay tax at the same average rate as a single person inheriting £50,000. This would mean that a man who had received a substantial inheritance (and paid a high rate of tax) marrying a poor girl with no inherited wealth would be entitled to a substantial tax refund, but such an incentive for intermarriage between wealth groups may well be thought desirable. Where the married couple is taken as the basic unit, problems would arise in the case of divorce. In particular, one would want to rule out situations where a rich man could marry a poor girl, reduce his tax liability, and subsequently divorce her without repaying the tax. Provisions would have to be included in the legislation to cover this eventuality: for example, an agreed apportionment of the joint lifetime wealth at the time maintenance was awarded. When the apportionment had been agreed, the tax could then be assessed on each party at the rate for a single person (if it were split equally no tax would have to be paid).

The integration of the tax-paying unit could be carried one stage further by basing the lifetime capital receipts tax on the family unit (incorporating dependent children as well as husband and wife). Such a basis was recommended by the Carter Commission for its combined income-inheritance tax. Until the age of majority, a child would be regarded as a member of the family unit (with some exceptions, such as where the child married or left the country), and any transfer of wealth from parents to children (or vice versa) would be ignored. At the juncture when the child left the family unit, he would be taxed on the total wealth owned, this being regarded as his initial lifetime receipts. A similar procedure could be followed with the lifetime receipts tax: at the age of (say) 18 an initial declaration of wealth could be made, the individual becoming liable for the tax from that point. There are certain problems with this procedure. In particular, a person might be taxed twice on gifts received before he left the family unit (since they would be taxed as accruing to the family unit, and as part of his wealth when he leaves the unit). This could, however, be overcome if he was allowed to choose to leave the family unit at an earlier age.

Treatment of Trusts

In his discussion of the treatment of settled property under a lifetime capital receipts tax, Stutchbury suggested that any interest conferred on an individual should be included in his lifetime receipts (where only a right to income was conveyed, the actuarial value should be included). If no beneficiary could be identified (as with discretionary trusts), he argued that the tax should be imposed separately on the trust fund, this being regarded as an independent tax unit.

There are a number of objections to this proposed treatment of trusts. In the case of life interests, the taxation of the actuarial value may appear the logical application of the receipts tax principle, but it would mean that settled property could be transferred on more favourable terms than property bequeathed outright to successive heirs and thus increase their importance as a means of avoiding tax. Moreover, we have seen that the ownership of property can convey benefits apart from income and these may remain even when that property is held in trust (e.g. where a trust holds shares in a family business), so that the actuarial calculation is not necessarily appropriate. The 1972 Green Paper discussing the treatment of trusts under a possible inheritance tax suggests that the present estate duty procedure could be retained, with the lifetime capital receipts tax being charged on the full capital value whenever a person became entitled to a life interest. This may appear rather severe, particularly where the interest is for a short, fixed term, but a solution less favourable to trusts than that of Stutchbury must be found.

In the case of discretionary trusts, Stutchbury's proposals would mean that a person wishing to convey property to his heirs (already in a high lifetime capital receipts bracket) could substantially reduce the tax payable by creating a series of discretionary trusts, since each time he would be starting afresh. In an extreme case, a series of ten trusts worth £10,000 could transfer £100,000 without any tax being paid. Moreover, the incentive for the donor to spread his wealth widely would be lost. An alternative solution for discretionary trusts would be to follow the practice introduced for estate duty in the 1969 Budget, whereby a person is taxed at death on a proportion of the fund equal to the proportion of its income in the previous seven years which had been paid to him. (Although the original intention of taking his lifetime rather than seven years as the relevant period would be preferable.) This would then provide the trustees with an incentive to spread the benefits from the fund widely, since this would reduce the tax liability. These provisions would not, however, be ideal, and could give rise to considerable inequity where a beneficiary lived only for a short period.* It is clear in fact that discretionary trusts do not admit of any straightforward treatment under a lifetime re-receipts tax (or for that matter under any form of wealth-transfer tax). This leads one to question whether they should be allowed to continue in their present form. There are undoubtedly cases where such trusts are set up for genuine reasons, but the vast majority set up in the 1950s and 1960s almost certainly had tax avoidance as their principal purpose.

Scope for Avoidance

In many cases, compliance with the lifetime receipts tax could be ensured quite straightforwardly: for example, where the transfer is subject to stamp duty and the transaction void unless submitted to Somerset House. As Stutchbury pointed out, this check 'works now perfectly satisfactorily in practice and there is no reason why similar machinery should not cope with the G.E.T. [Gratuitous Enrichment Tax]'. Where gifts were made in cash or kind, evasion might be rather easier, although it seems unlikely that large sums

---

*An extreme example of this has been given in the *British Tax Review* (1969): if the trustees of a settlement give a christening present to a new-born beneficiary, who then dies at the age of two days, the present may represent a large fraction of the income in those two days, and hence the whole fund would be deemed to pass – all on account of a silver spoon!

could pass unnoticed. Further scope for avoidance might be through transactions which were effectively transfers but not covered by the definition of gifts. A garage owner might, for example, sell his son a new Jaguar for £5. This 'sale' would be equivalent to a gift of two or three thousand pounds, and should be treated as such. Similarly a wealth transfer takes place when an indulgent father pays his son's debts or living expenses. For this reason, Stutchbury proposed to include in taxable receipts:

the enhancement in value of any property of an individual in consequence of any contract or arrangement . . . any payment or other consideration made or given to a third party with a view to the provision . . . of goods or services to, or the release . . . of a claim against, an individual . . . any arrangement whereby a liability of an individual . . . is released for less than its full amount, otherwise than in the ordinary course of a business carried on by that individual. [1968, p. 25]

Stutchbury also makes the interesting suggestion that, in order to weight the scales against avoidance or evasion, the person legally accountable for the tax (in the first instance) should be the donor rather than the recipient. He argues that a rich donor will not even be tempted to try a tax avoidance scheme if there is a chance (however remote) that he may be rendering himself liable to pay the tax after he has disposed of the wherewithal with which to pay it. There are also a number of other measures which could be adopted to reduce the possibilities for avoidance, such as the removal of the present concessions for timber.

The ingenuity of tax-avoiders should never be underestimated, and it has to be remembered that no completely satisfactory solution has been offered to the problems of discretionary trusts other than their prohibition; however, there are strong grounds for expecting that, with safeguards of the kind outlined, the scope for avoidance would be considerably less with the lifetime receipts tax than with the present estate duty. Moreover, recipient-based wealth transfer taxes have been in force for a long time in a number of European countries, and appear to operate successfully. The only major difference between these taxes and the capital receipts tax considered here lies in the lifetime cumulation, and this would not make avoidance any easier.

The Consequences of a Lifetime Capital Receipts Tax

The lifetime capital receipts tax would be the most effective way in which wealth-transfer taxation could contribute towards bringing about greater equality of inherited wealth. Most importantly, it would provide a clear incentive for donors to spread their wealth widely. Under the lifetime receipts tax, a man with £1,000,000 to leave could reduce the tax payable by £255,000 if he left it to ten people rather than in one single bequest; and if he divided it among a hundred people no tax would be payable at all (assuming that none had previously received any inherited wealth). If this incentive was ignored, and a family still sought to preserve its fortune intact, then the rates of tax would be higher than under the present estate duty and all gifts *inter-vivos* would be taxed. Finally, the introduction of the lifetime receipts tax would serve to make quite clear the purpose of taxation and the basis for redistribution.*

As in the case of the wealth tax, the principal objections made to a lifetime receipts tax are that its introduction would adversely affect the incentives for saving, work and enterprise, and that it would be expensive to administer.

Effect on Savings and Aggregate Demand

A person could respond to the introduction of the lifetime capital receipts tax in a number of ways. Firstly, he might decide to increase his saving as a result of the tax, so as to be able to maintain the net amount (after tax) received by his heirs. If his aim in saving was to provide 'comfortably' for his children, an increase in the effective rate of tax (owing to the fact that gifts would now be caught) means that he would have to save more to ensure that they received a specified after-tax amount. He might, however, react in the opposite way and reduce the amount which he saved to transfer to his heirs. In an extreme case he might decide that it was no longer worthwhile saving anything (since the after-tax

*One problem to which the lifetime receipts tax does not, however, offer a solution is that of 'generation-skipping', where property passes not from father to son but from grandfather to grandson. This requires more consideration.

transfer was so small) and spend it all himself. But even in this case there would not necessarily be a net increase in consumption, since we should expect there to be some reduction in the consumption of his heirs. An increase in grandfather's consumption would be a signal for retrenchment, and even if not heeded immediately, consumption would ultimately have to be cut when the expected bequest did not materialize. Moreover, whether he saved more or less there would no longer be an incentive under a lifetime capital receipts tax (or under an integrated gifts and estate tax) to pass on his wealth early to his heirs, and as a result they would face greater uncertainty about the amount they would inherit and the date at which they would receive it. Without the security of the money safely in their pockets they would be expected to save more and to consume less.

As far as these factors are concerned, therefore, the lifetime capital receipts tax could be expected to lead to some reduction in the consumption of the wealthy (either the donors or the prospective heirs). As such it would allow some reduction in other taxes or an increase in government expenditure (for example, on a capital element in the state pension), although the amounts involved would be small. This needs to be qualified, however, in that we have not yet allowed for the incentive provided by the tax for donors to spread their wealth widely. If the donor decided to divide his wealth among a number of beneficiaries, the amount of tax paid might be considerably less than at present, and his saving little affected. Again the effect on the recipients would be important. Those who had not previously expected to inherit would probably tend to increase their consumption by more than the reduction in the consumption of those whose expectations were disappointed. In an extreme case, where £1 million was divided equally among 10,000 people who had not previously inherited, it seems likely that each of the beneficiaries would spend his £100 quite quickly; whereas if the whole estate were inherited by one person, he would probably aim to keep a large part intact. These effects are, however, based on little more than guesswork, and in any event are likely to operate slowly.

There is also the possibility that the introduction of a lifetime receipts tax might lead to a capital flight – the 'standing room only in the Bahamas' objection discussed earlier in the context of a wealth tax. This risk seems rather smaller, however, under the life-time receipts tax than under the annual wealth tax. In particular, the benefit to be derived from a change of domicile (with the inher-ent personal costs) would be received not by the emigrant but by his heirs. The move would save him little during his lifetime, un-like the wealth tax where 1 % or more of his wealth would visibly disappear each year.

If we compare the effect on saving of a lifetime receipts tax with that of an annual wealth tax, we might expect the former to have a smaller effect, since all savings intended to be spent before death would escape taxation: a wealth tax falls on all savings (above the exemption limit) but a wealth-transfer tax only on that part which is given away or bequeathed. However, it has to be borne in mind that the wealth taxes actually proposed would not apply to the vast majority of those whose wealth was simply the result of spreading consumption over their lifetime. The people subject to the wealth tax would in general be those with substantial inherited wealth, and to this extent the effect of the wealth tax on life-cycle saving would be quantitatively unimportant. It seems, therefore, reason-able to assume that the lifetime receipts tax and the wealth tax would have much the same effect per £ of revenue on the level of demand. At the same time, the effect per £ of revenue would prob-ably be very small – as we have seen in the case of the wealth tax, the adjustments in consumption made by the wealthy would be relatively insignificant and the bulk of the tax would be paid out of reduced saving. As a result, even though the wealth tax would generate substantially more additional revenue than the lifetime receipts tax, it would not provide appreciably more scope for re-distribution through such measures as a capital element in the state pension. The chief advantages of the wealth tax would lie in the availability of revenue for the purpose of reducing the National Debt (which is discussed in the next chapter): the money could not be used for increasing expenditure without adding to demand.

Effect on Work Effort and Enterprise

One major objection levelled against reform of wealth-transfer taxation is that it would discourage work effort on the part of the donor and reduce the incentive for individual enterprise. Since the lifetime capital receipts tax would affect principally those who accumulated substantial amounts of wealth (a man saving £30,000 over his life and leaving it equally to his three sons would not be affected), the latter aspect would be the more important: the possible disincentive for entrepreneurs like Lord Nuffield who build up large enterprises from nothing.

The source of entrepreneurial motivation is an extremely complex subject:

The desire to build up capital possessions is not a simple thing. It is made up of various elements blended in various ways among different men. One element is the desire to be able to exercise the constructive force, which a strong man may find in himself, in conjunction with a large-scale undertaking: another is the desire for that power in society or, perhaps, in politics which great wealth confers: another is the desire for fame or notoriety: another the desire for a large income accruing without effort in later life: another the desire for posthumous glory in dying very rich . . . Alongside . . . there is the desire to hand on accumulated capital to his children. [Pigou, 1947, pp. 142–3]

The effects of a lifetime receipts tax would depend on which of these different elements were more important. Where the primary motive was that of controlling a large enterprise or the acquisition of 'power in society', a wealth-transfer tax would not act as a disincentive. Unlike a wealth tax, the lifetime capital receipts tax would leave the entrepreneur with his control undiminished throughout his lifetime (though this might, of course, be thought undesirable on other grounds). Similarly, a person's behaviour would not be affected if he was concerned with the 'posthumous glory in dying very rich', and if he disliked the idea of his wealth passing to the Exchequer, he could (under the reform considered here) reduce the duty payable by spreading his wealth widely. Only where the primary motivating factor is the last of the elements mentioned by Pigou – the 'desire to hand on accumulated capital to his children' – could the lifetime receipts tax be expected to have any major influence, and even in this case the effect might operate either way (as we have seen earlier). In fact there is little evidence that this has been an important force motivating entrepreneurs. As was observed by Wedgwood:

Actually, 'self-made men' do not as a rule seem nearly so anxious to leave their children large inheritances, as those who have themselves inherited the bulk of their fortunes. I suspect that the 'self-made man' despises the large inheritor just as much as the latter despises him. At any rate it is an interesting sidelight on the psychological effects of Inheritance taxation that Carnegie and Leverhulme were strong advocates of the Death Duties. [1939, p. 232]

Irving Fisher similarly remarked that 'the ordinary normal self-made American millionaire is rather disposed, I believe, to look on the inheritance of his millions by his children with some misgivings'.

In the case of the *recipient* of inherited wealth, a lifetime capital receipts tax might affect not only the motivation of the potential entrepreneur but also his opportunities to enter business. A small inheritance may allow a person to start out on his own and build up a successful enterprise, in a way which would not have been possible without the initial capital. The importance of this factor is hard to assess without detailed study of the origins of modern entrepreneurs, but it should be noted that the lifetime capital receipts tax considered here does not preclude a modest inheritance: only £3,000 tax is payable, for example, on a bequest of £20,000. Indeed, Stutchbury framed his proposal with this in mind: '£20,000 can buy someone control of a small business. The objective is to stop him getting much more than this.' From the point of view of the *motivation* of the heirs, the lifetime capital receipts tax could well have an incentive rather than a disincentive effect. As Alfred Nobel is reported to have said: 'I regard large inherited wealth as a misfortune which merely serves to dull men's faculties . . . I consider it a mistake to hand over to children considerable sums of money. To do so merely encourages laziness.' The view that the lifetime tax could act as an incentive is strengthened by the fact that wealth would no longer be passed on early to avoid tax as at present. This means that a potential heir in the prime of his working life would not be certain how much he would inherit and could not rely on the security of having it in the bank. One would expect this to lead him to work harder.

A comparison of the lifetime capital receipts tax and the annual wealth tax shows that the former has clear advantages in terms of the effects on enterprise. As far as motivation is concerned, the wealth tax would fall on all wealth accumulated in excess of £50,000, whereas there would always be the possibility of paying nothing under a lifetime capital receipts tax if the money was shared out widely (or left to charities). The lifetime capital receipts tax would leave the holder's income and power unaffected during his lifetime, whereas these would be reduced by a wealth tax. The timing of the tax payment would also affect the opportunities open to entrepreneurs: under a wealth tax, the tax could become payable at a critical stage in the company's growth, when the ability to plough back profits was essential, whereas under the lifetime receipts tax the tax would not become due until later. Insofar, therefore, as the encouragement of individual enterprise is thought desirable (and the control which it implies over a production acceptable), the lifetime capital receipts tax is to be preferred to the annual wealth tax.

Although the wealth-transfer tax would not necessarily act as a disincentive during the lifetime of the founder of an enterprise, it might raise serious problems for its continuance after his death. These problems, which arise particularly in the case of medium-sized private companies and farms, have been described by Sandford as follows:

Consider a family business of moderate size (say upwards of £50,000) of which the chairman, who was also the majority shareholder, dies. It is probable that the available non-trade assets of the deceased would be insufficient to meet estate duty liabilities. Other members of the family might be able to buy the shares, but possibly only at the cost of a substantial loan on the security of the business. A new interest might have to be sought, perhaps on unfavourable terms to the family, either in the form of a new large shareholder from outside the family or, more drastically, a complete takeover by another company. [1969, p. 157]

Whether it is desirable to encourage the retention of such companies in private hands is open to question. Quite apart from the equity arguments, there is no reason to suppose that the managerial or other abilities of the founder would be passed on with his capital. Rather than follow the present estate duty practice of allowing special concessions for private companies, it seems preferable to incorporate provisions for the state to accept holdings in private companies as payment for the lifetime receipts tax (although it is not clear how far this could be applied in agriculture).

Administrative Costs

The operation of the lifetime capital receipts tax would undoubtedly require more administrative resources than the present estate duty. A record would have to be kept of every individual tax unit's cumulative receipts, and this would have to be done for everyone ever receiving a transfer, even when it was not liable for duty, since he might later receive gifts or bequests sufficient to bring him above the exemption limit. The Inland Revenue would, therefore, have many more 'accounts' than at present. The adoption of the family unit rather than the individual would mean keeping track of marriages and divorces, and procedures would have to be developed for ensuring compliance in the case of gifts. However, there is nothing inherently impracticable about the proposal. As Sandford has pointed out, the Inland Revenue agreed as long ago as 1927 that a death duty 'at a rate graduated by reference to the amount of benefit received could be effectively administered'. The amount of wealth involved each year would be very much less than with an annual wealth tax, and it seems likely that the costs of administration would be considerably smaller. Moreover, the lifetime receipts tax would have the important advantage that the work load would only build up gradually, since the tax would not be made retrospective.* This is in sharp contrast to the annual wealth tax, where the valuation would place a heavy burden on the Inland Revenue from the outset. The lifetime receipts tax is, therefore, much less likely to be considered impracticable on administrative grounds.

Lifetime Capital Receipts Tax – Conclusions

As a means for achieving greater equality in the distribution of inherited wealth, the lifetime capital receipts tax would have definite advantages over other forms of wealth transfer taxation and over an annual wealth tax. It would fall directly on the total received by a person in gifts and bequests over his lifetime, and by

---

*The provisions for the transition from the present Estate Duty would clearly need to be carefully drafted.

including gifts *inter vivos* would be very much more effective than the present estate duty. Moreover it would provide a positive incentive for donors to leave their wealth to those who had inherited little, which means that, even if it raised little extra revenue, it would have a greater redistributive impact than a donor-based transfer tax. The introduction of a lifetime receipts tax would be unlikely in the short run to lead to a rise in consumption; it could happen in the long run as a result of the equalization of inherited wealth, but this is an inevitable consequence of any redistribution by whatever means it is brought about. A lifetime tax would be less likely than a wealth tax to lead to a capital flight or to have a disincentive effect on work effort or enterprise. It would cause some increase in the work of the Inland Revenue, but substantially less than an annual wealth tax.

Part III
Wealth For All

So far we have considered redistribution in terms of reducing the transfer of wealth by the rich. In this part of the book we examine measures designed to increase the social ownership of wealth and to increase the wealth in the hands of those who at present own little – in other words we are concerned with the uses to which the revenue raised from the top 5% could be put.

The wealth of the state can be increased in a number of ways. Chapter 10 considers proposals to reduce the National Debt through a capital levy and to increase the public ownership of physical assets through nationalization. After the First World War a capital levy was proposed by the Labour Party, but little has been heard of it in recent years. Was the idea rightly dropped? Further nationalization has remained part of Labour Party policy but its contribution to achieving greater equality of wealth-holding has been largely neglected. Would it in fact make any difference to the distribution of wealth or economic power? Would – as right-wing critics suggest – denationalization be more effective?

It is commonly argued that inequality in the distribution of wealth should be approached primarily through measures to increase the wealth of those at the bottom of the scale. *The Times*, for example, has suggested that 'The right way to approach the problem of the ownership of wealth is to encourage the creation of capital among people who have not in the past had the habit of capital formation or indeed the opportunity.' (28 September 1968.) In chapter 11 we describe a range of schemes intended for this purpose and examine whether they are likely to prove effective.

10. The Social Ownership of Wealth

The only part of the so-called national wealth that actually enters into the collective possessions of modern people is . . . the National Debt. – *K. Marx*

At present the net wealth in the possession of the state is a small fraction of total national wealth, reflecting the fact that the physical assets of the public sector (central and local government and the nationalized industries) are largely counterbalanced by its financial liabilities. In 1966 the assets of the public sector amounted to some £65,000 million, but its liabilities in the form of currency, money held in the National Savings Bank, Premium Bonds, Treasury Bills, quoted securities, etc., totalled in all £59,000 million. As a result, the net worth of the public sector was only £6,000 million, which was less than 4% of the total national wealth. Indeed, until recently the net worth of the state was negative, the value of its assets being less than its liabilities, which led J. E. Meade to comment that: 'As far as the management of real property is concerned, we live in a semi-Socialist state; but as far as the net ownership of property is concerned we live, not in a semi-Socialist state, but in an anti-Socialist state.' (1964, p. 69.)

The extension of the social ownership of wealth is often suggested as a means for achieving greater equality, but just how such an extension would contribute towards this end is not usually made explicit. To the extent that wealth in social ownership is held to be shared equally among all the population, an increase has a direct effect in reducing inequality. If everyone felt that he owned a 1/55 millionth share in the assets of the nationalized industries and was responsible for the same share of the National Debt, then he would gain from an increase in the net worth of the public sector. Expressed in this way, such a view has little appeal, since it seems unlikely that people do in fact feel this sense of identification with the wealth of the state. On the other hand, the greater the net worth of the public sector, the less important is private wealth in relation to the total value of capital, which in turn reduces the importance of inequality in private wealth-holding. If private wealth were only a small proportion of total national wealth, it might not matter particularly that the top 1% of wealth-holders owned more than their proportionate share. An increase in the net worth of the public sector would change, therefore, the balance between social and private property, and thus serve to diminish the importance of inequality in the latter. Moreover, an increase in the net worth of the state has consequences for the distribution of *income*. As it has been put by Meade:

> Suppose that by the wave of some . . . magic wand . . . the ownership of all property were transferred from private individuals to the State . . . profits now go to the State, which could use them to pay out an equal social dividend to every citizen. In one basic respect this system is the same as a system in which property is privately owned but is owned in equal amounts by every citizen. In both cases income from property is equally divided among all citizens. [1964, p. 66]

The net worth of the public sector can be increased by a reduction in its liabilities or by an increase in the assets in its possession, particularly in the hands of the nationalized industries. I examine these two approaches in turn.

The National Debt and a Capital Levy

So far I have not discussed what is meant by the highly ambiguous term 'National Debt'. Quite apart from its misleadingly being called the 'national' debt when most of it is owed to ourselves, the term has at least two interpretations. Firstly, it is conventionally applied to a large part (but not all) of the debt of the central government: in particular, marketable securities, Treasury Bills, National Savings and Tax Reserve Certificates. This definition does not correspond to any meaningful economic concept. It excludes the liabilities of local authorities and of the nationalized industries, both of which represent for our purposes part of the public sector, and it excludes such elements of central government debt as notes and coin. Moreover, it makes no allowance for the fact that much of this debt is held within the public sector itself (e.g. by the Bank of England). For these reasons, this first definition is unhelpful, and its continued use can be explained only by respect for tradition. The alternative definition of the National Debt is that followed by the Radcliffe Committee on Monetary Reform, whereby the term is applied to the total liabilities of the public sector – or the figure of £59,000 million in 1966 referred to earlier. This definition is clearly that best suited for our purposes and is adopted in what follows.

The National Debt could be reduced in a number of different ways, of which the most obvious is through taxation. In Part II we saw that a number of tax reforms would yield a larger revenue than could be used either for reducing taxation or for increasing expenditure while maintaining a stable level of aggregate demand. The redistributive wealth tax discussed in chapter 8 would have raised something like an extra £300 million in revenue, of which possibly some £250 million would have been available for reducing the National Debt. However, such a contribution could only lead to a very slow reduction in the size of the debt. To pay off the present National Debt would take at this rate over two hundred years! To make any major inroads into the problem, more far-reaching measures are necessary and the only real possibility is that of a capital levy.

In Britain we have in fact had two miniature capital levies since the Second World War: the Special Contribution imposed by Sir Stafford Cripps in 1948 and the Special Charge levied by Mr Jenkins in his 1968 Budget. The 1968 Special Charge was a retrospective charge on investment incomes for one year (1967–8), according to the following scale:

Chargeable investment income	Charge (%)
Less than £3,000	—
£3,000–£4,000	10
£4,000–£5,000	15
£5,000–£8,000	30
Above £8,000	45

Since the levy was additional to the normal income tax and surtax, investment income was in some cases being taxed at rates above 100%. A single person with an investment income of £25,000

would have paid income tax and surtax of £19,640 (assuming that
he had no earned income) and a special charge of £8,800 – making
an effective tax rate of 114% in all. (As a result the Chancellor had
to frame the legislation to make sure that people could not give
away income.)

In that it fell on those with substantial wealth, and was both
unanticipated and once-and-for-all, the 1968 Special Charge can
fairly be described as a capital levy. Its scale, however, was very
small, the revenue representing less than 0·1% of total personal
wealth. Even on a very large holding yielding taxable income of
10% the levy was only some 4% of the value of wealth (see Table
23). A once-and-for-all measure of this size is not going to have
any major lasting impact on the distribution of wealth.

Table 23: Redistributional Impact of the 1968 Special Charge

Wealth (£)	Special Charge as a percentage of wealth* assuming a (taxable) return of	
	5%	10%
50,000	—	0·5
100,000	0·3	2·1
200,000	1·0	3·3
500,000	1·8	4·0
1,000,000	2·0	4·2

*For a single person.
Source: own calculations.

Concrete proposals for a large-scale capital levy in Britain were
put forward by the Labour Party in 1922 (when it was considered
at length by the Colwyn Committee on National Debt and Taxation) and in a pamphlet by *Tribune* in 1951. The 1922 plan was
described by one of its advocates (Hugh Dalton) as follows:

The Capital Levy . . . would be a special emergency payment by all
individuals owning more than a certain amount of wealth. This payment would be graduated according to individual ability to pay . . . The
Levy would be imposed, not annually like the income tax, but once and
for all, although those liable to it would be allowed in certain cases to
pay, if they preferred, by instalments over a term of years. [Dalton,
1923]

Immediately after the levy was decided upon, those liable would be required to make a return of their total net worth to the Inland Revenue, which would then check the return and determine the levy payable. If the levy were anticipated, the wealthy would clearly have a strong incentive to spend, and this could create serious problems if the debate about the measure were prolonged. The form in which the levy could be paid would depend on the use to which the revenue was to be put. Under the Labour plan, the proceeds were earmarked for the reduction of the National Debt, and for this purpose payment in cash or government securities would obviously be acceptable. Acceptance of other forms of property, such as company shares or real assets, would place the burden of selling on the government (with the consequent risk of loss). If, however, the purpose was simply to increase the net worth of the public sector, the government might be quite willing to hold real capital or company shares (which would also convey some control over production).

To form some idea of what a levy would mean today, let us take the rates of levy proposed by the Labour Party in 1922 (adjusted for the increase in wealth since that date), which are shown in Table 24.

Table 24: Scale for a Capital Levy

Wealth (£)	Rate of levy on that range of wealth (%)	Average rate at lower end of wealth range (%)
Under 20,000	exempt	—
20,000–50,000	20	0
50,000 100,000	30	12
100,000–200,000	40	21
200,000–500,000	50	31
500,000 and above	60	42

Source: based on the Labour Party proposals (given in Dalton, 1923), adjusted for the increase in average wealth since that date. (The number of steps in the scale has also been reduced.)

On the basis of the Inland Revenue's figures for wealth-holding in 1968, it can be estimated that the yield of a levy at these rates would have been of the order of £7,000 million – or some 7% of total private wealth. This revenue would, however, only have been sufficient to redeem about an eighth of the National Debt, and the state ownership of wealth would only increase from 4% of total national wealth to 9%. Although it would be possible to increase the revenue by lowering the exemption limit and making the rates more progressive (the *Tribune* proposal had a top rate of 95%), it seems unlikely that the revenue could feasibly be increased beyond about £15,000 million.

Distributional Consequences of a Capital Levy

A capital levy on the scale described above would have an immediate impact on the current distribution of wealth, and would be borne almost entirely by the top 5% of wealth-holders. However, the effect would be fairly small: the share of the top 5% in personal wealth would only fall (on the basis of the Inland Revenue statistics) from 59% to 55%. Although as a percentage of total *nationa* wealth, the share of the top 5% would fall more sharply (reflecting the reduced importance of private capital in relation to social capital), this is scarcely the dramatic effect that a capital levy is often assumed to have. Even if the revenue were doubled from the top 5%, they would still own over half the total personal wealth (although this would be a smaller proportion of total national wealth). The capital levy would therefore fall a long way short of bringing about equality in the distribution of current wealth. The gap between the top wealth-holder and the average man would still remain enormous: the man worth £1 million before the levy would retain over half his wealth and would still have over two hundred times the wealth of the average man. With the rates proposed by the Labour Party in 1922, the capital levy would still leave great inequalities in the current distribution of wealth and, by its once-and-for-all nature, would not provide any means by which the remaining inequalities could be eliminated.

There are a number of other reasons why a capital levy might not adequately fulfil our equity objectives. Firstly, it might lead to serious problems of horizontal inequity arising from the fact that only certain types of asset would be acceptable as means of payment. If only cash and government securities were accepted, those who held less in this form than they were required to pay would have to sell other assets (and even where they held enough to pay the levy, they might well want to rearrange their portfolios). There would, therefore, be a tendency for the price of government securities to rise, and for that of other assets, such as company shares, to fall.* As a result, a person whose holding of company shares was assessed at £100,000 might find when he came to sell the shares to meet the liability that their value had fallen to £80,000. He would nonetheless have to pay the same levy as a person holding government securities worth £100,000 (the value of which had increased). The impact of the levy on the capital market would mean that people with the same wealth held in different forms would effectively be subjected to different amounts of tax. The significance of this problem depends on the width of the class of acceptable assets; if approved company shares and real property were acceptable, there would be less need for selling to pay the levy.

These problems become still more serious when we consider the relationship between the capital levy and the distribution of *inherited wealth*. The basis for the levy is the current distribution at some (arbitrary) date, and as such the redistribution involved is unlikely to be in full accordance with the objective of achieving greater equality of inherited wealth. As was pointed out by Sir Felix Schuster in evidence to the Colwyn Committee, 'a man who has saved all his life is much harder hit than a man who is beginning and who has got time before him when he can earn something for himself'. In terms of the life-cycle savings theory developed earlier, it would mean that a person who had saved for his retirement would be penalized, whereas a young person with the same inherited wealth would escape lightly. People of different ages with the same inherited wealth could be treated very differently. When we consider those not born at the time of the levy, problems of inter-generational equity arise still more acutely. It is not true to say that those born after the levy would be unaffected, since the amount they inherited would undoubtedly be reduced.

*If the reduction in the National Debt led to a fall in the level of taxation on unearned income (as a result of the saving on the interest cost) there would be a reverse effect. However, the reduction in taxation is not likely to be large – see below.

However, the levy would not fall on wealth accumulated after the levy and transmitted to the next generation: the sons of self-made millionaires would inherit just as much as before, and this growth in inequality would be unchecked by the levy. It seems fruitless, therefore, to contemplate a capital levy without proposals designed to prevent further development of inequality after the levy has been imposed. As Keynes pointed out: 'If this measure is to be on a scale which would take it out of the category of a mere modification of the incidence of taxation, it ought to be the last, rather than the first, step in any transition from individualistic capitalism to a new order of society.' (Keynes, 1927.)

The capital levy would have a lasting effect insofar as the interest paid on the National Debt would be reduced; and we should examine how far the reduction in interest payments and the consequent reduction in taxation would lead to a more equal distribution of income. The Minority Report of the Colwyn Committee on National Debt and Taxation concluded in 1927 that 'we think that it is beyond question that the internal debt involves on balance a transfer of wealth such as aggravates the existing inequality in distribution of income, and tends to increase the proportion of the national income which finds its way into the hands of nonproducers'. This raises two questions. Would the capital levy in fact allow taxation to be reduced? If so, could this reduction be used to further the aims of redistribution?

At the time of the Colwyn Committee, there was a great deal of discussion of the tax saving that would result from a levy designed to reduce the National Debt. The saving would clearly be less than the gross interest cost, since the interest is in general subject to income tax and surtax. Moreover, the reduction in private wealth would lead to a fall in the yield of estate duty. In his tract on the levy, Dalton estimated that the net saving would be some half the interest cost, although Lord Stamp's more detailed calculations produced an estimate of about 30%. Sir Paul Chambers, however, in a critique of the *Tribune* proposals went to the extreme of claiming that the net saving might actually be *negative*. He argued that those liable for the levy would not own all the debt cancelled by it, and that there would consequently be a rearrangement of portfolios. In order to meet their liability the rich would have to sell shares (say) to those not subject to the levy; and these people would be in a lower income tax bracket, so that the income tax collected would fall. As a result, Chambers claimed, the total tax lost might exceed the saving on the interest charges, as illustrated by the following example:

Before levy	After levy
Smith (not subject to the levy) holds government stock paying interest of 5%. Tax at standard rate = 2%.	Smith has bought shares from Jones and pays tax at standard rate = 4%.
Jones (subject to the levy) holds shares with yield of 10%. Income tax plus surtax = 8%.	Jones has bought from Smith government stock and hands it over to pay the levy. Saving on interest = 5%.

The net loss of tax is $(2\% + 8\% - 4\%) = 6\%$, which is greater than the saving on interest (5%).

There are, however, two reasons why this argument is not applicable today. Its validity depends on the existence of a large gap between the (taxable) income from government stock and that on other assets. Although this may have been the case in the 1950s, the reverse has been true in recent years: the yield on government securities has exceeded the average dividends paid on ordinary shares. Secondly, the argument makes no allowance for the effect of the levy on the relative yields of different securities. If the wealthy had to sell shares to pay the levy, share prices could be expected to fall (and hence the yield on shares to rise). This rise would increase the tax paid by Smith (in the example given) after the levy.*

It seems likely, therefore, that redemption of the National Debt *would* reduce its net interest cost, although this would amount to less than half of the gross saving. However, this by itself does not mean that taxation could necessarily be reduced or the revenue used for redistribution. We have also to examine the effect on the

---

*One further factor (not relevant at the time Chambers was writing) would be the reduction in capital gains tax revenue, although this would not be large enough to validate his argument.

level of aggregate demand, and, in particular, whether the imposition of the capital levy would lead to a fall in consumption. As in the case of the annual wealth tax, it is difficult to predict the response of the very wealthy, and the sheer size of the levy renders its effect even more problematic. In that the levy would substantially reduce the investment incomes of the rich their consumption would be diminished (although, as we have seen, a considerable part of the income would have gone in taxation anyway). To the extent that they tried to maintain their previous standard of consumption by drawing on capital, their estates would be reduced still further and more of the burden shifted on to their heirs. As I have suggested in the case of the wealth tax, the heirs could be expected to cut back their consumption as a result of their reduced 'expectations', so that the levy would be deflationary nonetheless. In broad terms it is likely, therefore, that a capital levy would lead to a fall in the level of aggregate demand, so that it would be possible for the government to use for redistributional purposes part of the revenue which it would have paid in interest on the National Debt, although the amount involved is virtually impossible to predict.

Economic Consequences of a Capital Levy

In theory, the once-and-for-all nature of the capital levy should mean that it has no effect on the incentives for saving, work or enterprise. If a person genuinely believed that it would not be repeated, his subsequent behaviour would not be affected, since wealth accumulated after the levy would be unaffected. It is essential in this respect that there should be no expectation of its being repeated. If this were thought at all likely (as in pre-war Germany, where the response used to be '*noch wieder die "Einmaligen"*'), it would be regarded as simply a tax on wealth carried out at irregular intervals, and would have rather similar effects to those of the annual wealth tax.

In practice, however, the consequences of a levy are rather difficult to forecast. Lady Hicks has written that: 'The economic effects of this [levy] cannot easily be foreseen. They depend to an enormous extent on the particular circumstances of the time and place – on political and fiscal circumstances and institutions, as well as on economic conditions.' (1968, p. 208.) It seems likely that the levy would have a disruptive effect on the economy and, in particular, on the working of the capital market. The announcement of a levy on the scale described above would undoubtedly cause a short-term fall in the price of many securities. In the initial dislocation, it would no doubt be difficult for firms to borrow, and there would be a great deal of uncertainty. In the medium run a levy designed to redeem the National Debt might well reduce the supply of capital to risky enterprises. Since the wealth of the very rich would be substantially reduced by the levy, such borrowing would have to come from the lower end of the wealth scale, and the premium required to induce them to invest in risky undertakings might be higher. In part, this is the inevitable consequence of the redistribution of wealth, but it would arise much more acutely in the context of a levy to redeem the National Debt, since the balance of government securities and other assets in personal wealth would be changed. As we have seen, where company shares are not an acceptable means of payment there might be a short-term fall in their price (and hence a rise in the cost to companies of borrowing share capital). In the longer term, however, the effect might work in the opposite direction. If people increased their saving to offset the effect of the levy, total personal wealth would rise towards its previous level and (given the reduced borrowing by the government) more would be available to the company sector.

We have also to consider the effect on the balance of payments, particularly in view of the fact that in many cases the levies carried out in Europe during the 1920s generated a substantial capital flight. When the levy was announced (or became imminent) there would clearly be a strong incentive for the rich to take their money out of the country. It might be possible for the government to prevent the outflow of funds through exchange controls, but it is questionable whether they could be fully effective. Even if capital movements by those subject to the levy were controlled, we have to allow for the reactions of foreign holders of wealth in Britain. Although they would not be subject to the levy, their confidence might be seriously affected, and this could lead to a considerable drain on the capital account of the balance of payments.

Administrative Problems of a Levy

The levy would provisionally be based on a person's own assessment of his wealth, but this would have to be checked by the Inland Revenue and a final valuation agreed. The Labour Party argued in 1922 that the problem would not be insuperable, pointing out that the Inland Revenue 'have a skilled and practised staff constantly engaged on this very work in connection with the death duties'. In their evidence to the Colwyn Committee, the Inland Revenue agreed that the levy was feasible but said that they regarded its carrying out as 'a task of the first magnitude'. Whether they would agree that it was feasible today seems rather doubtful. With the scale described earlier, the levy would mean handling some 650,000 returns – or over double the number processed annually for estate duty. The amount of wealth involved would be nearly twenty times greater. Moreover, in view of the magnitude of the levy it seems likely that the taxpayer would be even more anxious than usual to adopt any device that might reduce his liability, which would lead to long and complex negotiation and litigation. The problems of administration would undoubtedly rest crucially on public attitudes to the levy. There would have to be extensive appeal procedures to safeguard the individual, and if hostility to the levy led people to appeal out of protest, the administration would be both lengthy and costly.

A Capital Levy – Conclusions

A capital levy would lead immediately to a reduction in the wealth of those at the top of the wealth scale, and in this way narrow the gap between the top 1% and the average man; it would increase the social ownership of wealth, and hence reduce the importance of inequality in private capital. A levy would, however, fall a long way short of bringing about complete equality, and could not provide a permanent solution to the problem of inequality in wealth-holding. The execution of the levy would represent a major addition to the burden on the Inland Revenue. It is also possible that it would seriously dislocate the operation of the capital market, and give rise to an outflow of foreign capital. Moreover, there can be little doubt that the success of the levy would depend critically on its being publicly acceptable – the minority of the Colwyn Committee concluded, for example, that the levy was practicable provided that it was accepted with general goodwill. As they pointed out, the levy is most likely to be acceptable in situations like those of 1919 or 1946, where appeal could be made to the need to tax those who had profited from the war. It seems much less likely that the levy would be acceptable in the 1970s.

Nationalization

Nationalization has always been a leading aim of Socialist policy, and it formed a significant part of the programmes of both post-war Labour governments. The reasons given in support of national-ization have, however, varied a great deal, and in the present context it is important to examine exactly how nationalization may be expected to contribute towards greater equality of wealth-holding.

In recent years the arguments put forward for nationalization have been expressed primarily in terms of ensuring the efficiency of the industry concerned and of consistency with the objectives of national economic planning. R. Pryke has commented that: 'Al-though it would be wrong to ignore the contribution which ideology made towards the post-war Labour government's pro-gramme of nationalization, it was chiefly inspired by the belief that public ownership was essential if the industries were to be made efficient.' (1970, p. 43.) This emphasis is well illustrated by the arguments given for the renationalization of the steel industry in 1965. In the debate on the Queen's Speech, the Secretary of State for Economic Affairs said: 'we have considered the contribution which the steel industry will have to make towards economic growth, and we are satisfied that this can best be achieved by re-establishing public ownership and control'. The subsequent White Paper of April 1965 reiterated the importance of greater efficiency in the industry, and referred to the need for a coordinated invest-ment programme and the expansion of exports. The White Paper concluded that: 'An efficient and dynamic steel industry, fully coordinated into the Government's general economic plan, is of paramount importance to the country. The proposals ... are designed to enable the industry to realize its full potential in the national interest.' (Para. 44.)

Questions of equity do not, therefore, appear to have played a prominent role in the policy of the recent Labour government towards nationalization. Nonetheless, many of those who have argued in favour of nationalization have stressed the contribution it could make towards achieving greater equality. This contribution has two main aspects: a change in the balance between social and private ownership, and a change in the pattern of control over industry. These two changes are considered in turn.

Nationalization and the Social Ownership of Wealth

The effect of nationalization on the balance between private and social ownership depends on the means by which it is brought about. One possible method of nationalization is for the government simply to expropriate the investments of the shareholders in the firms concerned. In other words, the assets of the computer industry (say) would be transferred to a state corporation, and shareholders in I.C.L. and other computer firms would lose the amount they had invested. Such a method would not only cause a great loss of business confidence, but would also be grossly inequitable. It is hard to see why those who happened to have invested in a particular industry should be penalized while those with the same wealth invested in another are not. As was pointed out by R. Jenkins in his New Fabian Essay on 'Equality', there is: 'no possible justification for expropriating the owners of the railways, rich and not so rich, merely because they were railway shareholders, and leaving the fortunes of the cotton-owners unscathed.' (1952, p. 81.) Expropriation would offend the principle of horizontal equity according to which those with the same wealth (and otherwise in the same circumstances) should be treated equally. As it was put by H. Gaitskell: 'A proposal to confiscate the property of some people but not others for no relevant reason cannot be defended on the basis of any principle and is never likely to commend itself to a British electorate.' (1956.) Nationalization has, for this reason, been considered in terms of the industry's being compulsorily purchased from its owners rather than in terms of outright expropriation.

The basic principle of nationalization has, therefore, been fair compensation. If by 'fair' is understood an amount such that the owners are just as happy holding the government bonds issued as compensation as they were with the original shareholding, the distribution of wealth would be unaffected by nationalization, and there would be no change in the total capital in social ownership. The previous owners of the nationalized company would have exchanged their shares in the company for government debt of an equal value, so that their wealth would be unchanged in total; similarly, the state would have acquired real capital but would have increased its liabilities by an equivalent amount. On the assumption that compensation is fair, the nationalization of an industry would, therefore, be irrelevant as far as the distribution of wealth and the balance of public and private ownership is concerned. As Sir Hubert Henderson pointed out in the 1920s:

If the railways were nationalised the man who now gets dividends from shares in the Great Western Railway would receive instead interest on the government stock created to buy out the Great Western Railway. If the shares which he now holds are so many as to make him one of the idle rich, he will still be one of the idle rich after the change is made. If he is a parasite and a bloodsucker now, he will be equally a parasite and a bloodsucker afterwards. [1926, p. 9]

The irrelevance, as far as the distribution of wealth is concerned, of nationalization with fair compensation cannot be emphasized too strongly, since it is a subject that generates considerable confusion. This is illustrated by the following passage from Mr Jenkins's essay:

. . . too many sins should not be laid at the door of the compensation policy which has been pursued. While it did not penalise the individual shareholder, for it gave him a gilt-edged security equal in value . . . to the equity which he had lost . . . it did exclude the private investor as a class from the future profits of the industry which had been taken over. In a period of gradual decline in the value of money . . . this is a consideration of some importance. The prices of steel shares would have been rising rapidly in 1951 had it not been for nationalisation; the fixed-interest securities for which they were exchanged did not react in the same way. [1952, pp. 81–2]

Mr Jenkins cannot have it both ways. Either the compensation is fair, in which case there is no redistribution, or it is less than fair, allowing redistribution away from the shareholders in the nationalized firm (it is not as he suggests the private investors *as a class* who lose, but the shareholders in that particular company). Although nationalization excludes private investors from the future profits of the industry, fair compensation would require that the value of the gilt-edged securities be sufficient to compensate them for this loss. The compensation should have the same value as the stream of income and capital gains they would have received as shareholders (there being no more reason to exclude capital gains when assessing compensation than there is when assessing for income tax).* If, allowing for capital gains, the gilt-edged provided a lower return than would have been obtained from the shares, then compensation was not in fact fair and did penalize the shareholder. The same confusion is present in Mr Crosland's discussion of the argument that nationalization provides: 'a means of appropriating the property income of the capitalist. Given that we pay full compensation, it relies on (a) the difference between the yields on gilt-edged and equities, (b) the fact that nationalization precludes rising dividends and share values.' (1964, p. 328.) If the return on the gilt-edged stock paid as compensation is lower than that (including capital gains) on the equity of the company being nationalized, then we are not paying 'full compensation'.

So far I have not considered how 'fair' compensation is determined. In the past a number of methods of compensation have been adopted, of which the most common was the stock market valuation of the shares of the companies taken over. The question of the extent to which this represents a 'fair' basis for compensation was discussed at great length in the case of the first iron and steel nationalization. Aside from detailed problems about the date on which the valuation is to be based, the underlying principle is

---

*I am ignoring here the complications caused by uncertainty; it is possible that the compensation was thought fair at the time, but that prices rose more than anticipated.

open to question. The Labour spokesman argued in 1949 that the ruling stock market price represented the value at which a person was willing to sell the share to someone else, and that there was, therefore, no reason why he should not regard the same price as 'fair' when the share was being bought by the government. The Opposition, however, argued that the ruling price related only to small parcels of shares being sold by 'marginal' shareholders, and to support this they showed that between 1945 and 1948 the average premium above the stock market valuation for firms being taken over was 36% (a figure very similar to that found recently by H. B. Rose and G. C. Newbould in a study of the 1967 takeover boom). This is consistent with the finding in chapter 1 that the Stock Exchange value of the company sector as a whole falls considerably short of the value of its physical assets.

The difference between the Stock Exchange quotation and the value of a company may be attributable to two main factors. The first is that shareholders have different expectations regarding the future prospects of the firm. Those who do not sell their shares at the current price feel that the firm has better prospects than the shareholder who is willing to sell. Compensation at the current stock market price would not be regarded as fair, therefore, by the intramarginal shareholder who holds a rosier view of the firm's prospects. The value of the holding depends on the person's expectations of future profits and, to leave people as well off as before, those with different expectations should in theory receive different compensation. The second and probably more important factor is that the marginal share does not in general convey control over the firm. Those with a controlling interest in a company would be unlikely to regard compensation at the Stock Exchange quotation as fair. The situation has been described as follows:

The gross value of all the shares in an undertaking, calculated at the prices current on the Stock Exchange on any particular day, and the value of that undertaking to its owners are in fact two different and distinct things. The first is a paper calculation; the second depends partly upon the discounted value of expected future yield but rests more upon the present owners' personal interest in their property ... these two values have little in common with each other and can coincide only by accident. [Walker and Condie in Robson, 1952, p. 61]

Some allowance has to be made for these factors, but it is in practice very difficult to do so. The Coal Nationalization Act, for example, set up a tribunal consisting of two judges and an accountant which determined an overall compensation figure; but no statement was given of the means by which this figure was reached, and it seems unlikely that such a method would in general be thought acceptable. There are therefore considerable problems in determining 'fair' compensation. The stock market quotation is probably the only feasible solution, but it is ungenerous to intramarginal holders and therefore involves an element of expropriation. To this extent, the actual nationalizations carried out on this basis will have tended to increase the net worth of the public sector, but by the same token they will have involved horizontal inequity.

Nationalization and Control

Nationalization undoubtedly changes the balance of control over production in that it involves the exchange of government securities (which convey no such control) for the physical assets of the industry concerned. This means that the industry is under much more pressure to operate 'in the public interest'. The government not only appoints the management, but also is in a strong position to influence its pricing and investment policy. We have seen that one of the principal reasons given for the re-nationalization of the steel industry was that it would ensure an efficient industry 'fully co-ordinated into the Government's general economic plan'. This control is also significant in other areas: for example, the steel industry has probably shown more concern than private industry would have done for the social consequences of closing down plants in depressed regions and has been more responsive to the objections raised by trade unions.

While this transfer of control to the state is of great importance, it is not the only aspect which was stressed by early supporters of nationalization. They were also concerned that it should contribute towards providing *those employed in the industry* with greater control over their working environment. In 1912 *The Miners' Next Step* put forward a plan for a nationalized industry under workers' control, arguing that:

Today the shareholders own and rule the coalfields. They own and rule them mainly through paid officials. The men who work in the mine are surely as competent to elect these, as shareholders who may never have seen a colliery. To have a vote in determining who shall be your foreman, manager, inspector, etc., is to have a vote in determining the conditions which shall rule your working life. [Quoted in Coates and Topham, 1970, p. 23]

When Clause 4 of the Objects of the Labour Party was adopted in 1918 it called not just for common ownership of the means of production but for 'the best obtainable system of popular administration and control'. Similarly, the Guild Socialists saw nationalization as a means for achieving wider industrial democracy.

These views have not been given much weight by successive Labour governments. They were flatly rejected by Lord Morrison, who claimed that 'the stereotyping of the representation of classes and interests on the Boards of public concerns seems to me to be capitalist rather than Socialist in its philosophic basis'. In the series of nationalizations carried out by the Attlee government, the only step taken in this direction was the introduction of machinery for joint consultation. Under these provisions, the nationalized industries established joint advisory or consultative councils at national, regional and local levels. These consist of representatives of management, together with trade union officials and other representatives of the workers, and can consider questions such as safety, health, welfare and education as well as 'other matters of mutual interest'.

From their introduction, these provisions were much criticized as only a shadow of the original proposals for workers' control or representation. This criticism came not only from the left wing, but also from more unexpected sources. For instance, Mr Harold Macmillan said of the Coal Nationalization Act: 'This is not Socialism; it is state capitalism. There is not too much participation by the mine-workers in the industry; there is far too little.' Within its terms of reference, the joint consultation procedure is considered to have worked quite successfully in certain sectors (notably the electricity supply industry), but many commentators have expressed dissatisfaction. J. Hughes wrote in 1960 that:

in nationalised industry there has been considerable neglect of consultation from both sides . . . There has been a widespread failure to link the different levels of consultation adequately, or to open 'higher' levels to trained and informed participation by rank and file workers. All too often higher levels of consultation are the province of full-time official-dom and may degenerate into an unrewarding formality. At plant level . . . the joint consultation the worker sees is largely limited to vestigial influence on job environment. [1960, p. 30]

and other writers have seen joint consultation as little more than a technique of personnel management.

When the steel industry was re-nationalized under the Wilson government, it was not initially planned to go further than the incorporation of joint consultation machinery parallel to that in other nationalized industries. In the debate on the second reading of the Iron and Steel Bill, Mr Marsh said:

I know that some of my hon. friends feel strongly that the Bill should provide for a measure of direct worker participation in management . . . I do not think that the steel industry would necessarily be the right place for an experiment as far-reaching as this at a time when it faces a major structural re-organization. [*Hansard*, 25 July 1966]

This view contrasted markedly with that of the National Crafts-men's Co-ordinating Committee for the Iron and Steel Industry, which put forward proposals for worker representation at all levels. Under their plan, the national board would have had five (out of twelve) members appointed from a panel submitted by the trade unions; at group level the appointment of the chairman would have been subject to ratification by a group workers' council, and at plant level workers would have equal representation on the board of management. Pressure from this and other quarters led to a change in attitudes, and in May 1967 the British Steel Cor-poration submitted proposals to the T.U.C. for the appointment of part-time employee-directors. Subsequently, as an experiment, three were appointed from a list drawn up by the unions to each of the Group Boards (now the Divisional Boards), with the role of taking part in working parties, advisory committees, formal and informal meetings of functional and line managers, as well as attending Divisional Board meetings and providing liaison with the trade unions. There is now one employee-director on the national board. Although important, the British Steel Corporation scheme falls a long way short of the National Craftsmen's Committee's proposals. There is only a small number of employee-directors; they are not directly accountable to the workers; there is no participation in management at lower levels; there are no workers' councils with power to make or ratify appointments. *The Times* commented at the time (22 May 1967): 'There is room for experiment, and the nationalized industries are one admirable field for experiment. But experiments will be of little value unless they are less faint-hearted than those proposed by the Steel Corporation.'

It is clear from this brief description that the extent of worker participation in the management of the nationalized industries is at present very limited. The joint consultation procedures are strictly advisory in nature and although the British Steel Corporation scheme goes considerably further, it can hardly be said to represent a major step towards industrial democracy. In their present form the nationalized industries cannot, therefore, be said to have led to any significant redistribution of control in favour of those working in the industry, and if nationalization is to contribute towards this goal radical changes in their organization are necessary. Discussion of the room for such changes is outside the scope of this book, and would require detailed analysis of the experience of those countries where worker participation has progressed furthest (notably Yugoslavia and Israel) and of its relevance to large-scale industrial organizations.

Nationalization – Conclusions

One argument put forward for further nationalization is that it would help bring about greater equality of wealth-holding. The analysis in this section has shown, however, that in the form which nationalization has taken in Britain, its contribution would in fact be very limited. If 'fair' compensation were paid, the balance between the social and private ownership of wealth would be left unchanged; but if an element of expropriation were involved, it would be horizontally inequitable. Nationalization transfers control to the government and in this way reduces the power in the hands of private property. However, only limited steps have been taken towards providing those employed in the industries with more control over their working lives. If significant progress is to be made in this direction, much more attention needs to be given to the possibilities for the participation of workers' representatives in management at all levels.

Denationalization

Having considered the contribution which nationalization would make towards greater equality, we should discuss the consequences of the reverse policy of *denationalization*, particularly since this forms part of the programme of the present Conservative government. (It is also an integral part of Mr Powell's plan to halve income tax.)

As in the case of nationalization, the effects of denationalization depend on the manner in which it is carried out, and there are a number of possibilities. Under the first (which is that envisaged by Mr Powell), the government would sell the assets of the industry to a privately owned company (or companies). This would simply be nationalization in reverse, and if the price paid was a 'fair' one, we can deduce by the converse of the earlier argument that it would have no effect on the distribution of wealth. The sale of shares in Thomas Cook and Son Ltd would not change the balance between social and private ownership of wealth: the state would exchange its claim on physical assets, goodwill, etc., for financial assets, and the net worth of the public sector would be unaffected. If the price was less than 'fair', in the sense that the payment received by the government was less than the value of the assets, there would be a reduction in the net worth of the public sector, with a corresponding rise in personal wealth. The latter would accrue to the shareholders in the companies purchasing the assets, and as such is unlikely to be very equally distributed. Moreover, just as there are no grounds for expropriating the holdings of particular shareholders and not those of others with the same wealth, there is no reason why the government should provide a windfall to particular companies – there are questions of horizontal equity involved.

The determination of the fair price to be paid is very difficult –

even more so than in the case of nationalization, since there is no stock market quotation. The method to be adopted by the Conservative government is not at present clear. In the debate on the ending of state management of the Carlisle public houses (21 April 1971), an assurance was given that an independent valuation would be made. This procedure may work reasonably well in the case of a small-scale denationalization, but where a large sector is involved, any valuation would be to a considerable extent arbitrary. An alternative method would be to invite bids, but since the number of potential purchasers would almost certainly be small, there is a serious danger that the government would obtain less than a 'fair' price.

A rather different form of denationalization is that proposed by *The Times* in an editorial of 14 September 1968 entitled 'Give the shares to the people'. This suggested that every elector should be issued *at no cost* with shares in the nationalized industries. In this way, *The Times* argued: 'If British Telephone have an equity value of £1,000 million then each elector might receive some 35 £1 ordinary shares in the British Telephone Company. This would be a simple transfer of assets from the state to the citizens as beneficiaries of the trust.' As such, the transfer clearly *would* change the balance of ownership between private and social wealth, and would in effect be confiscation in reverse. The value of the state's physical assets would decline, and there would be an increase in total personal wealth. Since this increase would be equally distributed among the adult population, it would undoubtedly tend to reduce the degree of concentration in personal wealth-holding. One serious difficulty with this denationalization proposal as it stands is that it would be inflationary. The reaction of many people on receiving their shares in British Telephone would be to sell them at once and use the proceeds to increase their consumption. Denationalization could not therefore take place in this form unless accompanied by a substantial increase in taxation to offset the effect on the level of demand. *The Times* did in fact recognize that inflation might follow, and suggested that the shares should be made non-transferable for a certain period. This would serve to postpone the increase in demand, but an increase in taxation would eventually be necessary, and the redistributive effect of the measure would depend on the form in which the taxes were levied.

The country in which denationalization has been carried furthest is West Germany, where a number of major industrial undertakings have been partially transferred to private ownership, including Volkswagen and V.E.B.A. (an electricity and mining holding company). The measures introduced there represent a cross between the two schemes discussed here, in that the shares were sold, but at preferential rates (and they were also restricted to those with incomes below a certain limit). The partial denationalization of Volkswagen in 1961 has been described by K. Heidensohn as follows:

... shares amounting to 360 million D-marks (representing about 60 per cent of Volkswagen's share capital at that stage) were sold. Again the newly issued shares were sold at what experts regarded as well below the 'true' value at the time, and only to those whose incomes were not higher than £1,600 p.a. Some 1·5 million new shareholders emerged. Attempts were made ... to counter the early selling of the shares, because this would clearly have reduced the redistribution effects of the measure. A savings premium of 20 per cent was offered to investors who held their shares for five years ... VW share prices rocketed up. On the day the shares were introduced on the stock exchange their price doubled. [*Guardian*, 28 January 1971]

Denationalization along the lines of the *Times* proposal or on the Volkswagen model could clearly make a once-and-for-all contribution towards greater equality, although its precise effect would depend on the way in which taxes were adjusted to avoid the denationalization being inflationary. Moreover, it might have the additional consequence of introducing small savers to the holding of company shares and inducing them to hold their wealth in a form which probably enjoys better protection against inflation. In this respect it is interesting to note that four years after the denationalization of Volkswagen, two thirds of the original purchasers still retained their shares. There is, however, absolutely no reason why the transfer of capital assets to those with little wealth should be linked with the ownership of the nationalized industries. Precisely the same effect could be achieved through the establishment of a state unit trust with the shares being issued equally to all (and its portfolio being built up through the revenue from increased taxation). Alternatively, we could provide everyone with a uniform capital payment by including a capital element in the state pension – a possibility discussed in the next chapter.

Denationalization – Conclusions

Denationalization as proposed by Mr Powell and others would contribute nothing to achieving greater equality of wealth-holding. If the assets of the nationalized industry were sold for a 'fair' price the social ownership of wealth would be unchanged. In practice it is extremely difficult to determine a 'fair' price and there is a serious danger that it would be less than fair, which would reduce the net worth of the state as well as introducing further inequities in the distribution of personal wealth. If the shares were given equally to all, or sold on Volkswagen lines, it would serve to bring about greater equality of wealth, but there is no reason why this should be tied to the question of denationalization – the same effect could be achieved through other means without transferring control over the nationalized industries from public to private hands.

11. Spreading Personal Wealth

And do you expect me to turn my back on 35 per cent when all the rest are pocketing what they can, like sensible men? No such fool!
– *Sir George Crofts in* Mrs Warren's Profession

Most people in Britain have very little wealth apart from their personal possessions, their rights to a pension, and possibly their own house. For this reason, a number of schemes have been put forward to increase wealth-holding among those in the bottom 90%, and in this way to help narrow the gap between them and the top 1%. In this chapter I consider three main types of scheme: saving incentives, the extension of pension provisions, and union-negotiated capital growth-sharing schemes. Particular attention is given to the contribution that these schemes can make towards bringing about greater equality and the extent to which they provide a minimum level of wealth on which everyone can draw at some point in his life – a 'minimum inheritance' for all.

Saving Incentives

Saving incentive schemes have been put forward with a variety of motives, and it is important to consider exactly what they are intended to achieve. In the case of Save As You Earn (S.A.Y.E.), introduced by Mr Jenkins in his 1969 Budget, the primary motivation was undoubtedly that of its effect on the level of aggregate demand. In this sense S.A.Y.E. was seen as an alternative to raising taxes: to the extent that people voluntarily refrained from consumption the pressure on demand would be reduced without the need for higher taxation. At the same time the scheme may have been expected to have contributed to the redistribution of wealth by encouraging wealth-holding among the lower- and middle-income groups, and it is on this aspect that I concentrate here.

Insofar as saving incentive schemes lead to new saving by those who at present own little they tend to promote greater equality in the current distribution of wealth. In chapter 3 we saw that a person saving £100 a year throughout this working life, would accumulate £11,200 (at an after-tax real interest rate of $4\frac{1}{2}\%$.) As the S.A.Y.E. advertisements claim, he can 'make a *small* fortune' (my italics). The contribution which such schemes make towards greater equality in the distribution of *inherited* wealth is less certain. Clearly the 'small fortune' referred to in the advertisements is not the same as one inherited by a person from his father. The fact that a saving incentive scheme may lead small savers to acquire more wealth does not mean that there is any change in the distribution of inherited wealth: the saving induced by such a scheme transfers consumption from one year of a person's life to another, but does not represent an increase in his 'life chances'. If as a result of the scheme a person accumulates £11,000 while he is working, it is at the expense of consumption earlier in his life, and cannot be seen as being on a par with an inheritance of £11,000 (which costs him nothing). It does not in any sense provide him with a minimum level of inherited wealth. The only way in which a saving incentive scheme can be said to affect the opportunities open to a small saver is through offering him a higher rate of interest than he could previously obtain. If the scheme offers him a return of 6% rather than $4\frac{1}{2}\%$ (with the same degree of risk and ease of liquidation), this *can* be seen as equivalent in a sense to his receiving inherited wealth, since he can accumulate more over his life without any decrease in his consumption. The contribution which saving incentive schemes can make towards greater equality of inherited wealth lies, therefore, in their offering a higher rate of return than that previously available to small savers.

The return offered by saving incentive schemes is one important feature; another is the extent to which they offer protection against inflation (and accelerating inflation). Many of the assets held by those with little wealth – cash, bank deposits, National Savings, trustee and building society deposits – provide a return which is secure in money terms but not in real terms. As a result, many who believe that they are putting something by for their old age find when they reach retirement that the purchasing power of their savings has been eroded. Saving incentive schemes may, therefore, play an important role if they provide small savers with the opportunity of protecting themselves against inflation. This opportunity may take the form of providing assets whose value is based directly on price indices (such as the index-linked bonds available in a number of European countries) or assets whose value is indirectly related to prices (such as pensions payable as a percentage of earnings at retirement). Alternatively, it seems reasonable to suppose that a hedge against inflation would be provided by real assets, such as houses, and (in the long run) by assets whose income is derived directly from real assets, such as ordinary shares.

The form of the asset offered by saving incentive schemes is also relevant to the aim of achieving greater equality of the economic control conveyed by certain types of wealth. The chief assets which convey such control are equity shares and real capital, and if saving incentive schemes are to make any contribution in this direction, they must provide small savers with the opportunity to invest in this form. An 'indirect' holding of such assets will not achieve this objective where the associated control is not transferred to the saver: a unit trust, for example, would not satisfy this condition, since the voting rights of the shares would remain in the hands of the trust managers.

With these considerations in mind we can examine the contribution that would be made by specific saving incentive schemes: Save As You Earn and proposals for wider share ownership.

Save As You Earn

Save As You Earn is a contractual savings scheme under which a person has to save regularly for a minimum period of 5 years making regular payments ranging from £1 to £20 a month. At the end of 5 years, he receives a tax-free bonus of £12 for every £1 that he has been saving monthly and if he leaves it untouched for a further two years the bonus is doubled. This represents a return of 7% per annum after tax ($7\frac{1}{2}\%$ over the seven-year period). This is considerably higher than the return available to small savers from institutions such as the National Savings Bank (currently $3\frac{1}{2}\%$ after tax) or building societies (currently around 5% net of tax on share accounts).

In the assessments that have been made of the effectiveness of S.A.Y.E., attention has largely been focused on the extent to which it has given rise to an increase in total savings. It has been pointed out that the scheme may simply have caused a switch of savings from one institution to another, with S.A.Y.E.'s gain being the loss of other savings media. However, if the critical aspect of the scheme is the return offered, the effect on total saving is not relevant; and the more switching there is from other assets, the more effective S.A.Y.E. is proving to be in raising the return offered. In fact we have seen that the return after tax is definitely higher than that on other assets which are likely to be available for small savers. To see what difference this makes in quantitative terms, let us take a simple example. Suppose that the rise in the effective after-tax return is from 5% to 7%. For a man saving £10 per month from the age of 30 to the age of 60, this would increase the total accumulated (in real terms) from £4,800 to £7,000. The gain from the increased return is equal to £2,200. This hardly represents a small fortune! (The calculation assumes a long-term average rate of inflation of 3% with the maximum amount of permitted saving rising in line with prices.) If inflation miraculously stopped, the gain (in real terms) would be £3,850 rather than £2,200; if, on the other hand, the recent rates of inflation continued, the gain would only be less than £1,000. These figures almost certainly overstate the gain to the average person, who is unlikely to be able to save at this rate for thirty years – in the early part of his life a large part of his saving will take the form of buying consumer durables or paying off his mortgage. The gain provided to small savers in terms of an improvement in the rate of return is, therefore, quite limited; it will not lead to a dramatic increase in the amount of wealth that a person can accumulate.

It has also to be remembered that the return to S.A.Y.E. is fixed in money terms. This means that it offers no protection against inflation, the return remaining the same whatever the rate of price increase. With inflation at its present rate, the real return after tax is about -2%, which is undoubtedly less than most people expected when they invested in S.A.Y.E. In view of the inflexible nature of the investment (it can be withdrawn before the five years are up but the interest paid is then reduced to $2\frac{1}{2}\%$), this lack of inflation-proofing is particularly important.

In contrast to the benefit to small savers, that provided by

S.A.Y.E. to *surtax payers* is very considerable. For a person paying the standard rate of income tax, a return of 7% after tax is equivalent to a return of 12–12½% before tax; but for a person with a marginal tax rate of 60%, it is equivalent to 17½% before tax; and for a surtax payer in the top bracket, it is equivalent to around 70% before tax! *The Economist* in an article entitled 'Saye for surtax payers' pointed out that:

An analysis of existing national savings holders suggests that surtax payers are already well aware which side their bread is buttered on. While the savings banks get only a little over a third of their funds from the middle classes, for the tax-free savings certificates the proportion rises to two-thirds. Saye will appeal to the same group of people. [26 July 1969]

If the intention had been to limit the benefit to those with small wealth-holdings, it could easily have been achieved. For example, the S.A.Y.E. bonus could have been exempted from income tax but not from surtax. Alternatively, a fixed tax-credit could have been given for interest from S.A.Y.E., setting an upper limit on the amount by which a person's tax liability could be reduced. In this way, a surtax payer would have gained no more than (say) a standard-rate taxpayer who held the maximum amount.

The conclusion to be drawn from this analysis is that, although S.A.Y.E. has made some contribution to raising the return available to the small saver, it has only limited effectiveness as a means of bringing about greater equality of inherited wealth. The magnitude of the benefit is small; the surtax payer gains much more than the person with average earnings and the scheme does not incorporate any protection against inflation.

Wider Share Ownership

It has been argued that the disadvantages of S.A.Y.E. stem from its being based solely on a fixed-interest return, and that they would be avoided in a scheme designed to widen share ownership. On this view, encouraging share ownership would allow small savers to obtain on average a higher return and (in the long run) enjoy protection against inflation. Schemes to encourage wider share ownership could take the form either of the direct holding of shares by small savers or of indirect holding through unit trusts or other institutions. The former channel does not appear particularly promising in view of the paucity of information available to the small saver, the difficulties in diversifying a small holding, and the high transaction costs. The person with £250 to invest would be able to hold at most some ten different securities so that his eggs would be in a small number of baskets, and even if he followed the market closely the risks involved would be considerable. If he attempted to adjust his portfolio at all regularly he would face high commission charges. In February 1970 the minimum commission payable was doubled, so that people buying shares to the value of less than £320 at a time pay more than the normal commission of 1·25%.

The alternative to direct shareholding is investment in a unit trust or similar institution, which in large part overcomes the difficulties outlined above. They allow the small saver to hold a diversified portfolio without incurring prohibitive handling costs, and in effect provide him with investment advice. The extent to which the encouragement of unit trusts would represent a means of achieving greater equality depends on the return offered to the small saver. It seems reasonable to suppose that, on average, equity shares will provide a significantly higher return than assets such as building society deposits, and that in the long run they may be safer in real terms. Moreover, it is possible that unit trusts, with the expert management they offer, would allow the small saver to obtain a return which is better than the average for ordinary shares, so that the benefit would be still greater. (This assumption is, however, open to question. In a recent United States Senate hearing, a senator demonstrated that a portfolio picked by throwing darts performed no worse than the average unit trust!)

Given that unit trusts provide a means by which small savers can obtain a higher return than that obtainable on other assets, there is the problem of encouraging the wider holding of units. The survey referred to in chapter 2 showed that manual workers and pensioners accounted for over two thirds of the population but fewer than a third of unit trust holders. In order to reach those not at present investing in this way a Conservative Political Centre report *Everyman a Capitalist* recommended a number of years ago

the provision of tax advantages (similar to those introduced for
S.A.Y.E.) for unit trust contractual savings schemes satisfying
certain conditions, together with an extensive selling campaign.
More recently, the Wider Share Ownership Council has proposed
a part fixed-interest, part share-based contractual savings scheme
to be operated in much the same way as S.A.Y.E. (*The Times*,
22 February 1971). The effectiveness of such schemes, and of the
plans for promotion, has yet to be tested, and depends on the
precise terms of the return offered. It has to be borne in mind that
the fact that the return would not be fixed in money terms –
although clearly an important advantage in an inflationary world –
would make the scheme more difficult to put across.

Finally we should note that all these schemes for the indirect
holding of shares transfer the control associated with ownership
from the saver to the managers of the trust. This means that they
would not contribute towards achieving greater equality of control, and indeed the concentration of voting rights in the hands of
the trust managers might have the reverse effect.

Saving Incentive Schemes – Conclusions

Saving incentive schemes are important insofar as they raise the
return available to small savers, and we have seen that both
S.A.Y.E. and the plans for wider share ownership are likely to
have this effect. The amount of the benefit is, however, small and
(in the case of S.A.Y.E. at least) would be larger for the surtax
payer than for the small saver. Moreover, it has yet to be demonstrated that these schemes can attract a substantial proportion of
those with little wealth.

Pensions and Wealth

For many people, rights to a pension on retirement represent one
of their most valuable assets. In part this wealth is distributed very
equally: the National Insurance retirement pension is received by
everyone and its actuarial value is approximately the same for all.
However, the rights to occupational pensions are distributed
much less uniformly. A substantial minority of workers is not yet
covered by occupational schemes, and there are wide disparities

in the benefits provided (particularly in the degree of inflation-proofing). In this section I examine the contribution which would be made towards greater equality of wealth-holding by the reform of state and occupational pension provisions.

According to the survey carried out by the Government Actuary in 1967, about one third of male employees (and three quarters of female employees) were not covered by occupational pension schemes. The coverage of occupational schemes has been increasing over the past twenty years, but even when occupational schemes have reached their full development there is no guarantee that all workers will be sufficiently covered. Many small employers would consider that the establishment of their own pension fund was not feasible (and so their employees will have to fall back on the state reserve scheme), and the self-employed are unlikely to be adequately covered.*

The schemes in operation differ widely in their conditions – the method of finance, the degree of transferability, and the method by which pensions are determined. The last factor is of especial importance when assessing the value of the rights to an occupational pension and the degree of protection against inflation. Where the pension is calculated in cash terms (for example, £10 annual pension for each year of membership), there is no protection against inflation. With an investment covering such a long period, this consideration is of crucial importance: since 1925 (when a person now retiring would have paid his first contributions) prices have risen by over three-and-a-half times. A pension which appears quite reasonable in cash terms today may be totally inadequate when the person comes to retire. Schemes under which the pension is determined on the basis of terminal salary (e.g. 1/80th for every year worked) will protect the value of the pension up to retirement (provided that salaries keep up). The Government Actuary's survey showed that a quarter of all schemes were of this type; but this overall figure masks a sharp contrast between the situation for non-manual workers (three quarters of whom were

---

*There are special income tax provisions for savings by the self-employed towards pensions, but they do not provide much benefit to the person with low income. They are very helpful to the barrister, but much less so to the window-cleaner paying little or no tax.

covered by terminal salary schemes) and manual workers (for whom the proportion was much lower). Protection up to the point of retirement by itself is still not sufficient, since without further adjustments the purchasing power of the pension will be eroded by inflation *during retirement*. Some schemes provide for augmentation of pensions after retirement, but few do so on a predetermined basis, with the result that the pensioners lack the security of knowing that the real value will be maintained. The present structure of occupational pensions contains, therefore, considerable disparities in treatment, and only for a very few does it provide adequate protection against inflation.

Pension Reform

With the aim of securing greater equality of pension provision and of providing 'inflation-proofing', the Labour government put forward in 1969 proposals for National Superannuation, and these were going through Parliament at the time of the 1970 general election. This scheme would have provided earnings-related pensions for all employees, protected against inflation. The pension paid would have been based on national average earnings at the time a person retired, so that it would have been similar to a terminal salary scheme. It would, however, have gone further, in that the pension would have been protected against inflation *after retirement*. Every two years there was to have been a review of pensions in payment, and the government would have been committed to increasing them in line with the rise in prices.

The contribution that National Superannuation would have made to reducing inequality in wealth-holding depends on the relationship of the return offered to that obtainable on other forms of saving. Critics of the scheme claimed that it would have been a 'bad buy' for most employees and Mr A. Seldon went so far as to say that the return would have been only half that obtainable from private schemes. (*Sunday Telegraph*, 2 February 1969.) These claims were not, however, based on any detailed examination of the scheme, or any actuarial calculations of the benefits to be derived. If such calculations are made, they show that for a married couple the after-tax (money) return would have been about $8\frac{1}{2}\%$ for a person with average earnings, a return which is considerably higher than that offered by institutions such as the National Savings Bank and slightly higher than that from S.A.Y.E.* This estimate of the return is based on the assumption that the average rate of increase of money earnings would be the same as that in the 1950s and 1960s (6% per annum). If earnings were to rise at a faster rate, the money rate of return would be correspondingly higher. The return is therefore completely in-flation-proofed (at a real after-tax return of about 5%). This certainty of the real return distinguishes the pension proposal from the assets at present available to small savers, all of which involve some uncertainty about the real return. National Super-annuation would, therefore, have provided not only a higher return but also a degree of security which cannot be matched by other assets.†

The proposals of the Conservative government for pension re-form have been outlined in the White Paper *Strategy for Pensions*. It is proposed that the present two-tier system be retained. Every-one will receive the basic flat-rate state pension, although this will be financed wholly by earnings-related contributions (rather than by the present largely flat-rate contributions). Earnings-related pensions on top of the basic state pension will be provided through (recognized) occupational schemes or – for those not covered by such schemes – through the new state reserve scheme. To be recog-nized, an occupational scheme must satisfy a new Occupational Pensions Board that it meets certain minimum conditions; these conditions are specified in general terms in the White Paper, but the Board will have 'discretion to conduct their affairs flexibly' (p. 10). The new state reserve scheme (which will replace the

*It is very difficult to compare this return with that derived from occu-pational schemes, since the latter do not in general provide the same kind of benefits. A comparison with the type of private scheme closest in form to National Superannuation (a terminal salary scheme) suggests that there are no grounds at all for expecting the latter to be twice as good (as argued by Mr Seldon), and in some respects the occupational schemes are clearly worse.

†The return provided by National Superannuation would have been higher for those with below-average earnings, and to this extent the scheme would have been redistributive. Against this must be set the fact that those with higher earnings would have had a larger stake in the benefits from the higher return.

present graduated pension) will be based on earnings-related contributions, which will be paid into a fund administered by an independent board of management. The reserve pension will consist of
two parts: a fixed entitlement based on the contributions paid, and
a variable bonus which 'will depend mainly on the investment
performance of the fund' (p. 23).

These proposals have wide-ranging implications, but our concern here is with the contribution that they will make to greater
equality of wealth-holding. As far as the basic pension is concerned
the change will increase the effective rate of return to lower-paid
workers and will guarantee the value of the pension in terms of
purchasing power. Both of these will have an important equalizing
effect. The proposals for the second tier of pensions (the primary
concern of the White Paper) are however much less satisfactory.
We have seen that the Labour plan for National Superannuation
had the merit of providing a return higher than that on other
assets available to small savers and it was well protected against
inflation. By contrast, the proposed state reserve scheme will only
guarantee a return of 4% (provisional figure). It provides in addition bonuses which 'might be expected to offset, or offset to a substantial extent, the effect of rising prices' (p. 40); however, as the
White Paper emphasizes, 'this cannot be guaranteed because the
level of bonuses must depend on the net amounts of the profits
emerging'. The employee is in effect being offered an investment
in a state unit trust, and while experience suggests that the real
return might be quite high, it cannot be claimed that the scheme
would provide the same degree of security as National Superannuation. The proposals designed to improve occupational pensions, particularly those relating to the protection of the value of
pensions after retirement and the preservation of pension rights on
changing jobs, are clearly steps in the right direction. However,
while they may help ensure a higher pension in old age, they do not
necessarily guarantee a reasonable return to the pensioner (which
is what concerns us here). For example, a scheme might be recognized even though it provides no augmentation after retirement if
the level of the pension was above the minimum. In such a case
there would be no inflation-proofing. Similarly, the proposed
legislation for the preservation of pension rights does not require

that the real value of rights be maintained. This would mean that employees changing jobs could find that the return on their contributions remained unprotected. As *The Times* editorial commented at the time (15 September 1971): 'there will need to be a substantial improvement in their quality if occupational schemes are permanently to have the large place in the British pension system that is now offered to them. The White Paper does nothing to hinder their improvement, but it does little enough to encourage it.' Indeed, as far as the effect on wealth-holding is concerned, the contribution of the White Paper is well described by the title of *The Times* editorial: 'This plan could and should be better'.*

A Capital Element in the State Pension

A possible major reform of the state pension scheme referred to in earlier chapters is the inclusion of a capital element in National Insurance. Many occupational schemes provide such a benefit (for example, the British Steel Corporation scheme provides a lump sum on retirement equal to three times the annual pension), and there are good grounds for extending this provision to the state scheme. It would ensure that everyone could look forward to a minimum capital sum at retirement. Old people would enjoy greater flexibility in planning for retirement, and have a reserve to cover unforeseen expenditure. The benefit provided would, of course, depend on the amount of the capital payment. For the purposes of illustration, it is assumed that the payment would be twice the annual pension, which would have been some £520 per person in January 1971 (although the amount would not be fixed

*Given that the extension of private pensions forms an important part of Conservative policy, it is clear that the reform of occupational pensions is an area in which more active trade union policy seems called for. Unions should, for example, be concerned to ensure that pension schemes provide benefits and preserved rights which are fully protected against inflation. A further question which could well be examined by the trade unions is that of control of the pension funds. As T. Lynes has recently pointed out: 'is it not time that the occupational pensions ceased to be regarded as a fringe benefit conferred by benevolent employers, and came to be recognized for what they are – deferred pay? The money invested in an employer's pension fund belongs, morally, to the workers, not to the employer. Yet these funds are almost invariably controlled by the employers or their appointees.' (Lynes, 1970(b), p. 137.)

in cash terms but related to prices or – preferably – to average earnings). In 1970 the number eligible for such a payment would have been around 650,000, giving a total cost of about £340 million.

The idea of a capital element in the state pension scheme has some similarity with the proposal for a 'negative capital tax' put forward by C. T. Sandford, under which everyone would receive a 'coming of age' bonus at the age of 21 (the age limit would presumably now have to be lowered to 18). The introduction of the bonus at this age would, however, involve serious transitional problems, since no government could simply introduce the scheme and give nothing to those aged over 18! The inequity involved could be reduced if there were some kind of sliding scale, so that (say) those aged 28 or younger would get half; but even this is unlikely to commend itself to older voters. If the capital payment were made at the age of 65, however, the transitional problems would be much less severe. The scheme could be introduced by starting payments for those aged 80 or over and working back, so that in the next year it would be paid to those aged (say) 77 and over and so on. (If it was felt that the scheme would be unfair on families where the husband died young, a similar capital element could be included in the widow's benefit.) During the transition period the cost would be higher than when in full operation.

The redistributional effect of such a reform depends on the means by which the cost would be financed. If a person were to receive at the age of 65 only the actuarial value of the contributions he had paid, the scheme would not represent anything more than compulsory saving (on the assumption that the return was no higher than he could obtain elsewhere); on the other hand, if he did not contribute at all to its finance, the capital payment would genuinely be equivalent to inherited wealth. I assume here that the cost would as far as possible be raised from the reformed taxes on wealth discussed earlier.* As we have seen, however, the scope for

---

*It could be objected that this represents a departure from the 'insurance principle' embodied in National Insurance. It has however to be remembered that an actuarial return to contributions is a more complex notion than Lord Beveridge envisaged when he laid down this 'principle', and that the present National Insurance scheme has departed from it in many important ways (as have private schemes).

this is limited by considerations of the effect on the level of aggregate demand: the capital payment would undoubtedly add to consumption (in the near future if not immediately), whereas taxes on wealth are likely to be paid largely out of saving. The bulk of the cost would have, therefore, to be met from National Insurance contributions or general taxation, and it is assumed that the former method would be adopted. If the balance to be raised, after allowing for the extension of taxation on wealth transfers and capital gains, were met by graduated National Insurance contributions beginning at earnings of £18 a week* (as with the increases announced in April 1971), the person with below-average earnings would undoubtedly gain over his lifetime as a whole. The current distribution of wealth would also become more equal, in that the wealth of those over 65 would be considerably increased (unless they all decided to spend it at once on a round-the-world cruise). The impact of the capital payment may be gauged from Table 25, which shows the savings (apart from owner-occupied houses) of retirement pensioners in 1965. About three quarters of the married couples, and two thirds of the single pensioners, owned less than the amount they would receive under the reform considered here.

Table 25: Savings of Retirement Pensioners

Savings	Married couples	Single men	Single women
less than £125	40%	50%	54%
£125–£500	23%	19%	19%
£500–£1,000	13%	12%	11%
£1,000–£2,000	9%	8%	7%
£2,000 and over	15%	11%	9%

Source: Ministry of Pensions and National Insurance (1966), Table II.6.

Pensions and Wealth – Conclusions

Reform of the pension system could make two important contributions towards reducing inequality in wealth-holding. Firstly, it could ensure that everyone held part of his wealth in a form which

*Where it is assumed that these amounts would rise over time with the average level of earnings.

gave a return protected against inflation. At present neither the National Insurance pension nor (in general) occupational schemes give such a guarantee, although it would have been provided by the Labour proposals for National Superannuation and will be partly provided by the Conservative plan. Secondly, the introduction of a capital element in the state pension would ensure that everyone could look forward to receiving £500 or so when he reached retirement – it would effectively provide a 'minimum inheritance' for all.

Capital Growth-Sharing Schemes

The past few years have seen considerable growth of interest in a number of Western European countries in the possibility of including a capital element in wage negotiations. In West Germany definite steps in this direction have been taken, and proposals have been actively discussed in Italy and the Netherlands. These schemes differ in a number of major respects, but share a common origin in the recognition by trade unions of the failure of collective bargaining to achieve a number of their objectives, particularly that of a more equal distribution of wealth. In Britain, where it seems unlikely that any successful long-term incomes policy can be operated without some new approach, these ideas have not received the attention they merit.

The Continental Proposals

The Continental proposals have been described in detail in a recent report published by the Organization for Economic Co-operation and Development (O.E.C.D., 1970). The schemes have a number of common features. They are intended to provide workers with the opportunity of acquiring rights to capital assets. Their acquisition would be financed primarily by employers' contributions (perhaps facilitated by tax concessions), with the amount to be determined by collective bargaining between management and unions. At the same time, there are important differences between the proposals. The main distinction is between those where the amount of the employer's contribution would be predetermined (referred to as 'investment pay' schemes) and those where the employer's contribution would depend on the retained profits of the firm (referred to as 'capital growth-sharing' schemes). Under the investment pay schemes, part of the wage increase negotiated by a union would not be paid out immediately but saved for some specified period. As such, the schemes are rather similar to a contractual savings scheme or an occupational pension. Under capital growth-sharing, on the other hand, the unions would negotiate a percentage of the retained profits which would be paid each year into a workers' investment fund (the amount would not, therefore, be known in advance). Each worker would receive a share of the annual allocation to the fund, which he could withdraw after a specified number of years, perhaps when he retired. Capital growth-sharing represents, therefore, a combination of compulsory savings with a profit-sharing agreement.

These ideas have been most widely accepted in West Germany, and many of them originated with German trade union leaders. Saving incentive schemes, similar to S.A.Y.E., were established in the 1950s and extended in 1961 with the 'Act for Promoting Workers' Participation in Capital Formation', which offered relief from tax and social insurance contributions for wages voluntarily set aside by workers and invested in certain assets (and blocked for a number of years). These provisions fell a long way short of being a fully-fledged investment pay scheme, since both the employer's setting-up of the scheme and the worker's participation in it were voluntary decisions, and schemes determined by collective bargaining did not qualify. In 1964, Herr Georg Leber of the Construction Workers' Union put forward a plan whereby employers would pay 1·5% of wages into a fund (managed jointly by unions and employers), which would be deposited in a worker's name and accumulated until he retired. He suggested that the funds could be invested in a number of ways, and it would have been open to firms to pay by transferring shares or loan capital (on which dividends or interest would be paid). This led to a second Act in 1965, which extended tax concessions to schemes established by collective bargaining and where the employer paid all the contributions (although approval was not extended to jointly-managed funds of the kind envisaged by Leber). In Germany it is chiefly investment pay schemes that have received attention, but in the

Netherlands prominence has also been given to capital growth-sharing. In 1964 the three Dutch trade union federations published a joint report advocating both capital growth-sharing and investment pay schemes. These proposals have met with some hostility from the employers' organizations but interest has been shown by a number of political parties. Finally, in France legislation was passed in August 1967 introducing (with effect from January 1969) a scheme of compulsory profit-sharing, where the worker's share of the profits is blocked for five years. This scheme is similar in many respects to the capital growth-sharing plans in the Netherlands, but differs in that it is not linked to wage negotiations. The scheme is obligatory for all companies employing more than a hundred workers and the amount of the payments is laid down by the government.

Capital Growth-Sharing in Britain?

In Britain there have been a number of schemes with features similar to those proposed on the Continent. As long ago as 1889, the South West Metropolitan Gas Company introduced a scheme whereby workers received a share of the profits, part of which was invested in the company. At the present time a number of firms operate schemes which allocate shares to their employees or allow them to be purchased on favourable terms, among them I.C.I., Tate and Lyle, Rugby Portland Cement and Courtaulds. These differ from the Continental proposals, however, in that they have not been reached by collective bargaining and that the shares are held directly by the workers (there being no workers' investment fund). The trade unions play no role, therefore, in such schemes; and indeed a recent report on such employee shareholding schemes commented that 'with one exception companies do not appear to have thought it worthwhile to consult trade unions, although in some cases they informed them as a matter of courtesy'. (Wider Share Ownership Council, 1968.) Moreover, the schemes most similar in form to those proposed on the Continent are small in scale: in one scheme, for example, unskilled workers only received twelve 5s. shares each year. The introduction of the Continental proposals in Britain would, therefore, represent a major innovation; and in this section I examine how they might work and their advantages and disadvantages. In doing so, I concentrate on capital growth-sharing schemes similar to those proposed in the Netherlands.

In concrete terms, the introduction of capital growth-sharing means that unions would bargain not just about pay, hours, conditions of work, but also about a share of the retained profits. An agreed percentage (say 25%) of 'excess profits' – understood as profit after allowing for taxes, depreciation and a 'reasonable' return on capital – would be transferred each year to a workers' investment fund. What is considered a 'reasonable' return on capital is likely to be a highly controversial question, since it is virtually impossible to suggest any general rules by which it could be determined. As the O.E.C.D. report observed:

. . . this question will loom large in the detailed negotiation. The whole issue of the appropriate return to private equity shareholders is at stake. Deep cleavages of opinion between unions, managers and shareholders, on what is a fair return, are very near the surface and agreement might prove extremely difficult. [O.E.C.D., 1970, p. 58]

A scheme where the workers received a proportion of excess profits in the form of cash would be little different from the profit-sharing schemes operated by a number of companies (of which perhaps the best known is John Lewis). What distinguishes the capital growth-sharing proposal is the fact that the payment would not be in cash but in the form of a share of the workers' investment fund. The precise form in which the payments would be made by employers to the fund is a further possible source of disagreement. If all transfers had to be in the form of cash, serious liquidity problems might arise for some companies, and it has been argued that they should be allowed to pay by transferring their own shares. This latter proposal would mean that the companies had in effect automatic access to new equity finance. This would not only raise a number of detailed problems, such as the method of valuation to be adopted, but it would also mean that the workers' investment fund had less control over the use to be made of the accumulated contributions. The fund could always sell the shares with which they were paid, but this would give them less influence over the allocation of investment funds. In what follows it is assumed that the employers' contributions would be paid partly in cash and partly in the form of shares.

The workers' investment fund would be controlled by representatives of the workers (either union officials or directly elected members). Their chief task would be the management of the portfolio held by the fund. In doing so, they would probably want to aim at holding a wide variety of different assets: shares, government bonds, and (possibly) advances to members for such purposes as house purchase. In particular, the fund would not want to maintain large holdings in the firms in which its members were employed. No worker wants to put all his eggs in one basket: if his employer should run into a bad spell, so that earnings fall, he does not want to find that his entitlement to the workers' investment fund has also fallen. It would not have been much consolation to the workers made redundant by Rolls-Royce if the workers' investment fund had held shares in the company. It is important here to distinguish between the annual amount of the capital growth-sharing payment, which will inevitably depend on the success of the firm, and the *security of the capital accumulated* through past capital growth-sharing payments. The latter depends on how the fund is invested and, given that payments are made by the employer in either cash or shares which can be sold on the Stock Exchange, it need not include any shares in the company (even where the fund only covers workers in the one company).

The individual worker would receive from the fund each year share certificates corresponding to his allotment of that year's capital growth payment. The allocation between workers could be based on earnings and length of service, or could be equal for all. It is a central aspect of the scheme that these claims would not (other than in exceptionable circumstances) be encashable until the end of a 'freezing period', and it is assumed here that they could not be cashed until retirement (or death in service). In this respect the scheme has similarities to an occupational pension, and one could view capital growth-sharing as a method of extending occupational pensions to those groups of workers (particularly manual workers) who are not yet covered. Capital growth-sharing would, however, differ in the method by which the benefit payable at retirement was determined. It would be related to the value of a share in the fund, which would be likely to rise more or less in line with the general level of share prices (depending on the investment skills of the managers). Although it is hard to predict with great confidence, this would probably provide good protection against inflation *in the long run*; in this respect capital growth-sharing would be clearly superior to occupational schemes where benefits are fixed in cash terms.* The qualification about the long run is, however, important, since the value of the fund might fluctuate considerably. A person retiring in December 1970, for example, would probably have done rather worse in money terms than someone retiring two years earlier. In practice the workers' investment fund would have to maintain a stabilized buying-in price for its shares (in the manner in which insurance companies determine bonuses on with-profits policies): the fund would smooth out fluctuations in share prices, so that the short-run risk would not be borne by the individual worker.

Effect on the Distribution of Wealth

In assessing the impact of capital growth-sharing on the distribution of wealth, we have first to examine whether it would in fact represent a real increase in the workers' remuneration. This depends on two factors, the first being the extent to which the scheme would be negotiated at the expense of a lower rate of wage increase. The Continental trade unions envisage that the share of excess profits would be a net addition to the workers' pay: that the introduction of capital growth-sharing would proceed parallel to wage negotiations and not as a substitute for wage increases. In practice it seems likely that the introduction of the scheme would involve the unions' acceptance of a somewhat slower rate of growth of money wages in the year in which the scheme is introduced – there would have to be something in it for management. There would effectively be a once-and-for-all reduction in the level of wages. Nevertheless, this reduction would be less than the value of the payments under capital growth-sharing, so that the total amount received by the workers would increase.

The second consideration is the extent to which the benefit from

*Half of the manual workers at present covered by occupational pensions are in schemes of the fixed cash-benefit type.

capital growth-sharing would be offset by price increases: price increases would clearly reduce the real gain to be derived by the union from capital growth-sharing. For those not covered by the capital growth-sharing agreement – workers in other industries and pensioners – any increase in prices would, of course, represent an overall reduction in their real standard of living. In fact it is argued by the proponents of capital growth-sharing that it would have quite the reverse effect and prices would be lower than they otherwise would have been. This claim is based on the view that the amount to be paid under capital growth-sharing would not be known in advance, and would not therefore enter into the employers' calculation of labour costs (it is assumed that firms price on the basis of a mark-up on labour and raw material costs). As the O.E.C.D. report put it: 'There is no clear, specific, quantifiable increase in labour costs, therefore the entrepreneur cannot know by how much he needs to increase his prices in order to recoup his contributions.' (1970, p. 115.) From this standpoint, capital growth-sharing is held to be less likely to affect prices than an investment pay scheme, where the amount to be paid is known in advance. If this is correct, the introduction of capital growth-sharing would by itself have no effect on prices, while the reduced rate of wage increase in the year of its introduction would tend to lower them.

This argument ignores, however, any indirect effects that capital growth-sharing may have on prices. If prices remained unchanged, net profits (after allowing for the capital growth-sharing payment) would be reduced, which would affect the availability of capital for expansion, both from retained earnings and from new issues of shares (if the dividend were reduced and the share price depressed). It is here that the compulsory savings element is important. If the firm could borrow automatically from the workers' investment fund (as where payment could be made through the transfer of shares), this source might replace funds previously obtained from new issues or retained earnings. In that case, the effect on the firm's pricing policy would depend on the relative cost of capital from the two sources, and in particular on the rate of return allowed under the capital growth-sharing scheme in calculating 'excess' profits. If this allowed a dividend equal to that being paid before the introduction of the scheme, then it is quite possible that the workers' investment fund might represent a 'cheaper' source of finance than new issues on the Stock Exchange, and the firm's rate of expansion might actually be increased. If, on the other hand, the unions drove a hard bargain over the definition of excess profits, firms might have to increase their prices to raise the capital needed for expansion.

So far we have considered whether there would be pressures on the firm leading it to want to raise its prices, but its ability actually to do so would depend on a number of factors, including the extent to which capital growth-sharing schemes were being introduced by its competitors. A scheme which applied to only a small number of firms would be less likely to lead to a rise in prices than one covering a whole section of industry. Secondly, the effect on the level of aggregate demand has to be considered, and it is here that the advantages of the compulsory savings element have been especially emphasized. Whereas a shift in the distribution of income away from profits towards wages would normally be expected to lead to a rise in consumption, in the present case this would probably be prevented by 'freezing' the workers' entitlement until retirement. To the extent that workers could reduce other forms of saving, the freezing might not be effective; however, it seems reasonable to suppose that the scope for this would be limited. When allowance is made for the reduction in the rate of wage increase in the year in which the scheme is introduced, the net effect would almost certainly be to reduce demand. Firms could not therefore raise their prices in the expectation of increased demand. In the longer term, the effect is more difficult to predict. If about 1/40th of the labour force retired each year, some 5% of the fund would be paid out annually when the scheme reached maturity.* With an annual income of (say) 15%, this would represent a propensity to consume out of profits of $33\frac{1}{3}\%$, which is probably not a great deal higher than that of the average

*This figure is reached on the basis of the following highly simplified calculation: If the labour force covered by the scheme is constant in size and the rights of an individual worker are compounded at a rate equal to the rate of increase of payments into the fund, those about to retire own rights worth twice those of the average worker, or $2 \times 1/40$th of the fund $= 5\%$.

shareholder. When we allow for the reduction in the level of (ordinary) wages, it is unlikely that in the long run the introduction of capital growth-sharing would lead to a significant rise in consumption.

In broad terms, it appears therefore that it might be possible to introduce capital growth-sharing without its leading to higher prices. Shares in the workers' investment fund would represent (at least in part) a real addition to the income of workers in that industry and a real redistribution of wealth away from the shareholders. Moreover, the magnitude of such a redistribution could be substantial. If workers received 25% of company retained earnings the annual addition to the fund would be some £750 million at present, or nearly half the annual net increase in life assurance and superannuation funds.

The introduction of capital growth-sharing is likely on this basis to lead to a redistribution from shareholders to workers; however, we must also consider the distribution of the gains among different groups of workers. This depends in large part on the coverage of the schemes: if capital growth-sharing were brought about by union negotiation it seems inevitable that, initially at least, the schemes would only apply to a limited range of firms or industries. The gains would not, therefore, be uniformly distributed, and if prices did in fact increase, those in firms not covered by schemes would be worse off. Capital growth-sharing would no doubt spread in time to most unionized industries, and the process could be accelerated in less organized industries by bodies such as the Wages Councils. (Tax concessions could also be used to encourage the spread of schemes.) There are certain sectors where capital growth-sharing is not possible: those where there is no profit, such as the civil service, teaching, hospitals, and those where profits are subject to direct control by the government – the nationalized industries and agriculture. For these sectors an investment pay scheme would be more appropriate and the same may also be true of smaller private employers. Even, however, if capital growth-sharing (or investment pay) schemes eventually covered all employees, there might remain major differences in the benefits derived. Under capital growth-sharing, allotment of new shares to each worker would depend on the profit made by the firm in which he was employed, and a worker in a declining industry with low profits would receive much less than a worker in, say, the chemical industry. This problem could be overcome if all employer contributions were pooled and shared equally among all employees, but such an arrangement could clearly not be introduced without government intervention.

The final distributional aspect of capital growth-sharing of importance is the extension of control by workers over the firms in which they are employed. Workers' control could be brought about directly through legislation or industrial action, but capital growth-sharing provides an indirect means of giving workers a significant degree of control through the workers' investment fund. Where payments were made in cash, the fund managers could have a direct say in investment decisions; where the contributions were paid in the form of shares, the fund could still have considerable influence through the substantial shareholdings which it would gradually acquire. Although we have seen in chapter 2 that the control over industry offered by such holdings is rather limited it is nonetheless significant, and would put the workers' investment fund on a par with other shareholders and with institutions such as pension funds, insurance companies and unit trusts.

Arguments Against Capital Growth-Sharing

One of the principal arguments raised against capital growth-sharing in discussion of the Continental proposals is that it would lead to a reduction in the level of investment. In reply to this objection, the trade unions have emphasized that total investment funds would not be seriously affected (and might well increase in the short run). That part of the capital growth-sharing payment made by transferring shares would be directly available to the firm for reinvestment, and the remainder (except for payments made to retiring members) would be available to the capital market as a whole. The *availability* of investment funds is not, however, the only relevant factor and it could be argued that growth-sharing would also affect the *inducement to invest*. In part this turns on the cost of capital, which we have seen to depend on the amount allowed for a 'reasonable' return on capital under the capital growth-sharing agreement. If the unions did not drive too hard a bargain, the effective cost of capital borrowed from the workers' investment fund might be less than that of capital raised by new issues on the Stock Exchange, and the firm could therefore undertake *more* investment. It was argued by the O.E.C.D. report that:

If all investment funds have to come from the market, the manager may be under restraints similar to those of the entrepreneur, but with self-financing, managers may undertake investment in projects which do not have a rate of return high enough to have attracted funds from the market. If part of the profits are to be taken away from shareholders, it does not follow therefore that managers will be reluctant to undertake investment activities if the funds are available to them . . . The crucial determinant becomes the rate of return set by management on its own use of internal funds or the rate of return accepted as a minimum by the Workers' Investment Fund. [1970, p. 123]

In this context, there is no presumption therefore that capital growth-sharing would necessarily discourage investment and whether it would do so depends on the precise terms of the agreement.

A second objection is that the introduction of capital growth-sharing would lead to a capital flight, so that a country introducing such a scheme unilaterally would experience a drain on the capital account of the balance of payments. This argument has been examined by a Dutch economist, who concluded that:

As far as the large public companies are concerned, this does not appear likely. As soon as the profit-sharing concerned is discounted in stock prices and the shares show a yield comparable with that of other stock . . . they automatically become a desirable investment again. It is unlikely, therefore, that there will be any appreciable flight of capital. [O.E.C.D. Supplement 1970, p. 136]

In considering this question, we should distinguish between a flight of investible resources and a reduction in the willingness of foreign companies to invest. The first depends on the reaction of shareholders. If the argument quoted above is correct, there would be a once-and-for-all fall in stock market values as capital growth-sharing was introduced, causing a capital loss to existing shareholders. Once this had taken place and the effect of capital growth-sharing had been fully discounted, the allocation of investment funds would not be affected. The second factor would depend on the investment decisions of foreign (typically American) corporations, which, like their native counterparts, might well decide to invest more, particularly if it were felt that the profit-sharing element would reduce industrial stoppages.

Finally, it could be objected that the fact of a worker's having rights to accumulated capital growth-sharing would inhibit labour mobility. Whether or not this objection is valid would depend on the conditions under which the rights of the worker would be protected if he changed his job. It is the clear intention of the Continental proposals that these rights should be guaranteed: a person leaving the industry covered by a fund would retain his shares in the fund. Moreover, the value of these shares would rise as the income and capital gains accumulated, so that they are likely to be well protected against inflation. In this respect, capital growth-sharing would be much superior to the many occupational pension schemes which allow no transfer or only preserve the cash value of contributions, and it is not likely seriously to hinder labour mobility.

Capital Growth-Sharing – Conclusions

It seems likely that the capital growth-sharing scheme discussed here would lead to a substantial redistribution away from shareholders towards workers. By increasing the real income of the workers it would effectively lead to greater equality of inherited wealth, providing them with a capital sum at retirement in addition to their wages, and it would certainly lead to more equal holdings of current wealth. However, the benefits would not necessarily be shared very equally among different groups of workers. The establishment of the workers' investment fund would provide employees with the same degree of (possibly latent) control over production as enjoyed by such institutions as insurance companies and pension funds. The compulsory savings element in the scheme would ensure that there would not be a reduction in the level of saving, and the inducement to invest might well be increased.

There are, therefore, good grounds for investigating further the scope for capital growth-sharing in Britain. There are already schemes of this type, although they tend to be small in scale, and in some cases were introduced in opposition to union demands (the South Metropolitan Gas Company scheme of 1889 included a clause by which the bonus was forfeited if the person went on strike). Despite such inauspicious precedents, there is much in the idea of capital growth-sharing that merits trade union attention, and if arrived at through collective bargaining such schemes could provide a means for the substantial redistribution of wealth.

Part IV
Conclusions

12. A Programme for Reform

In the Introduction I emphasized the importance of clarifying the objectives of reform, and this has been one of the main aims of the analysis. In particular, I have stressed the need to distinguish between the distribution of inherited wealth – the amount received by a person through inheritance during the course of his life – and the distribution of current wealth among everyone alive today. *Inherited wealth* represents the 'start' which a person has in life, and inequality in its distribution has fundamental consequences for the structure of our society. At present a handful of people inherit £1 million or more, while the majority inherit virtually nothing. If instead everyone inherited £5,000, our society would be very different. Inequality in the *current distribution of wealth*, on the other hand, leads to unequal incomes, and concentrates control over the economy in a few hands. The reduction of inequality in the distribution of income is the aim of the income tax system; however, one important element of income – capital gains – is at present taxed at a much lower effective rate. Since capital gains accrue especially on assets (company shares and real property) which are held predominantly by the rich, this has led to greater concentration of investment incomes. Company shares are also important from the standpoint of the distribution of control, and the achievement of greater equality in this respect requires not just the redistribution of wealth but also the spread of ownership of these assets.

As a means of achieving these ends, I would propose the following programme for reform:

1: Replacement of Estate Duty by a Lifetime Capital Receipts Tax
Under a lifetime receipts tax, the total of bequests and gifts received over a person's lifetime would be taxed at a steeply progressive rate. Such a tax would make a major contribution towards a more equal distribution of inherited wealth. It would be very difficult for a rich family to maintain its wealth intact for a

long period, since – unlike the present estate duty – all gifts *inter vivos* would be taxed.* In that the tax would be levied on the amount received (rather than the amount given away) and would be cumulated over a lifetime, it would provide a strong incentive for donors to pass their wealth to those who had inherited little. A millionaire would pay no tax at all if he shared his wealth equally among a hundred people who had previously inherited nothing. In this respect, the lifetime receipts tax would be superior to the alternative of supplementing the present estate duty by a gifts tax. Moreover, the lifetime receipts tax would serve to ensure that the basis for taxation, and the extent of redistribution, were clear to all; unlike estate duty, it would not entail the 'sham' of high apparent rates of tax coupled with easy means of avoidance. As a means for bringing about greater equality in inherited wealth the lifetime receipts tax has definite advantages over an annual wealth tax, and is likely to operate more quickly. It would be less costly to administer and would not involve the same risks of capital flight or adverse effects on incentives.

2: The Reform of Capital Gains Taxation

All realized capital gains should be subject to the full rates of income taxation (accompanied by the introduction of a five-year averaging period). This reform would ensure that capital gains were taxed at the same rate as other forms of income, and would make it much more difficult for people to acquire large fortunes through capital gains (as in the property boom of the 1950s). The increase in the effective rate of tax would in the long run lead to a substantial increase in revenue. The chief possible disadvantage of the reform is that the incentive to invest in risky enterprises might be reduced, although the existence of such a disincentive has not been demonstrated. The reform of capital gains taxation has the major advantage over the alternative of introducing an annual wealth tax that its administrative costs would be considerably

*It is this feature which is the main difference between the lifetime capital receipts tax proposed here and the inheritance tax considered in the government Green Paper of April 1972. The latter would not include gifts (other than those made within seven years of death) and would be a much less effective means of redistributing wealth.

smaller, and there is no reason why it should be more likely to have adverse effects on savings or work effort.

3: Pension Reform

For many people rights to a pension represent one of their most important assets. It is therefore of great importance that these should provide a return which is guaranteed in terms of purchasing power, so that people's savings are not eroded by inflation. At present neither the National Insurance pension nor the majority of occupational schemes provide such a guarantee, and there are serious doubts whether the government's proposals for changes in occupational pensions and for a state reserve scheme will adequately deal with this problem. It is essential that reforms be introduced to ensure that occupational schemes and the state reserve scheme provide for the real value of benefits to be maintained both before and after retirement (as would have been the case with the Labour Party proposals for National Superannuation). In addition, reform of the state pension scheme should introduce a capital element to be paid as a lump sum at retirement, as is now provided by some occupational schemes. The inclusion of such a capital payment would give everyone the prospect of receiving £500 (say) at the age of 65 – there would be a 'minimum inheritance' for all. It would be introduced gradually so that those who had passed the age of 65 when the scheme was introduced would also benefit. It would be financed partly from the extra revenue raised by the tax reforms outlined above and partly from National Insurance contributions falling primarily on those with above-average earnings.

4: Trade Union Negotiations for Capital Growth-Sharing

On the Continent considerable interest has been shown in schemes in which a share of company-retained profits would accrue to the employees and be held in a workers' investment fund until they retire. These schemes differ from those which have been tried by some companies in this country in that they would be larger in scale, would involve a fund administered by the workers, and would be introduced through collective bargaining. Such schemes could lead to a substantial redistribution from shareholders to workers (although the benefits would be shared rather unequally between workers in different industries); and would transfer an important element of control to the workers' investment fund. The negotiation of a capital growth-sharing scheme would be less likely to lead to a rise in prices than an ordinary wage increase, and could represent an important feature of a long-term incomes policy. Although capital growth-sharing could not be introduced immediately the idea deserves careful consideration by the T.U.C. and others.

5: Nationalization and the Control of Industry

The analysis of chapter 10 showed that nationalization has failed not only to contribute materially towards a more equal distribution of the ownership of wealth but also to make significant progress towards greater equality in the distribution of control. The introduction of employee-directors by the British Steel Corporation represented an advance, but cannot be described as providing 'industrial democracy'. Serious consideration must be given to the possibilities of extending the scope for employee participation in the nationalized industries.

Each of these measures would by itself contribute towards greater equality; however, the programme should be seen as a concerted whole, designed to meet the different dimensions of inequality which we have seen to exist in Britain today. The introduction of the lifetime capital receipts tax would be aimed at reducing the transmission of wealth between generations; and this would be supported by the capital payment in the state pension, which would effectively provide everyone with a minimum inherited wealth. Pension reform and capital growth-sharing would allow those with little wealth to protect themselves against inflation, and would lead to a more equal distribution of current wealth (and hence of income). The reform of capital gains taxation would make it more difficult to acquire substantial fortunes through capital gains. The establishment of workers' investment funds under capital growth-sharing and changes in the organization of the nationlized industries would lead to a more equal distribution of economic power.

Plans for a redistribution of wealth are often attacked on the grounds that they are simply taking from the rich with no benefit to those with little wealth. It is argued that taxing the rich provides little help to the poor, since only a small part of the revenue can be used to increase wealth-holding at the bottom without adding to the level of aggregate demand. This objection does not apply to the proposals made here. One of the merits of the lifetime capital receipts tax is that it is not simply a tax on the rich – it also provides an incentive for them to spread their wealth widely. With the present estate duty there is no such incentive. Moreover, the increased taxes on the wealthy would be accompanied by measures to increase wealth-holding: pension reform, the capital element in the state pension, and capital growth-sharing.

There will no doubt be those who feel that the proposals put forward here are too revolutionary. To them I must point out that similar schemes are in force or are actively being discussed in other countries. In no other major Western country do gifts escape tax free; in Canada the Carter Commission has proposed that capital gains should be taxed in full as other income; in the Netherlands and West Germany concrete proposals have been put forward for capital growth-sharing, and the French have since 1969 had a compulsory profit-sharing scheme for all large firms. In international terms, the proposals are far from revolutionary, and indeed in the context of the extreme degree of inequality in Britain they can be more reasonably criticized as being too limited in their scope.

Notes on Sources and Further Reading

The purpose of these notes is to describe the chief sources on which I have drawn, and to make suggestions for further reading. The notes are arranged under chapter headings, since this facilitates reference from the text and broadly corresponds to a division according to subject matter. Works cited are referred to in the notes by the author's surname and date of publication, and the full reference is given in the bibliography at the end; where necessary, works by the same author published in the same year are distinguished by letters: e.g. Lydall (1955a).

For those interested in further general reading in this field, I would suggest the following few books:

MEADE, J. E., *Efficiency and the Ownership of Property* (1964). This is a short and clearly written analysis of the factors influencing the distribution of income and wealth, and of the role that could be played by tax and other reforms.

PEN, J., *Income Distribution* (1971). A very readable account of the distribution of income in Britain and of the alternative theories explaining inequality.

SANDFORD, C. T., *Taxing Inheritance and Capital Gains* (1967). A brief but stimulating discussion of the possibilities for fiscal reform.

WEDGWOOD, J., *The Economics of Inheritance* (1939). Now dated, but an interesting and detailed analysis of the role of inheritance in Britain.

Chapter 1

Total personal wealth. (Table 1, p. 7.) These figures are based on the estimates made at the Department of Applied Economics, Cambridge, by J. R. S. Revell and A. Roe. For a brief introduction to the work see Revell (1966). The basic method of estimation is described in detail in Revell (1967), who discusses the question of the positive net worth of the company sector. The figures quoted in Table 1 and in the text are obtained from Roe (1971).

Distribution of wealth. (p. 11.) A clear and concise account of the difficulties involved in obtaining information about the distribution of wealth is given in Lydall and Tipping (1961), who present estimates relating to the period 1951–6.

Oxford Institute of Economics and Statistics savings surveys. (p. 9.) These are described in Lydall (1955a).

Of the figures given in the text, Table 2 is derived from the *Inland Revenue Statistics 1970*, which contains brief notes on the deficiencies of the estimates. The adjusted estimates given in Table 3 are my own calculations, and the methods are described in more detail in Atkinson (1971). The adjustments made are in a number of cases parallel with those of Lydall and Tipping (1961), although they made no allowance for state pensions. The estimates relate to the population over the age of 25 (in contrast to those given in Table 2) and exclude the wealth of those aged under 25 (and where the age of the decedent is not stated). In adjusting for the missing settled property and occupational pensions, it is assumed that these would be distributed in the same way as other wealth included in the Estate Duty statistics. The allowance for the actuarial value of the rights to state pensions is based on the present value of prospective benefits at an interest rate of 5%. The investment income estimate given by the *Economist* was published on 15 January, 1966. The figures given in Table 4 for the top investment incomes are taken from the *Inland Revenue Statistics 1970*, Table 43. The assumptions about the investment income from wealth are essentially arbitrary, although it is useful to bear in mind that the average dividend yield on the *Financial Times* – Actuaries' Ordinary Share Index in 1967 was 5.2%. Further research on the investment income approach is badly needed.

Comparison with other countries. (p. 19.) The basic sources used in the comparison with the United States in the text are the articles by Lydall and Lansing (1959), from which Figure 1 is taken, and by Lampman (1959). The question is also discussed in Lydall and Tipping (1961) and in the monograph by Lampman (1962), which is a full-length study of the changes in the share of the top 1% in the United States over the course of this century. There is very little material allowing comparisons to be made with other countries. On West Germany, see Kisker (1964).

Changes in the distribution of wealth over time. (p. 21.) Table 5 is taken from Revell (1965), which is based in part on earlier work by Langley (1950), Campion (1939) and Daniels and Campion (1936). (The table is also given in Meade (1964), p. 27.) The interpretation of the trends in the distribution is discussed in the article by Revell, and the treatment in the text owes a lot to his analysis.

Chapter 2

The material in this chapter is derived from a number of different sources.

Income. (p. 31.) The definition of income was discussed very clearly in the Minority Report of the Royal Commission on the Taxation of Profits and Income, which drew in turn on Simons (1938). The readings edited by Houghton (1970) contain convenient extracts from these authors.

Portfolios of the rich. (Table 6, p. 30.) The information about the portfolios of the wealthy is derived from Revell (1962), and the figures from the survey of investors were given in *The Times*, 23 September 1970. Table 7 is taken from Lydall and Tipping (1961). (A more recent estimate of the concentration of the ownership of different assets is seriously needed.)

Distribution of income from wealth. (Table 8, p. 38.) The figures are given in Meade (1964), and the sources are described there. As is explained in Meade's Appendix I, there are a number of difficulties in estimating the relevant share of profits, and the figure of 20% is taken for illustrative purposes only.

Wealth and the control of industry. (p. 38.) The studies of the concentration of industrial shareholding are by Florence (1961) and Brown (1968). The figures on the owners of quoted ordinary shares (Table 9) are given in Revell and Moyle (1966) for 1957 and 1963. Those for 1970 are preliminary and as yet unpublished, and were made available to me by A. Roe of the Department of Applied Economics, Cambridge.

Separation of ownership and control. (p. 40.) The separation of ownership and control in the modern corporation has been discussed a great deal in recent years. For a number of different views, see Marris and Wood (1971).

Chapter 3

In this chapter I have drawn on three main sources.

Life-cycle factors. (p. 49.) The analysis of the role of life-cycle factors in explaining inequality in the overall distribution of wealth is based on Atkinson (1971), and the figures given in Table 10 and in the text are from the same source. The reader is referred to the article for details of the method of calculation and discussion of the reliability of the results. For a discussion of the empirical evidence with regard to life-cycle savings behaviour see Lydall (1955b).

Yield on equities. (p. 53.) The basic source is the index published by the stockbrokers de Zoete and Bevan. Their figures were used by Carrington in his articles in *The Times* (14–18 October 1968) and by Merrett and Sykes (1966). This latter article contains a more detailed discussion of the return to equities over the period 1919–66. Table 11 was taken from Carrington's articles, and Table 12 from the de Zoete and Bevan pamphlet *Equity and Fixed Interest Investment 1919–1971*, which they very kindly made available to me.

Property fortunes. (p. 56.) This material is largely derived from Marriott (1967).

Chapter 4

As pointed out in the text, the subject of inheritance has been almost entirely neglected in recent years (with the notable exception of the work of C. D. Harbury). There was, however, considerable interest in the 1920s and I have drawn heavily on the work of J. Wedgwood (1939), H. Dalton (1925) and Sir Josiah Stamp (1926).

Factors influencing the transmission of wealth. (p. 59.) The evidence from the University of Michigan surveys of the savings behaviour of the rich is described in Barlow et al. (1966). Wedgwood (chapter 4) discusses the role of primogeniture and equal division. The reader is also referred to Meade (1964), chapter 5, where there is a very clear discussion of the role of differential family size and of assortative mating. For a mathematical treatment, see Stiglitz (1969).

Quantitative importance of inheritance. (p. 68.) The basic studies in this field are those by Harbury (1962) and Wedgwood (1939). The method used in their investigations is clearly described in Harbury's article, where there is also a summary of Wedgwood's results. As is explained in Harbury's article, the results are subject to a number of qualifications. In particular, they are based on the gross values of estates as admitted for probate and therefore exclude a considerable amount of settled property. A further study using the Estate Duty statistics is that by Fijalkowski-Bereday (1950), which is the source of the evidence about charitable bequests on page 64. The survey of agricultural estates is reported in Denman (1957).

Chapter 5

In the first part of this chapter I have drawn on a number of sources, and I should mention in particular Tawney (1964), Benn and Peters (1959), von Leyden (1963), Barry (1965), and Donnison (1970). Although the general subject of equality has received a great deal of attention, little of the literature appears to have been directly concerned with the questions considered in this chapter.

The general subjects discussed in the second part of this chapter are treated in a number of economic textbooks. The specific question of the relationship between the distribution of wealth and savings, work effort, etc., is less well covered. On the question of savings, see Wedgwood (chapter 1) and Lampman (1957). There is a good discussion of the factors influencing work effort in Brown and Dawson (1969). The final section on the 'quality of life' owes a great deal to Crosland (1964).

Chapter 6

The general subject of the taxation of wealth is covered in most text-books on public finance. The better known British textbooks include Prest (1967), Sandford (1969), Hockley (1970), Williams (1963), and Hicks (1968). The first three of these contain descriptions of the present British system of taxation. A more specialized book on wealth taxation is that by Tait (1967). These books contain further discussion of the methods to be adopted in analysing the effects of taxation and the basis for comparing taxes.

In the section describing some of the taxes in force in other countries, I have drawn on a number of sources. I should refer in particular to Tanabe (1967), Wheatcroft (1965) and the symposium on wealth taxation in the journal *Public Finance* (1960). The report of the Carter Commission – Carter (1966) – should also be referred to; for a summary of its proposals for wealth transfer taxation see Jantscher (1969).

Chapter 7

Death duties. (p. 113.) A more detailed history of death duties in Britain is given in Soward and Willun (1919) and in the *Midland Bank Review* (1954).

Estate duty. (p. 114.) The chief provisions of the current Estate Duty are conveniently summarized in Lynch (1968), which lists the main amendments over the period 1894–1968. The major changes made in the Finance Act 1969 are discussed in Silberrad (1969) and Wheatcroft (1969a). For a fuller (legal) description of Estate Duty, see the latest edition of *Dymond's Death Duties*. The *British Tax Review* contains a number of articles on Estate Duty.

Impact of estate duty on the distribution of wealth. (p. 118.) The effectiveness of Estate Duty in achieving redistribution is considered in Tait (1960) and (1967). The latter reference contains a discussion of Estate Duty avoidance, which is also treated in Titmuss (1962) and Meacher (1971). For illustrations of the methods that can be used, see Argent (1964).

Revenue from death duties. (Table 16, p. 126.) Table 16 is based on the statistics for the revenue from Estate and other duties published by the Inland Revenue, and on the estimates of total personal wealth given by Campion (1939), Langley (1950), Lydall and Tipping (1961), and the

Inland Revenue (1970). The estimate of the value of gifts avoiding Estate Duty uses a modified version of the method suggested by Tait (1967), Appendix II. The figures quoted for discretionary trusts are from Revell (1967). The survey of the payment of Estate Duty on agricultural estates is reported in Denman (1957).

The income tax treatment of investment income and the long-term capital gains tax are described in Prest (1967) and Hockley (1970), although the situation will be changed in forthcoming Budgets. The history of the capital gains tax legislation up to 1970 is well summarized in the *Midland Bank Review* (1971). The effective rate of tax on capital gains is further discussed in Merrett (1965).

The quotation on p. 119 is from Henderson (1926); the quotation from Queen Victoria on p. 122 is given in Tait (1967), p. 92.

Chapter 8

In this chapter I have drawn heavily on a number of articles written during the early 1960s on the subject of a wealth tax: Peacock (1963), Stewart (1963), Balogh (1964), Tress (1963), and Wheatcroft (1963). (The last of these articles deals in particular with the administrative problems of a wealth tax.) More recently proposals for a wealth tax have been made by Stutchbury (1968), *Economist* (22 January 1966) and a Labour Party study group (1969). The paper by the Confederation of British Industry on the subject of a wealth tax was reported in *The Times* (22 August 1969).

The estimates of the revenue given on page 141 were based on the Inland Revenue estimates of the distribution of wealth (*Inland Revenue Statistics 1970*, Table 123).

The incentive to work. (p. 146.) The evidence about work incentives is derived from Break (1957), Daniel (1968), and Brown and Dawson (1969). The latter contains a good summary of the issues.

Reform of capital gains taxation. (p. 157.) The discussion of the reform of capital gains taxation draws on both the Minority and Majority Reports of the Royal Commission on the Taxation of Profits and Income (1955), and in particular on chapters 4 and 8 of the Majority Report, chapter 2 of the Minority Report, and the Memorandum of Evidence by the Board of the Inland Revenue. For further discussion of the issues, see Turvey (1960), Ilersic (1962) and Merrett (1964).

Chapter 9

The treatment of wealth-transfer taxation in this chapter owes a great deal to the influence of Meade (1964), Sandford (1967) and Stutchbury

(1968), all of whom have made proposals for a lifetime capital receipts tax. Although the proposals made here are more detailed, and differ in a number of respects, they are very much in the spirit of those made by these earlier writers.

Integrated gift and estate tax. (p. 163.) The discussion of gift and estate taxes, and the possibility of an integrated gift and estate tax, draws on the interesting discussion in Shoup (1966) and Wheatcroft (1965).

Lifetime capital receipts tax. (p. 168.) The economic effects of a lifetime capital receipts tax are discussed in Meade (1964) and Sandford (1967).

Taxing wealth transfers as income. (p. 172.) The taxation of wealth transfers as income was discussed by Simons (1938) and incorporated by the Canadian Royal Commission in their proposals for tax reform (Carter (1966)). For a thorough discussion of these proposals, see Jantscher (1969).

Chapter 10

Capital levy. (p. 196.) The possibility of a capital levy has not been discussed a great deal in recent years, and much of the literature dates from the 1920s when the Labour Party proposals were under active discussion. The Labour Party proposals are described in Dalton (1923), and examined in detail in the report of the Colwyn Committee (1927). The idea was revived in a *Tribune* pamphlet in 1951, and at that time was attacked in an article by Chambers (1951). For a description of the levies used in a number of Western European countries, see Robson (1959).

Nationalization. (p. 207.) In discussing the impact of nationalization on the distribution of wealth I have drawn on the treatment of this question in Shanks (1963) and Robson (1952). The question of the definition of 'fair' compensation does not appear to have received a lot of attention. For discussion of the compensation criteria applied in practice, see Eastham (1948), Joy (1950) and Robson (1952). In the section on nationalization and control I have drawn on Coates and Topham (1970), and on the chapters on joint consultation in Robson (1952) and Shanks (1963). The quotation from *The Miners' Next Step* is taken from Coates and Topham, p. 23. The plan of the National Craftsmen's Committee for worker representation in the steel industry is given in Coates (1968), pp. 147–56. The evidence about the attitudes of workers to participation and the consequences of increased participation is surveyed in the recent book by Pateman (1970), which contains an extended analysis of the question.

Denationalization. (p. 216.) Although this is at present a popular slogan, very little has been written on this subject. There is, however, a statement of Mr Powell's views in Powell (1970), chapter 5.

Chapter 11

Savings incentive schemes. (p. 220.) These schemes have been very little discussed, and there has been no detailed analysis of the effectiveness of Save As You Earn. The chief features of the scheme are described in Hockley (1970), chapter 19. Schemes to encourage wider share ownership are discussed in the Conservative Political Centre Report *Everyman a Capitalist*, and Wider Share Ownership Council (1968).

Pension schemes. (p. 226.) The chief source of information about occupational pension schemes is the survey carried out periodically by the Government Actuary (the most recent is that covering 1967 – Government Actuary (1968)). The contribution that would have been made by National Superannuation to a reduction in inequality is discussed in Lynes (1970a) and Atkinson (1970), where the main features of the schemes are described. The proposal for a 'negative capital tax' is made in Sandford (1969).

Capital growth-sharing schemes. (p. 234.) In this section I have drawn heavily on the papers given at a conference organized by the O.E.C.D. in 1967, and on the final report prepared by D. Robinson and S. Barkin (O.E.C.D. (1970)). The schemes are also discussed in Pen (1971) and in the book sponsored by the Wider Share Ownership Council (1968).

References

ARGENT, H. D., *Death Duty Mitigation*, 2nd edition, Business Publications Ltd, 1964.

ATKINSON, A. B., 'National Superannuation: Redistribution and Value for Money', *Bulletin of the Oxford University Institute of Economics and Statistics*, August 1970.

ATKINSON, A. B., 'The Distribution of Wealth and the Individual Life-Cycle', *Oxford Economic Papers*, July 1971.

BALOGH, T., 'A Note on the Wealth Tax', *Economic Journal*, March 1964.

BALOGH, T., *Labour and Inflation*, Fabian Tract, 1970.

BARLOW, R., BRAZER, H. E. and MORGAN, J. N., *Economic Behaviour of the Affluent*, Brookings Institution, 1966.

BARRY, B., *Political Argument*, Routledge and Kegan Paul, 1965.

BELL, C., *Civilization*, Penguin, 1938.

BENN, S. I., and PETERS, R. S., *Social Principles and the Democratic State*, George Allen and Unwin, 1959.

BERLIN, I., 'Equality', in F. Olafson (ed.), *Justice and Social Policy*, Spectrum Books, 1961.

BREAK, G. F., 'Income Taxes and Incentives to Work: An Empirical Study', *American Economic Review*, September 1957.

BROWN, C. V., and DAWSON, D. A., *Personal Taxation, Incentives and Tax Reform*, PEP Broadsheet 506, 1969.

BROWN, M. B., 'The Controllers of British Industry', in K. Coates (ed.), *Can the Workers Run Industry?*, Sphere, 1968.

CAMPION, H., *Public and Private Property in Great Britain*, Oxford University Press, 1939.

CAMPION, H., and DANIELS, G. W., *The Distribution of National Capital*, Manchester University Press, 1936.

CARTER, K. LeM., (chairman), *Report of the Royal Commission on Taxation*, Queen's Printer, Ottawa, 1966.

CHAMBERS, S. P., 'The Capital Levy', *Lloyds Bank Review*, January 1951.

COATES, K. (ed.), *Can the Workers Run Industry?*, Sphere, 1968.

COATES, K., and TOPHAM, T., *Workers' Control*, Panther, 1970.

Colwyn Committee on National Debt and Taxation, H.M.S.O., 1927.

CROSLAND, C. A. R., *The Future of Socialism*, revised edition, Cape, 1964.

DALTON, H., *The Capital Levy Explained*, Labour Publishing Company, 1923.

DALTON, H., *Some Aspects of the Inequality of Incomes in Modern Communities*, Routledge, 1925.

DANIEL, W. W., 'Personal Taxation and Occupational Incentives', *Banker*, 1968.

DENMAN, D. R., *Estate Capital*, George Allen and Unwin, 1957.

DONNISON, D., 'Liberty, Equality and Fraternity', *Three Banks Review*, December 1970.

DUE, J. F., 'Net Worth Taxation', *Public Finance*, 1960.

EASTHAM, J. K., 'Compensation Terms for Nationalised Industry', *Manchester School*, January 1948.

ELIOT, T. S., *Notes towards the Definition of Culture*, 1948.

FIJALKOWSKI-BEREDAY, G. Z., 'The Equalising Effects of Death Duties', *Oxford Economic Papers*, June 1950.

FLORENCE, S., *Ownership, Control and Success of Large Companies*, Sweet and Maxwell, 1961.

GAITSKELL, H. T. N., *Socialism and Nationalization*, Fabian Tract, 1956.

GLASS, D., (ed.), *Social Mobility in Britain*, Routledge and Kegan Paul, 1954.

GOVERNMENT ACTUARY, *Occupational Pension Schemes – Third Survey by Government Actuary*, H.M.S.O., 1968.

HARBURY, C. D., 'Inheritance in the Distribution of Personal Wealth', *Economic Journal*, December 1962.

HENDERSON, H. D., *Inheritance and Inequality*, 'Daily News' pamphlet, 1926.

HICKS, U. K., *Public Finance*, 3rd edition, Cambridge University Press, 1968.

HOCKLEY, G. C., *Monetary Policy and Public Finance*, Routledge and Kegan Paul, 1970.

HOLLINGSWORTH, T. H., 'A Demographic Study of the British Ducal Families', *Population Studies*, July 1957.

HOUGHTON, R. W. (ed.), *Public Finance*, Penguin, 1970.

HUGHES, J., *Nationalised Industries in the Mixed Economy*, Fabian Tract 328, 1960.

ILERSIC, A. R., *The Taxation of Capital Gains*, Staples, 1962.

INLAND REVENUE, *Inland Revenue Statistics 1970*, H.M.S.O., 1970.

JANTSCHER, G. R., 'Death and Gift Taxation in the United States After the Report of Royal Commission', *National Tax Journal*, March 1969.

JENKINS, R. H., 'Equality', in *New Fabian Essays*, Turnstile Press, 1952.

JOY, N. V., 'Fair Compensation under the British Labour Government', *Political Science Quarterly*, no. 4, 1950.

KEYNES, J. M., *Evidence to Colwyn Committee on National Debt and Taxation*, vol. II, 1927.

KISKER, K. P., *Die Erbschaftssteuer als Mittel der Vermögensredistribution*, Duncker und Humblot, 1964.

LABOUR STUDY GROUP, *Labour's Economic Strategy*, Labour Party, 1969.

LAMPMAN, R. J., 'Recent Thought on Egalitarianism', *Quarterly Journal of Economics*, 1957.

LAMPMAN, R. J., 'Changes in the Share of Wealth Held by Top Wealth-Holders, 1922–1956', *Review of Economics and Statistics*, November 1959.

LAMPMAN, R. J., *The Share of Top Wealth-Holders in National Wealth 1922–1956*, National Bureau for Economic Research, 1962.

LANGLEY, K. M., 'The Distribution of Capital in Private Hands in 1936–1938 and 1946–1947', *Bulletin of the Oxford University Institute of Economics and Statistics*, December 1950.

LEYDEN, W. von, 'On Justifying Inequality', *Political Studies*, February 1963.

LOCKE, J., *Two Treatises of Government*, 1694.

LYDALL, H. F., *British Incomes and Savings*, Oxford 1955(a).

LYDALL, H. F., 'The Life Cycle in Income, Saving and Asset Ownership', *Econometrica*, April 1955(b).

LYDALL, H. F., and LANSING, J. B., 'A Comparison of the Distribution of Personal Income and Wealth in the United States and Great Britain', *American Economic Review*, March 1959.

LYDALL, H. F., and TIPPING, D. G., 'The Distribution of Personal Wealth in Britain', *Bulletin of the Oxford University Institute of Economics and Statistics*, February 1961.

LYNCH, T. D. (ed.), *Direct Taxation in the United Kingdom*, The Institute of Chartered Accounts of Scotland, 1968.

LYNES, T., *Labour's Pension Plan*, Fabian Tract 396, 1970(a).

LYNES, T., 'National Superannuation – What Next', *General Federation of Trade Union News*, October 1970(b).

MARRIOTT, O., *The Property Boom*, Hamish Hamilton, 1967.

MARRIS, R. L., and WOOD, A. (ed.), *The Corporate Economy*, Macmillan, 1971.

MCKENDRICK, N., 'Josiah Wedgwood: An Eighteenth Century Entrepreneur in Salesmanship and Marketing Techniques', *Economic History Review*, no. 3, 1959–60.

MEACHER, M., 'Inequalities of Wealth', in P. Townsend and N. Bosanquet (eds.), *Labour and Inequality*, Fabian Publications, 1972.

MEADE, J. E., *Efficiency, Equality and the Ownership of Property*, George Allen and Unwin, 1964.

MERRETT, A. J., 'Capital Gains Taxation: The Accrual Alternative', *Oxford Economic Papers*, July 1964.

MERRETT, A. J., 'The Capital Gains Tax', *Lloyds Bank Review*, October 1965.

MERRETT, A. J., and SYKES, A., 'Return on Equities and Fixed-Interest Securities: 1919–1966', *District Bank Review*, June 1966.

MIDLAND BANK REVIEW, 'Sixty Years of Death Duties', August 1954.

MIDLAND BANK REVIEW, 'Taxation of Capital Gains', February 1971.

MILL, J. S., *Principles of Political Economy*, Routledge, 1891.

MINISTRY OF PENSIONS AND NATIONAL INSURANCE, *Financial and other circumstances of Retirement Pensioners*, H.M.S.O., 1966.

MONTAGU, Lord, *The Gilt and the Gingerbread*, Sphere, 1968.

O.E.C.D., *Workers' Negotiated Savings Plans for Capital Formation*, Final Report and Supplement, Paris, 1970.

PATEMAN, C., *Participation and Democratic Theory*, Cambridge University Press, 1970.

PEACOCK, A. T., 'Economics of a Net Worth Tax for Britain', *British Tax Review*, November–December 1963.

PEN, J., *Income Distribution*, Allen Lane The Penguin Press, 1971.

PIGOU, A. C., *A Study in Public Finance*, 3rd edition, Macmillan, 1947.

POWELL, E., *Income Tax at 4/3 in the £*, Tom Stacey, 1970.

PREST, A. R., *Public Finance in Theory and Practice*, 3rd edition, Weidenfeld and Nicolson, 1967.

PRYKE, R., 'Public Enterprise and the Economics of Large Scale Production,' *Annals of Public and Collective Economy*, January–March 1970.

REFORM COMMITTEE OF THE SOUTH WALES MINERS, *The Miners' Next Step*, 1912 (reprinted in *Archives in Trade Union History and Theory*, Centre for Socialist Education, Nottingham, 1965).

REVELL, J. R. S., 'Assets and Age', *Bulletin of the Oxford Institute of Economics and Statistics*, August 1962.

REVELL, J. R. S., 'Changes in the social distribution of property in Britain during the twentieth century', *Actes du Troisième Congrès International d'Histoire Économique*, Munich, 1965.

REVELL, J. R. S., 'The Wealth of the Nation', *Moorgate and Wall Street Journal*, Spring 1966.

REVELL, J. R. S., *The Wealth of the Nation*, Cambridge University Press, 1967.

REVELL, J. R. S., and MOYLE, J., *The Owners of Quoted Ordinary Shares*, Chapman and Hall, 1966.

ROBINSON, J., *Economics: An Awkward Corner*, George Allen and Unwin, 1966.

ROBSON, P., 'Capital Levies in Western Europe After the Second World War', *Review of Economic Studies*, October 1959.

ROBSON, W. A. (ed.), *Problems of Nationalized Industry*, George Allen and Unwin, 1952.

ROE, A., *The Financial Interdependence of the Economy 1957–1961*, Chapman and Hall, 1971.

ROSE, H. B., and NEWBOULD, G. C., 'The 1967 Take-Over Boom', *Moorgate and Wall Street Journal*, Autumn 1967.

ROYAL COMMISSION ON THE TAXATION OF PROFITS AND INCOME, *Final Report*, H.M.S.O., 1955.

SABINE, B. E. V., *A History of Income Tax*, George Allen and Unwin, 1966.

SANDFORD, C. T., *Taxing Inheritance and Capital Gains*, 2nd edition, Hobart Paper, 32, 1967.

SANDFORD, C. T., *Economics of Public Finance*, Pergamon Press, 1969.

SANDFORD, C. T., *Realistic Tax Reform*, Chatto and Windus, 1971.

SELDON, A., *Pensions for Prosperity*, Hobart Paper 4, 1960.

SEN, A. K., *Collective Choice and Social Welfare*, Oliver and Boyd, 1970.

SHANKS, M., (ed.), *Lessons of Public Enterprise*, Cape, 1963.

SHOUP, C. S., *Federal Estate and Gift Taxes*, Brookings Institution, 1966.

SILBERRAD, J., 'The Estate Duty Provisions of the Finance Act 1969', *British Tax Review*, May–June 1969.

SIMONS, H. C., *Personal Income Taxation*, University of Chicago Press, 1938.

SOWARD, A. W., and WILLUN, W. E., *The Taxation of Capital*, Waterlow and Sons, 1919.

STAMP, Lord, 'Inheritance as an Economic Factor', *Economic Journal*, September 1926.

STEWART, M., 'The Wealth Tax', *Bankers' Magazine*, 1963.

STIGLITZ, J. E., 'Distribution of Income and Wealth Among Individuals', *Econometrica*, July 1969.

STUTCHBURY, O., *The Case For Capital Taxes*, Fabian Tract 388, 1968.

TAIT, A. A., 'Death Duties in Britain', *Public Finance*, 1960.

TAIT, A. A., *The Taxation of Personal Wealth*, University of Illinois Press, 1967.

TANABE, N., 'The Taxation of Net Wealth', *International Monetary Fund Staff Papers*, 1967.

TAWNEY, R. H., *The Acquisitive Society*, G. Bell and Sons, 1921.

TAWNEY, R. H., *Equality*, 5th edition, George Allen and Unwin, 1964.

TITMUSS, R. M., *Essays on 'the Welfare State'*, George Allen and Unwin, 1958.

TITMUSS, R. M., *Income Distribution and Social Change*, George Allen and Unwin, 1962.

TRESS, R. C., 'A Wealth Tax is a Wealth Tax', *British Tax Review*, November–December 1963.

TREVELYAN, G. M., *History of England*, Longmans, Green and Co., 1943.

TURVEY, R., 'Equity and a Capital Gains Tax', *Oxford Economic Papers*, June 1960.

WEDGWOOD, J., *The Economics of Inheritance*, Penguin, 1939.

WHEATCROFT, G. S. A., 'The Administrative Problems of a Wealth Tax', *British Tax Review*, November–December 1963.

WHEATCROFT, G. S. A. (ed.), *Estate and Gift Taxation: A Comparative Study*, Sweet and Maxwell, 1965.

WHEATCROFT, G. S. A., 'Some Estate Duty Problems in Relation to Accumulating and Discretionary Trusts', *British Tax Review*, May–June 1969(a).

WHEATCROFT, G. S. A., 'Inequity in Britain's Tax Structure', *Lloyds Bank Review*, July 1969(b).

WIDER SHARE OWNERSHIP COUNCIL, *Sharing the Profits*, Garnstone Press, 1968.

WILLIAMS, A., *Public Finance and Budgetary Policy*, George Allen and Unwin, 1963.

de ZOETE and BEVAN, *Equity and Fixed Interest Investment 1919–1971*, 1971.

Index

Accumulation of wealth
  accumulated versus inherited wealth, 45–7, 68–73
  equality, 81
  inheritance, 59–61, 68–73
  life-cycle, 48–52, 58
  motives for, 47–56, 60–61, 187–8
  and rate of return, 46, 53–6, 58
  self-made millionaires, 56–8, 187–8
Age and distribution of wealth, 51–2
Aggregate demand and taxation, 89–91, 106–8, 138–42
Annual wealth tax,
  see Wealth tax
Argent, H. D., 262
Assortative mating, 65–7
Atkinson, A. B., 52, 262
Averaging of fluctuating incomes, 158, 173
Avoidance of taxation, 105
  see also Estate duty; Lifetime capital receipts tax

Balogh, Lord, 84, 262
Barkin, S., 261
Barlow, R., Brazer, H. E., and Morgan, J. N., 262
Barry, B., 262
Bell, Clive, 95, 262
Benn, S. I., and Peters, R. S., 262
Bequests,
  see Inheritance
Berlin, I., 77, 79, 262

Beveridge, Lord, 232
Break, G., 151, 262
British Steel Corporation, 214–15
Brown, C. V., and Dawson, D. A., 147, 262
Brown, M. B., 40, 262
Burke, E., 94

Campion, H., and Daniels, G. W., 16, 262
Cannan, E., 59
Capital element in state pension, 107, 141–2, 149, 231–4
Capital flight, 90–91
  capital growth sharing, 244
  capital levy, 205
  lifetime capital receipts tax, 185–6
  wealth tax, 152–3
Capital gains, 34
  income tax, 32, 130–33, 250
  property boom, 57–8
  return from shares, 36–7, 54–5
Capital gains tax
  accumulation of wealth, 58
  in Britain, 99, 131–4, 250
  reform of, 157–62
Capital growth sharing, 234–9
  arguments against, 243–5
  defined, 235
  effect on distribution of wealth, 239–43
  in other countries, 234–6, 261
  investment, 243–5
  prices, 239–42

Capital levy
  administrative problems, 206
  distributional consequences, 200–204
  economic consequences, 204–5
  proposals for, 198–200, 260
  reduction of the national debt, 197–9 passim
  scale for, 199
  tax saving from, 202–3
Carrington, J., 53–5
Carter Commission, 112, 253
  taxation of transfers as income, 172–5 passim
Carter, K., 262
Chambers, Sir Paul, 202–3, 262
Charities
  bequests to, 64
  treatment under estate duty, 115
  treatment under lifetime capital receipts tax, 170
Coates, K., 262
Coates, K., and Topham, T., 213, 262
Collective bargaining, 234–5, 237, 251–2
Colwyn Committee on national debt and taxation, 198–207 passim
Company shares
  capital gains, 35–7
  capital growth sharing, 235–44
  composition of wealth, 14–15, 30–31
  income, 34–5, 54–5
  ownership and control, 28–9, 38–44
  total personal wealth, 6–8
  wider share ownership, 224–6

Composition of wealth, 30–31
  see also Wealth
Confederation of British Industry, 139–53 passim
Consanguinity in inheritance tax, 111n, 177
Control of industry
  capital growth sharing, 243
  institutional shareholdings, 41–3
  nationalization, 212–15
  ownership of wealth, 28–9, 38–43
  redistribution of wealth, 93
Crosland, C. A. R., 40, 85, 94–5, 210, 262

Dalton, H., 84, 118, 198–9, 263
Daniel, W. W., 148, 263
Death duties,
  see Estate duty
Denationalization
  and the distribution of wealth, 216–19
  in West Germany, 218
  Mr Powell on, 216, 260–61
Denman, D. R., 72–3, 127, 263
Department of Applied Economics, Cambridge, 42
Department of Land Economy Cambridge, 72
Distribution of income
  distribution of wealth, 18–19, 31–8
  in the U.K., and compared with U.S., 19–20
  social ownership of wealth, 196
Distribution of wealth
  by age groups, 49–52
  changes over time, 21–4, 255

comparison with other countries, 19–21, 255
and distribution of income, 18–19, 31–8
estate duty, 22–3, 118–20, 258
estate duty method of estimating, 10–14
investment income method of estimating, 14–16
Division of estates,
see Inheritance
Donnison, D., 79, 84, 263
Duc, J. F., 147, 263

Earned and unearned income,
see Income Tax
Eastham, J. K., 78, 263
Economist, 15, 93, 129, 136, 255
Education
human capital, 26
Eliot, T. S., 94, 263
Emigration, 124
Enterprise,
see Incentive to work
Equality
case against greater, 78–85, 88–96
case for, 78–9, 96
and social justice, 79–84
and social ownership of wealth, 195–6
utilitarian argument, 84–5
Equity, 128
lifetime standard of, 85–7
see Horizontal equity
Estate duty
avoidance, 12, 22, 105, 120–28, 258
comparison with United States, 116–17
history, 113–15, 258

impact on distribution of wealth, 22–3, 118–20, 126–8, 258–9
method of estimating wealth distribution, 10–14
rates of duty, 115–18
revenue, 118, 126–8, 258–9
Estates,
see Inheritance
Evasion, 105
estate duty, 121
lifetime capital-receipts tax, 182–3
wealth tax, 154–5

Fair compensation, 208–12, 216–17
Family businesses, 122, 189
Fijalkowski-Bereday, G. Z., 64, 263
Fisher, Irving, 188
Florence, S., 39–40, 263

Gaitskell, H. T. N., 208, 263
Galbraith, J. K., 25
Gambling winnings, and lifetime capital receipts tax, 170
Generation skipping, 184n
Gibbon, E., 163
Giffen, Sir Robert, 14
Gifts
charitable, 64n
estate duty avoidance, 12, 22–3, 121–2
reform of wealth-transfer taxation, 163–8, 178
taxation of, 101–2, 110–12, 114
Gladstone, W. E., 113
Glass, D., 66, 263
Government Actuary, 227, 261, 263

Gratuitous enrichment tax, 169, 182

Green paper on inheritance taxation, 175–9

Growth
and nationalization, 207
and wealth tax, 144–5

Guardian, The, 218

Harbury, C. D., 68–71, 263
Heidensohn, K., 218
Henderson, Sir Hubert, 61, 119, 209, 263
Hicks, U. K., 104, 263
Hockley, G. C., 263
Hollingsworth, T. H., 66, 263
Horizontal equity, 87–8
capital-gains taxation, 161
capital levy, 200–202
denationalization, 216
investment income taxation, 130–31
nationalization, 208–9, 212
wealth taxation, 151–2, 156
wealth-transfer taxation, 164–5
Houghton, R. W., 263
Housing and owner occupation, 7, 33–4, 37
Hughes, J., 213, 263

Ilersic, A. R., 78
Incentive to invest
adverse effects of redistribution, 92–3
capital growth sharing, 243–5
Incentives for saving, 220–26
in West Germany, 235
Save As You Earn, 222–4, 261
wider share ownership, 224–6, 261

Incentive to work
adverse effects of redistribution, 91–2, 96, 257–9
capital gains tax reform, 162
capital levy, 204
effects of wealth tax, 146–9, 153–4
evidence, 259
lifetime capital receipts tax, 186–9
Incidence of taxation, nominal and effective, 103–4, 119–20, 142–3
Income
averaging of fluctuating income, 158, 173
definition of, 31–2, 255–6
income from wealth, 31–8
and ownership, 27
see also Distribution of income
Incomes policy, 84, 234, 252
Income tax, 15, 32
earned and unearned income, 99, 129–30, 134, 259
and 'hidden' wealth tax, 129–30
integration with wealth-transfer tax, 172–5
pension provisions, 227n
Inflation
estate duty, 115–16
pensions, 33–4, 227–31 *passim*
property boom, 57
protection from, 44, 223, 227–31 *passim*, 245
taxation of investment income, 55, 130–34
Inheritance
changing role of, 70–73
division of estates, 59–60, 62–5
in three families, 73–6

marriage and family size, 60, 65–8, 257
primogeniture, 29, 60–68 *passim*, 72
quantitative importance of, 45–7, 59, 68–73, 76, 257
Inheritance taxation, Green Paper on, 175–9
see also Wealth transfer taxation
Inland Revenue, 11, 13, 16, 21, 37, 94, 116, 138, 263
Institutional sharcholdings, *see* Control of industry
Integrated gift and estate tax, 101–2, 110–11, 163–8, 260
Investment income
  discriminatory taxation of, 129–30, 259
  method of estimating distribution of wealth, 14–16
  special charge, 197–9
  yield on equities, 54–5, 255–6
Investment pay schemes, 234–5, 242

Jantscher, G. R., 172, 174, 263
Jenkin, Fleeming, 104
Jenkins, R. H., 208–10, 263
Johnson, Dr, 92
Jouvenel, B. de, 94
Joy, N. V., 264

Keynes, J. M., 47, 50, 90, 93, 161, 202, 264
Kisker, K. P., 83, 264

Labour mobility, 245
Labour party
  a capital levy, 198–9
  a redistributive wealth tax, 149

Lampman, R. J., 19, 89, 264
Langley, K. M., 264
Leber, G., 235
Legitim, Law of, 62
Leyden, W. von, 78–9, 264
Life-cycle savings, *see* Savings
Lifetime capital receipts tax, 168–70
  administration, 190–91
  avoidance, 182–3
  comparison with annual wealth tax, 186, 188–9
  compared with Green Paper, 177–8
  definition of tax-paying unit, 179–81
  in other countries, 111–12
  rates of, 170–72
  savings and aggregate demand, 184–6
  treatment of trusts, 181–4
  and work incentives, 186–9
Locke, J., 80, 264
Lydall, H. F., 48, 264
Lydall, H. F., and Lansing, J. B., 19, 20, 264
Lydall, H. F., and Tipping, D. G., 9, 13n, 31, 264
Lynch, T. D., 264
Lynes, T., 231, 264

Macmillan, H., 213
Managerial Capitalism, 40–41
Marriage and inheritance, 60, 65–8
Marriott, O., 56–7, 264
Marris, R. L., and Wood, A., 264
Marsh, R., 214
Marshall, A., 89, 99
Marx, K., 45, 195

McKendrick, N., 264
Meacher, M., 265
Meade, J. E., 36, 38, 168–9, 195–6, 265
Merrett, A. J., 154, 265
Merrett, A. J., and Sykes, A., 55, 265
Midland Bank Review, 265
Millard Tucker Committee on the taxation of trading profits, 158
Mill, John Stuart, 26, 88, 265
Ministry of Pensions and National Insurance, 233, 265
Montagu, Lord, 125, 265
Morrison, Lord, 213
Mortality multiplier, 10, 12, 15, 21, 127
Motives for saving,
  see Saving

National Craftsmen's Co-ordinating Committee for the Iron and Steel Industry, 214
National debt, 195–7
  capital levy, 198–207
  effects of reduction in, 202–4
  wealth of state, 195–6
National Economic Development Committee, 144
Nationalization
  arguments for, 207–8
  and control, 212–15
  fair compensation, 208–12, 216–17, 260
  social ownership of wealth, 208–12, 260
  worker consultation, 213–15
National Savings Bank, 229
National Superannuation,
  see Pensions

Negative capital tax, 232, 261
Net worth,
  see Wealth
Nobel, Alfred, 188

Organization for Economic Co-operation and Development, 234–44 *passim*, 265
Ownership, 3, 25–9, 256
Oxford Institute of Economics and Statistics, savings surveys, 9, 19, 48, 254–5

Pateman, C., 265
Pay As You Earn, 101 n
Peacock, A. T., 136, 143, 148, 265
Pen, J., 3, 265
Pensions
  capital element, 107, 141–2, 149, 231–3
  Conservative proposals, 229–31
  distribution of wealth, 5, 11, 13–14, 17, 226–8
  funds, control of, 42–3, 231 n
  income from wealth, 33–4
  National Superannuation, 228–30
  occupational, 5, 28, 228–31
  pension reform, 228–34
  trade union policy, 231
  see also Saving, motives for
Personal wealth,
  see Wealth
Petty, Lord Henry, 82
Pigou, A. C., 187, 265
Powell, E., 216, 265
Prest, A. R., 165, 265
Primogeniture, 29, 60, 62, 65–72 *passim*, 92
Progressive taxation, 100 n

Property,
  see Ownership *and* Wealth
Property boom, 56–7
Pryke, R., 207, 265

'Quality of Life', 94–6, 258
Queen Victoria, 122
Quick succession relief, 115

Radcliffe Committee on Monetary
    Reform, 197
Reform Committee of the South
    Wales Miners, 265
Revell, J. R. S., 6–7, 21, 30, 125,
    127, 265
Revell, J. R. S., and Moyle, J.,
    39–40, 266
Risk taking
  capital gains taxation, 161
  capital levy, 205
  different assets, 35–6
  inflation, 36, 57
  redistribution, effects of, 92–3,
    96
  wealth tax, effects of, 145–6
Robinson, D., 261
Robinson, Joan, 40–41, 133, 266
Robson, P., 211, 266
Roe, A., 7, 266
Roosevelt, F., 83
Rose, H. B., and Newbould,
    G. S., 211, 266
Royal Commission on the Taxa-
    tion of Profits and Income,
    32, 131, 157–61, 266

Sabine, B. E. V., 82, 266
Sandford, C. T., 116, 169, 170n,
    189–90, 232, 266
Save As You Earn, 53, 94, 222–4,
    261

Saving
  capital growth sharing, 241
  capital levy, 204
  estate duty, effect of, 119
  for bequest motive, 60–61
  life-cycle saving, 48–52, 58, 256
  lifetime capital-receipts tax,
    184–6
  motives for, 47–56
  redistribution, effects of, 88–91,
    96
  wealth tax, 139–42, 152–4, 186
  see also Incentives for saving
Seldon, A., 42, 228, 266
Self-made millionaires,
  see Accumulation of wealth
Sen, A. K., 79n, 266
Shanks, M., 266
Shares,
  see Company shares
Shoup, C. S., 112, 266
Sidgwick, H., 88
Silberrad, J., 266
Simons, H. C., 128, 173, 266
Smith, Adam, 5, 105
Social justice,
  see Equality
Soward, A. W., and Willun, W. E.,
    113, 266
Special charge, 16, 197–9
Special contribution, 197
Stamp, Lord, 202, 266
Stewart, M., 266
Stiglitz, J. E., 266
Strategy for pensions, White
    Paper, 229
Stutchbury, O., 133, 136, 169–70,
    181–3, 188, 266
Succession, Law of, 62–3
  see also Inheritance
Sunday Telegraph, The, 228

Surtax, 128
  replacement by a wealth tax,
    142–9

Tait, A. A., 127, 266
Tanabe, N., 267
Tawney, R. H., 26, 84, 267
Taxes
  basis for comparing, 106–8, 198
  nominal and effective incidence,
    103–4, 119–20, 142–3
    see Capital gains tax; Estate
    duty; Income tax; Lifetime
    capital receipts tax; Wealth
    tax
Times, The, 64, 125, 127, 193, 215,
    226, 231
  and denationalization, 217–19
  life-cycle savings, 49–51, 53
Titmuss, R. M., 42, 267
Tocqueville, A. de, 62
Trades Union Congress, 149
Trade-union policy, 231 n
Transmission of wealth,
  see Inheritance
Tress, R. C., 267
Trevelyan, G. M., 95, 267
Trusts
  discretionary, 27, 123, 127,
    181–3, 259
  estate-duty avoidance, 12, 22,
    123–5, 182
  lifetime capital receipts tax,
    181–4
  wealth estimates, 12–13
  wealth tax legislation, 156
Turvey, R., 267

Valuation, 3–8, 12
  capital levy, 200–201
  company shares, 6–8, 211–12

denationalization, 217
nationalization, 209–12
wealth tax, 138, 154–6

Wage negotiations,
  see Collective bargaining
Wealth
  composition of, 15, 30–31
  definition of, 3
  and control, 38–44
  of the state, 195–6
  total personal, 6, 11, 13–15, 17,
    50, 254
  see also Distribution of wealth;
    Accumulation of wealth
Wealth tax
  administration, 94, 110, 136,
    138, 154–7, 259
  comparisons between taxes, 99–
    103
  defined, 99–100
  'hidden', 129–30
  in Britain, 135–42
  incentive to work, 146–9, 153–4,
    188–9
  in other countries, 108–10, 153,
    258
  rates of taxation, 109–10, 136–8
  risk taking, 100, 145–6
  savings, 139–42, 152–4, 186
Wealth-transfer taxes
  consanguinity, 111 n, 177
  defined, 100–102
  in other countries, 110–12, 164–
    5, 258
  integrated gift and estate tax,
    100–102, 110–12, 163–8
  integration with income tax,
    112, 172–5
  see also Estate duty; Lifetime
    capital receipts tax

Wedgwood, J., 57, 62, 64, 70–72, 75–6, 88, 267

Wheatcroft, G. S. A., 105, 124, 156, 267

Wider share ownership, 224–6

Wider Share Ownership Council, 226, 236, 267

Williams, A., 267

Work effort,
  see Incentive to work

Workers' control or representation
  capital-growth sharing, 243
  nationalization, 212–15

Yield
  multiplier, 14
  see also Income from wealth

de Zoete and Bevan, 54, 267

More About Penguins and Pelicans

Penguinews, which appears every month, contains details of all the new books issued by Penguins as they are published. From time to time it is supplemented by *Penguins in Print*, which is a complete list of all titles available. (There are some five thousand of these.)

A specimen copy of *Penguinews* will be sent to you free on request. For a year's issues (including the complete lists) please send 50p if you live in the United Kingdom, or 75p if you live elsewhere. Just write to Dept EP, Penguin Books Ltd, Harmondsworth, Middlesex, enclosing a cheque or postal order, and your name will be added to the mailing list.

In the U.S.A.: For a complete list of books available from Penguin in the United States write to Dept CS, Penguin Books Inc., 7110 Ambassador Road, Baltimore, Maryland 21207.

In Canada: For a complete list of books available from Penguin in Canada write to Penguin Books Canada Ltd, 41 Steelcase Road West, Markham, Ontario L3R 1B4.

Income Distribution

Jan Pen

Professor Pen takes here a new broad look at an area of economic theory well known for the heat of the disagreements it provokes. He presents a survey of how income is distributed between individuals and between factors of production, guiding the general reader clearly through some advanced parts of economic analysis and even introducing the expert to much relevant material.

Income Distribution throws light on several unfamiliar facets of the subject, such as the mathematical concepts underlying the statistical regularities of personal distribution; the manner in which wages reflect social as well as economic evaluations; the link between the decreasing share of the very rich with the decreasing share of capital; and the criteria for 'improving' distribution. In asking how equal we can make income distribution without harming economic growth and democracy, Professor Pen explicitly discusses the power structure, incomes policy, profit-sharing, capital-sharing, the curious British tax system, negative income tax and much else.

'A very handy compendium of the main facts and theories about income distribution'
– Samuel Brittan in the *Financial Times*

Economics of the Real World

Peter Donaldson

A sense of economic failure is in the air. The British economy may be working better than ever . . . without booms and slumps, without mass unemployment: yet government after government fails to achieve simultaneously full employment, stable prices, and economic growth.

Explaining why this is so, the author of *A Guide to the British Economy* describes here how a mixed economy is managed and (given the underlying market mechanisms) what can and what cannot be the subject of economic policy. More basically he argues that economics itself is strangely remote from the urgent problems of ordinary people and that policy-makers confuse ends and means. What matters, in his view, is not growth, but growth of what, for whom and at what cost; not full employment, but the nature of work; not just more wealth, but its more equitable distribution.

For *this* is the real world – a world of values and people – neglected by orthodox economics and evaded by policy-makers. Why? Because, suggests Peter Donaldson, if the real issues are to be tackled, there has to be a revolution in our whole outlook on economics and society.

Poverty and Equality in Britain

J. C. Kincaid

If you are complacently satisfied that the British system of social security is the finest in the world, this important book by Dr Kincaid may shake you.

Quoting estimates that suggest that 2,000,000 people in Britain are living in acute poverty, he argues that their poverty is a direct consequence of inadequate social-security schemes, that the Welfare State does nothing effective to iron out inequality, and that the services offered are far less egalitarian and more punitive than is generally supposed.

In the belief that poverty and inequality are integral components of a competitive social order, the author urges us to re-think our ideas about the poor. Working-class militancy, in his view, lacks political expression: if the unions were prepared to take action over the sores that fester in our society 'neither a Labour nor a Conservative Government would dare treat the old, the sick and the unemployed as they do at present'.

Poverty: The Forgotten Englishmen

Ken Coates and Richard Silburn

Is poverty in Britain a thing of the past? Too many of our
countrymen regularly do without the minimum considered
necessary for a healthy diet; they live in houses that are
overcrowded, insanitary and ludicrously expensive to keep
warm and comfortable; their children attend schools in
which teaching is a near-impossibility.

Ken Coates and Richard Silburn look again at what is
meant by the word 'poverty'. They conclude that vast
numbers of Englishmen, living in slums throughout the
country, are, for most of their lives, living in acute poverty.
What this actually involves is spelled out by means of a
detailed survey of one slum – St Ann's, an area of
Nottingham which has now been cleared but remains
typical of hundreds of such districts.

The book continues with a study of welfare services and
why they fail to alleviate or remove poverty, and finally
there is an analysis of the frequent failure of slum-
clearance schemes.

Originally published as a Penguin Special, this Pelican
attacks a problem – that of modern urban poverty –
neglected by western society.

'Writing with compassion, style, wit and an almost
complete lack of jargon, (they) present us with inescapable
facts which must remould our thinking and our actions'

– *The Times*